THE MORAL PHILOSOPHY
OF JOHN STUART MILL

The Moral Philosophy of John Stuart Mill

Toward Modifications of Contemporary Utilitarianism

MARK STRASSER

Longwood Academic
Wakefield, New Hampshire

© 1991 by Mark Philip Strasser

Published in 1991 by Longwood Academic, a division of Hollowbrook Communications, Inc., Wakefield, New Hampshire 03872-0757.

Printed on acid-free paper.

Library of Congress Cataloging in Publication Data:

Strasser, Mark Philip, 1955-
    The moral philosophy of John Stuart Mill : toward modifications of contemporary utilitarianism / by Mark Strasser
    p. cm.
Includes bibliographical references and index.
ISBN 0-89341-681-9 (alk. paper)
    1. Mill, John Stuart, 1806-1873--Ethics. 2. Ethics, Modern--19th century. 3. Utilitarianism--History--19th century. I. Title.
B1608.E8S77   1991
171'.5'092--dc20   91-15218
                                        CIP

*This book is dedicated
to Jeff, Leslee, and Dossie Ann*

ACKNOWLEDGEMENTS

Since this manuscript is a revised version of my doctoral thesis at the University of Chicago, I would like to offer special thanks to my committee: Profs. Gewirth, Adkins and Korsgaard. I have a huge debt of gratitude to Profs. Gewirth and Adkins, not only for their very insightful comments, great patience, and general support during the writing of the thesis, but also for their intellectual support and guidance throughout my graduate career. Prof. Korsgaard became a member of my thesis committee after the work had progressed relatively far. Nonetheless, her valuable criticisms and comments greatly enhanced my understanding of Mill and of utilitarianism in general.

I owe many thanks to friends and colleagues for their help on the numerous earlier drafts of this book as well as for their encouragement and general emotional support: Drs. Robert Audi, Michael Davis, Susan Hekman, Rachel McCleary, Mark McPherran, Don Sievert and Dabney Townsend as well as Mr. Gordon Giles, Mr. Mark Stansbury, Mr. Alan Strasser and Mr. Wyatt Benner.

Dr. L. Wayne Sumner was kind enough to allow me to see parts of his book before it was available to the general public. Dr. Carl Wellman offered careful, detailed, voluminous criticisms of this manuscript, enabling me to make it much better than it otherwise would have been. Through both written and oral comments, Dr. Henry West improved my understanding of Mill to an extent which I am only beginning to appreciate. I, of course, take sole responsibility for those parts of this book which are still in need of correction.

TABLE OF CONTENTS

INTRODUCTION

Every society must decide what its citizens should be forced to do, allowed to do, and prevented from doing. In *On Liberty*, John Stuart Mill argues that society should allow its citizens to make many of the decisions which affect their own lives. Yet, in *Utilitarianism*, he argues that the principle of utility is the ultimate principle of morality and that those acts which maximize humankind's utility are morally best. Critics argue that Mill is contradicting himself, since a society which allows its citizens to make many decisions for themselves will be allowing people to act in disutility-producing and thus immoral ways.

Mill solves this apparent difficulty by distinguishing between those activities which should be free from the interference of others and those activities which should be free *both* from the interference of others *and* from the interference of the agent's own conscience. By pointing to conscience as an additional regulator of action, Mill can offer consistent and convincing arguments which show why society must protect a multitude of activities from the interference of others, even if the pursuit of those activities would be morally wrong. He thus accounts for the protection of a great many freedoms while upholding a variety of our considered moral judgments.

Charging that Mill's moral system is plagued by a variety of internal inconsistencies, Mill's critics cite as evidence his confusing comments about imperfect duties and supererogatory actions, his seemingly contradictory comments about the role of the principle of utility, his potentially misunderstood claim that mental pleasures are intrinsically better than physical pleasures, etc. All of these can be included coherently and plausibly within one moral system. For the most part, Mill's position is not self-contradictory, his critics' comments notwithstanding. Those inconsistencies which his system does have do not establish the bankruptcy of either Mill's ethical theory or of utilitarian ethical theory in general.

Before we can understand how Mill demonstrates that society must protect individual rights from the interference of others, we must understand how Mill accounts for rights. To understand how he accounts for rights, we must understand both his notion of justice and some basic tenets of his theory. Chapter 1 shows that Mill argues for both the intrinsic and the extrinsic superiority of the higher pleasures, *and that for moral and political purposes both types of superiority should be considered.* That way, he can show that utilitarianism is compatible with the intrinsic superiority of the higher pleasures and also compatible with the denial that the intellectual pleasures of a few are morally preferable to the non-intellectual pleasures of a multitude.

Chapter 2 examines Mill's atypical act-utilitarianism. He takes a rather broad view of which consequences should be referred to as the effects of a particular action. Further, when judging whether an action or attitude is utility-producing, he considers whether it will promote the long-term interests of humankind rather than, for example, the long-term interests of a particular society. Finally, when Mill evaluates acts, he judges them in light of whether they promote a sufficient amount of utility rather than in light of whether they maximize utility.

It is important to understand that Mill is a type of act-utilitarian rather than a type of rule-utilitarian because, otherwise, one will neither understand many of the criticisms of Mill's work nor his responses to those criticisms. For example, because act-utilitarians believe that the action which will maximize utility is morally most worthy, they are rightly accused of morally countenancing some lies and thefts. If one could produce net utility by performing a theft, and if one's not performing the theft would produce hardship, then Mill would claim that the theft was both right and just. Indeed, he believes that this aspect (that, for example, some thefts are morally permissible) is a strength rather than a weakness of his position.

Chapter 3 discusses whether one can calculate which actions will promote utility. Mill never gives more than a vague suggestion about how to perform these calculations. Nonetheless, we can make reasonable predictions about the consequences of many of our actions. Further, utilitarians may not need to *know* which actions will be productive of utility — Mill sometimes suggests that actions which are foreseen to be utility-producing are morally praiseworthy. Thus, an action which fails to produce utility because of certain unforeseeable events might nonetheless deserve praise.

Chapter 4 examines various interpretations of Mill's moral theory. In each of these formulations, the costs of the sanction which would be imposed if the action were wrong are considered when determining the moral worth of the action. For example, one's seeing a boring movie would not be morally wrong if the disutility produced by the imposition of the sanction, e.g., a fine or pangs of conscience, would outweigh the disutility produced by the movie-viewing. Some interpretations (represented by Copp's view) include the costs of the sanction within an act-utilitarian framework, some (represented by Lyons's view) include them within a rule-utilitarian framework, and some (represented by Dryer'sview) include them within a hybrid which combines the two. These interpretations do not reflect Mill's position and are not particularly morally palatable.

Although critics are correct that Mill distinguishes between his theory of moral worth and his theory of moral obligation, they have not understood the basis upon which he makes that distinction. Chapter 5 discusses Mill's criterion for determining how much utility one must produce in order to fulfill one's moral duty. *Mill links the level of net utility which the agent is morally required to produce to the level of progress of the society in which she lives.* In backward societies, one may only have the duty to produce a minimal amount of net utility. In more progressive societies, however, one may have the duty to produce much net utility. By making this link, Mill accounts for an increasing range of obligations as societies continue to progress. Further, he assures that most individuals will not feel that their moral system imposes unfair burdens (since the moral demands made by the system will not exceed what the individual's own society deems reasonable). Mill's system is neither a maximizing act-utilitarian position in which the agent fulfills her moral obligation only if she *maximizes* (foreseeable) utility nor a minimizing act-utilitarian position in which she fulfills her moral obligation as long as she *promotes* net (foreseeable) utility, but a compromise between the two.

For Mill, an action is wrong if and only if a properly developed conscience would punish it. A properly developed conscience will impose sanctions if one does not promote the requisite amount of utility. Yet, this means that agents who promote (foreseeable) disutility deserve to have sanctions imposed against them, even if they acted with the best of intentions and motivations. Chapter 6 examines the difference between two different functions of conscience — imposing pangs of guilt and pangs of regret. By making this distinction, Mill can account for many of our considered moral judgments, both about how agents should act and about how they should feel.

Some critics argue that Mill and utilitarians in general cannnot offer a coherent moral theory because everything within utilitarianism can be reduced to the obligation to maximize utility. These critics charge that utilitarianism cannot account for imperfect duties (duties which can be satisfied when and for whom one chooses) and supererogatory actions (actions which one is praiseworthy for performing but not blameworthy for failing to perform), and then claim that "valid" moral systems must be able to differentiate among perfect duties, imperfect duties, and supererogatory actions. Chapter 7 discusses how Mill meets these objections. By distinguishing between his theory of moral worth and his theory of moral obligation, Mill has no difficulty in making these standard deontological distinctions.

One of Mill's most important contributions involves his offering a principle to help determine which actions can (properly) be interfered with or punished by society. *Mill does not say that all actions which society should protect are morally permissible actions.* He relies on conscience to do some of the punishing which society cannot do. Even if society should not impose sanctions against an agent for a particular action, the agent's conscience should do so if that action was morally wrong.

Mill's claim that society should protect certain immoral actions might seem surprising. Societies are supposed to promote the good of humankind. Insofar as immoral actions are harmful, one would expect Mill to require that society prevent or punish such actions. Yet, there are cases in which society's punishing certain immoral actions would produce even greater disutility than would the protection of those actions. For example, society's punishing someone for uttering disutility-producing statements would (in many cases) be much more costly than would society's protecting the utterance of those statements.

Quite simply, Mill says that there are some (foreseeably) disutility-producing actions which, although wrong, do not merit censure from others. He can thus maintain that there is a self-regarding sphere (a sphere of actions which, even if they are disutility-producing, are not appropriately subjected to blame from others), that the principle of utility is the ultimate moral principle, and that all (foreseeably) disutility-producing actions are immoral (although not necessarily blameworthy by others).

One cannot overestimate the importance of the distinction between actions which do not deserve censure *from others* and actions which do not deserve censure *at all.* Mill refutes the charge that he and utilitarians in general are unable to account for the protection of individual rights by pointing out that a disutility-producing action's deserving blame from conscience does not establish that the action deserves blame from others. Chapter 8 discusses a variety of Mill's arguments which show why society must prevent others from interfering with the exercise of certain rights, even if the individual's own conscience should prevent or punish the exercise of those rights.

Chapter 9 examines Mill's view that society should punish all (foreseeably) disutility-producing actions, if not directly (e.g., by jailing the agent), then indirectly (by developing within the agent a conscience which will punish all wrong actions). In those cases in which an individual exercises his right to do wrong and performs a (foreseeably) disutility-producing action, society has contradictory functions. It must protect the individual in his performance of the action, because he has a right to perform it, and also punish him, because all wrong actions deserve some form of punishment.

Mill argues persuasively that society should protect the exercise of a variety of individual rights from the interference of others and he thereby establishes that individuals have a moral right to do moral wrong, at least on one definition of a 'right'. Many rights theorists accept Mill's analysis, arguing that the notion of a right which he employs is not only theoretically acceptable, but is actually theoretically *required.*

Other theorists argue that a right to do wrong is a contradiction in terms. Were Mill to use their definition of a right, he would have to show that society should protect the agent who exercises his right to perform foreseeably disutility-producing (i.e., wrong) actions, both from the interference of others *and from the interference of the agent's own conscience.* This latter set of critics argues that unless Mill can somehow do this, he will be unable to demonstrate that individuals have as many moral rights as most people believe.

Even if this latter set of critics is correct, Mill's theory may nonetheless escape unscathed, since he may not need to demonstrate that individuals have rights. Chapter 10 examines whether moral systems must contain rights. If rights are not inherently valuable and are necessary only insofar as they protect or assure certain objects, then Mill may not need to account for rights. If the existence of rights is, at least arguably, disutility-producing, then his inability to account for rights may be a credit to his system rather than a debit against his system. In any event, most criticisms of Mill's utilitarianism are, when correct, correct for the wrong reasons. Further, Mill can acknowledge the truth of some of these criticisms without at all impugning his moral or political system.

In short, Mill is offering a utilitarian system in which that action which maximizes utility is morally best. When figuring out which action maximizes utility, we must consider both the quality and the quantity of the pleasures produced. We need not figure out exactly how much utility a particular action will produce in order for us to know whether we should perform it.

Yet, Mill does not believe that an agent must maximize utility in order to act rightly. He instead links the level of utility which the agent is obligated to produce to the society in which she lives. An agent who does not produce even that amount of utility acts wrongly.

Mill argues that not all wrong actions are appropriately punished by the State or by society. An agent has a right to perform those actions which the State and society should not prevent her from performing. An agent who exercises her right to perform a wrong action deserves to be punished not by the State or by society, but by her own conscience.

When explicating his theory, Mill interpreters have either under-appreciated or misunderstood the above facets of his position (among others). That is due, at least in part, to their tendency to concentrate on his *On Liberty* and *Utilitarianism*. The difficulty which arises from doing this is *not* that those are unimportant tracts and thus to be valued lightly, but that these important works are consistent with several possible interpretations. It is only when Mill's other works are considered that some of these possible interpretations can be rejected.

Mill interpreters face at least two difficulties — Mill does not *concisely* spell out his system (and thus one cannot understand it by simply reading one or two of his works) and Mill does not *explicitly* lay out his system (and thus one could not be assured that one would understand his moral system even if one had read all of his works). However, these difficulties notwithstanding, one should not assume that Mill's position cannot be understood nor that all interpretations of his work are equally valid or plausible. The account offered here captures the spirit of Mill's writings and is more plausible than any of the alternative interpretations.

This book is intended for individuals interested in moral theory, especially for those interested in Mill's moral theory. It is not assumed that the reader has great familiarity with Mill's writings, although even people who have that familiarity will find this account important for several reasons:

First, it demonstrates that Mill's system is or at least *can be made to be* much more coherent than most critics admit. While Mill does not explicitly and concisely spell out his position, he nonetheless offers numerous claims throughout his works which are most plausibly accounted for and explained by the system outlined in this book.

Second, it shows how Mill can convincingly differentiate between those actions which deserve punishment from society and those actions which only deserve punishment from the agent herself. He thus protects a great many actions from external interference, while still maintaining that individuals have a moral duty to promote a certain amount of utility. Further, he can also thus show how *self-*

regarding actions are within the moral realm and nonetheless are not appropriately regulated by the State or by society.

Third, it helps to explain why commentators who have neglected or misunderstood the role of conscience in Mill's moral theory have had such difficulty in understanding his moral view. By including conscience as an additional moral regulator, Mill can offer a consistent and coherent *utilitarian* position which recognizes the importance of the promotion and protection of a variety of liberties.

Fourth, it helps us to understand how Mill, by relying on conscience so heavily, casts light upon, if not solves, many of the problems which currently plague both deontological and utilitarian moral theories. While Mill may not have been as explicit as we would have liked, he has nonetheless offered us a plausible system which deserves to be taken much more seriously than many currently widely-respected theories.

CHAPTER ONE

The Higher and Lower Pleasures

As a utilitarian, Mill believes that actions are right insofar as they promote happiness and wrong insofar as they promote unhappiness. However, his view is much more complex than that. For example, he denies both that one must maximize utility in order to act rightly and that one's merely promoting utility will morally suffice, and instead offers a position which is a compromise between the two. People who act rightly will promote significant amounts of utility (especially if they live in progressive societies). At the same time, since they will not need to maximize utility in order to act rightly, they will not feel that their moral system imposes unfair and unreasonable demands upon them.

Mill's non-standard utilitarian position allows him to account for supererogation. Further, and perhaps more importantly, it allows him to maintain that there is a whole sphere of non-utility-maximimizing actions which are not appropriately prevented or punished by others. He thus can be a champion of liberty and individuality while at the same time offering a utilitarian position.

Mill defines utility in terms of happiness which, in turn, is defined in terms of pleasure. However, not all pleasures are of equal worth. His attempt to distinguish between the higher and the lower pleasures has sparked much debate, both about whether such a distinction is tenable and, if so, about what the ramifications of such a distinction are. Mill *can* make a qualitative distinction between pleasures in a way which will both promote his utilitarian ideals and which will give the appropriate weight to the mental pleasures. By distinguishing between intrinsic and extrinsic superiority, he can maintain that intellectual pleasures have greater intrinsic worth than bodily pleasures, while nonetheless valuing them morally and politically only insofar as their pursuit will promote the general good.

Mental Versus Bodily Pleasures

Mill defines happiness as pleasure and the absence of pain; unhappiness as pain and the absence of pleasure.[1] However, this definition does not address the qualitative distinction between pleasures. Mill argues that while utilitarians "have fully proved their case" by placing "the superiority of mental over bodily pleasures chiefly in the greater permanency, safety, uncostliness, etc. of the former — that is, in their circumstantial advantages rather than in their intrinsic nature," they could in addition have claimed that the mental pleasures are qualitatively better than the bodily pleasures. It is "quite compatible with the principle of utility to recognise the fact, that some *kinds* of pleasure are more desirable and more valuable than others."[2]

Mill talks about the greater *intrinsic* value of the mental pleasures because he may thereby permanently lay to rest any notions that utilitarianism is a doctrine worthy only of swine.[3] He offers a method by which to determine which of two pleasures is intrinsically superior. Suppose that one of two pleasures "is, by those who are competently acquainted with both, placed so far above the other that they prefer it, even though knowing it to be attended with a greater amount of discontent, and would not resign it for any quantity of the other pleasure which their nature is capable of." In that case, Mill claims that we would be "justified in ascribing to the preferred enjoyment a superiority in quality, so far outweighing quantity as to render it, in comparison, of small account."[4]

Even if Mill is correct that people who have experienced both mental pleasures and bodily pleasures tend almost universally to choose the former, that does not help us know *why* they so choose. Perhaps they so choose because they are trying to secure some other good and believe that the mental pleasures are a means to that further good. Or, perhaps they so choose because the mental pleasures are more intense than, although of the same kind as, the physical pleasures. That competent judges consistently choose mental pleasures over bodily ones does not establish the *intrinsic* superiority of the former type of pleasure.

Indeed, we cannot quite be sure what is indicated by competent judges' universally choosing one pleasure over another, since competent judges might choose the same pleasure for *different reasons*. Perhaps some judges choose pleasure₁ for its own sake. Others choose it because it is more likely to lead to some greater pleasure. Still others prefer it because of the greater intensity of that pleasure.

When we talk about qualitative differences between pleasures, we might talk about $pleasure_1$'s being an intrinsically better (better$_I$) pleasure than $pleasure_2$ or about $pleasure_1$'s being an extrinsically better (better$_E$) pleasure than $pleasure_2$, e.g., a pleasure which is better because it has some desirable effect or promotes some desirable end. Mill argues that the higher pleasures have both types of qualitative superiority and that both should be included within our moral and political calculations.

Suppose that we lived in a world in which the qualified judges universally chose the *bodily* pleasures. Many theorists who believe that the bodily pleasures are 'lower' would argue that the judges were mistaken and that their mistaken judgment would not change the intrinsic superiority of the mental pleasures.[5] However, if a pleasure can be intrinsically superior to another pleasure even if people tend to prefer the latter, then we cannot use people's preferences even as an *infallible test* to establish which pleasures are intrinsically superior to which.[6] Thus, even if some pleasures are intrinsically better than others, Mill would be wrong were he claiming that we could infallibly identify those pleasures by seeing which pleasures people tended to prefer.

Mill might adopt a different tack and claim that competent judges' choosing certain pleasures over others does not *establish* the intrinsic superiority of the former pleasures, but does *provide evidence* for their intrinsic superiority. That claim is less suspect, although competent judges' universally choosing certain pleasures over others would not provide evidence for their intrinsic *rather than* extrinsic superiority. However, our asking the judges certain questions might help us determine whether they thought the pleasures intrinsically superior, extrinsically superior, or superior in both respects. While this would not be an infallible way to resolve the issue, it would at least be suggestive.[7]

The Possibility of Making Qualitative Distinctions

Critics debate whether it is even coherent to say that one pleasure is qualitatively better than another.[8] When arguing about the *possibility* of distinguishing qualitatively among pleasures, they do not critically examine Mill's method of so distinguishing. Thus, even if one can distinguish between higher and lower pleasures, that does not establish that Mill's distinction is either tenable or desirable. (Obviously, if the distinction *cannot* be made, then Mill's distinction is not tenable.) Here, we will examine the tenability of Mill's distinction within his moral and political system.

Mill claims that "it is an unquestionable fact that those who are equally acquainted with, and equally capable of appreciating and enjoying both, do give a most marked preference to the manner of existence which employs their higher faculties."[9] Even if intellectual pleasures are "placed so far above [physical pleasures] that [competent judges] prefer [them] even though knowing [them] to be attended with a greater amount of discontent," and even if competent judges "would not resign [a mental pleasure] for any quantity of the other pleasure which their nature is capable of," we would nonetheless *not* be "justified in ascribing to the preferred enjoyment a superiority in quality."

Suppose that competent judges prefer reading the writings of one philosopher (philosopher$_1$) to the writings of another philosopher (philosopher$_2$) and, further, that the writings of philosopher$_1$ are much more difficult to read. Competent judges might (almost) always choose the writings of philosopher$_1$, "even though knowing [them] to be attended with a greater amount of discontent [e.g., because their being so difficult causes the reader so much frustration]." Yet, Mill would claim that the pleasures derived from reading the writings of philosopher$_1$ would be better quantitatively *but not qualitatively* than the pleasures derived from reading the writings of philosopher$_2$, i.e., the pleasures of reading the two philosophers are of the same *kind*.

Or, suppose that competent judges almost always choose to eat chocolate chocolate fudge ice cream rather than vanilla ice cream "even though knowing it to be attended with more discontent [e.g., because the ice cream is more difficult to get out of the carton or because it costs more or because it melts more quickly]." We have not thus established that there is a difference in kind between the pleasures derived from eating the different flavors of ice cream, since the former may be a more intense pleasure *of the same kind* as the latter. So, too, the pleasure derived from reading the writings of philosopher$_1$ may be a more intense pleasure of the same kind as the pleasure derived from reading the writings of philosopher$_2$. However, if people might universally choose pleasure$_1$ over pleasure$_2$ because pleasure$_1$ is a more intense pleasure of the same kind, then even if Mill is correct that competent judges almost always choose intellectual pleasures over bodily ones, he does not thereby establish a difference in *kind* between the pleasures.

Mill would respond to the charge that judges might be choosing in light of intensity rather than quality by pointing out that when he is distinguishing between the higher and lower pleasures he is doing so "apart from the question of intensity."[10] If one had offered a competent judge a choice between a very intense, lower pleasure and a very mild, higher pleasure in order to test Mill's theory, one would have used an unfair and inaccurate test.

When Mill discusses the higher and lower pleasures, he is distinguishing between "the pleasures of the intellect, of the feelings and imagination and of the moral sentiment" on the one hand and the pleasures "of mere sensation" on the other.[11] He believes "the pleasures derived from the higher faculties to be preferable *in kind* . . . to those of which the animal nature, disjoined from the higher faculties, is susceptible."[12] He further believes that utilitarianism is compatible with the 'fact' that competent judges find the mental pleasures inherently better than the physical pleasures. He approves of the Epicurean response to the charge that their theory is worthy only of swine. "Epicureans have always answered, that it is not they, but their accusers, who represent human nature in a degrading light; since the accusation supposes human beings to be capable of no pleasures except those of which swine are capable." Were humans only satisfied by swinish pleasures, "the rule of life which is good enough for the one would be good enough for the other. The comparison of the Epicurean life to that of beasts is felt as degrading, precisely because a beast's pleasures do not satisfy a human being's conceptions of happiness."[13]

When Mill offers his higher/lower pleasure distinction, he does *not* argue that his is the only possible distinction in kind. Rather, he argues that it is *a* distinction in kind and that the mental pleasures are superior.

There are a variety of criteria by which one *might* make *qualitative* distinctions between pleasures. (It is an empirical question whether other kinds of pleasures might also be deemed 'higher'.) For example, one might argue that intensity is a criterion by which one can make qualitative distinctions between pleasures.[14]

Yet, Mill does not argue that the mental pleasures are more intense than the bodily pleasures. He simply claims that:

a.   competent judges will tend to prefer the mental pleasures to the bodily pleasures,

b.   the preference is based on the "pleasures inherent in [the mental pleasures] themselves,"[15] and

c.   utilitarianism is compatible with a world in which the above happens to be true.

Mill's higher/lower pleasure distinction might seem to be based on an unwarranted assumption, viz., that competent judges would indeed consistently choose the mental pleasures over the bodily ones. Such an assumption is by no means easy to grant. Were we to survey all academicians (or all people of letters, or all writers, artists, etc.), we would not find that almost all of them almost always choose the mental pleasures over the bodily ones, but would instead find that they sometimes choose one type of pleasure and sometimes choose the other. Indeed, ironically, we (as competent judges?) would probably look askance at someone who always chose the mental pleasures over the bodily ones and would claim that such a person would need to restructure his priorities at the very least.[16]

Yet, Mill can deflect the charge that competent judges do not always choose the higher pleasures. One of his criteria for establishing that a particular pleasure is higher than another is that it is "one to which all or almost all who have experience of both give a decided preference — *irrespective of any moral obligation to prefer it* [my italics]."[17] He writes, "On a question which is the best worth of two pleasures or which of two modes of existence is the most grateful to the feelings, *apart from its moral attributes and from its consequences* [my italics], the judgment of those who are qualified . . . must be admitted as final."[18] The higher pleasures are those which are almost universally deemed preferable by competent judges *when the consequences of the pleasures' being pursued have been bracketed.*

We consider the hypothetical survey discussed above. When these people are asked to choose between pursuing a higher and a lower pleasure, they are presumably considering a variety of factors *in addition* to the inherent worths of the pleasures, e.g., the relative intensities of the pleasures, the consequences of pursuing one pleasure rather than another, etc. Even were the judges to choose the lower pleasures on some occasions, that would not invalidate Mill's claim.

Merely because Mill can explain why competent judges sometimes choose the lower pleasures does not establish that he is correct about what competent judges would indeed say or do in a 'fair' test. That is an empirical question which need not be answered here, especially since utilitarianism can accommodate both the existence and the non existence of higher pleasures.

On the Judgments of Competent Judges

Mill admits that judges *whom he considers competent* do not always agree about which pleasures are more desirable, pointing out that "many who are capable of the higher pleasures, occasionally, under the influence of temptation, postpone them to the lower." Such practices are "quite compatible with a full appreciation of the intrinsic superiority of the higher," since people often "from infirmity of character, make their election for the nearer good, though they know it to be less valuable; and this no less when the choice is between two bodily pleasures than when it is between bodily and mental."[19]

Mill's comment might seem surprising for at least two reasons. If he admits that judges sometimes make mistakes, then there is a possibility that the *majority* of the judges might make a mistake. In that case, would he claim that the less valuable pleasure would somehow be (or become) the higher pleasure (because it had, indeed, been chosen by the majority)? Or would he admit that the majority had, indeed, made a mistake and that the "less" valuable pleasure was, indeed, less valuable?

Perhaps Mill would claim that we cannot look at what the majority of current competent judges would say when comparing pleasures. Rather, we must look at what past, present, and future competent judges would say or have said about these pleasures. Such a tack would allow him to claim that the majority of judges currently living might "from infirmity of character" make the wrong decision (and nonetheless the 'correct' pleasure would still remain higher). However, we then would not know whether the majority of currently living, 'competent' judges are making a mistake when they choose the *intellectual* pleasures as the higher pleasures.

If we can conceive of the majority's choosing the wrong pleasure, then we implicitly have an independent criterion of correctness which is not based on the actual choices of those judges. If we appeal to the 'past, present, and future judges' criterion, then we have simply pushed the problem one step back — we then need to ask whether the majority of past, present, and future judges could make a mistake, and, if so, what independent criterion should be used to verify the correctness of their judgments.

Mill argues that "the judgment of those who are qualified by knowledge of both [pleasures], or, if they differ, that of the majority among them, must be admitted as final."[20] We could use a different test, e.g., take a general survey, but it would obviously be unhelpful to ask individuals to evaluate pleasures which they had never even experienced. Given our alternatives, the most sensible method is to see what 'competent' judges say. Their judgment must be accepted as final, not because that judgment is infallible, but because there is no better test which we might instead employ — "there is no other tribunal to be referred to"[21] which would be as good as the "tribunal" of competent judges.

Mill's own position seems undermined when he claims that just as we should not be surprised by people's sometimes choosing the less desirable bodily pleasures over the more desirable ones, we should not be surprised by people's sometimes choosing the (less desirable) bodily pleasures over the (more desirable) mental pleasures. Supposedly, the bodily pleasures only differ in degree. We can understand how people could make such mistakes. However, were the pleasures to differ in kind, we might not expect that these kinds of wrong choices would be made. If Mill is correct that bodily pleasures only differ *quantitatively* from other bodily pleasures, whereas mental pleasures differ *qualitatively* from bodily pleasures, then people's making quantitative mistakes when choosing among bodily pleasures should not help us to understand how people can make qualitative mistakes and choose bodily pleasures over mental ones.

The above criticism implicitly suggests something like the following: Individuals will never even be tempted to make mistakes *between* kinds -- they will only make mistakes *within* kinds. As soon as an individual recognizes that one of her choices is a higher pleasure and the other a lower pleasure, she will immediately choose the former.[22] Yet, Mill does not picture the difference between *kinds* of pleasures in that way. The "rule for measuring quality against quantity [is] the preference felt by those who, in their opportunities of experience ... are best furnished with the means of comparison."[23] Quality is only one of several factors which will influence one's choice of pleasures. Since the determination of the higher and lower pleasures is "apart from the question of intensity,"[24] a mistake might easily be made when comparing an intense lower pleasure with a mild higher one.

Not only do judges sometimes make mistakes, they sometimes lose their competency to judge. "Capacity for the nobler feelings is in most natures a very tender plant, easily killed, not only by hostile influences, but by mere want of sustenance." People "lose their high aspirations as they lose their intellectual tastes, because they have not time or opportunity for indulging them." They "addict themselves to inferior pleasures, not because they deliberately prefer them, but because they are either the only ones to which they have access, or the only ones which they are any longer capable of enjoying."[25] Once we have weeded out all of the incompetent judges, we can determine "which is the best worth having of two pleasures, or which of two modes of existence is the most grateful to the feelings, apart from its moral attributes and its consequences,"[26] by looking at what the majority of competent judges say.

When weeding out incompetent judges, we must use some standard for competency — we need some way to determine when a judge has been exposed to enough higher pleasures or to higher pleasures often enough for her to be able to judge them appropriately. Presumably, the first 'taste' of poetry will not be sufficient to make the neophyte a competent judge. Yet, if we wait for the neophyte to start choosing the higher pleasures rather than the lower ones before we are willing to call her a competent judge, we will be 'stacking the deck' in favor of the higher pleasures. By the same token, if we start to disqualify formerly competent judges solely on the ground that they are no longer choosing the higher pleasures, we are again building in a bias in favor of the higher pleasures.[27]

In pointing out that judges can become incompetent relatively easily, Mill is not trying to 'stack the deck'. (Were he doing that, he would not worry about how to settle disagreements among competent judges.) He is simply offering an observation. People who were once competent judges may lose their ability to make the relevant distinctions if they do not continue to partake of the relevant pleasures. (Presumably, this applies to both higher *and* lower pleasures.) Individuals who (because of financial difficulties, for example) are no longer able to take the time to pursue the mental pleasures of reading poetry or philosophy will likely lose their discerning judgment.

Mill denies that "any one who has remained equally susceptible to both classes of pleasure ever knowingly and calmly preferred the lower."[28] Yet, it merits emphasis that since such an individual is choosing what promotes her *own* happiness, we should not assume without argument that the pursuit of the higher pleasures will promote the *general* happiness.

The principle of utility (as a moral principle) does not decree that our action is morally best if we maximize the happiness of an individual at the expense of the happiness of many others; rather, it decrees that our action is morally best if we maximize the general happiness. Indeed, it is crucial for an understanding of Mill's position that the above point be understood and appreciated. Mill's distinction between higher and lower pleasures "is by no means an indispensable condition to the acceptance to the utilitarian standard, for that standard is not the agent's own happiness, but the greatest amount of happiness altogether."[29]

Fortunately, individuals who pursue the higher pleasures will benefit both themselves and society. "[I]f it may possibly be doubted whether a noble character is always the happier for its nobleness, there can be no doubt that it makes other people happier, and that the world in general is immensely a gainer by it."[30]

Mill is making two *different* arguments for the higher pleasures:

(1) The individual is happier by pursuing the higher pleasures. While admitting that such a contention "may possibly be doubted," Mill makes quite clear that it should not be. "But the bare enunciation of such an absurdity as this last [that the individual would not be happier by pursuing the higher pleasures], renders refutation superfluous."[31]

(2) Society benefits by individuals' pursuing the higher pleasures. Indeed, Mill argues that *one (morally) should not pursue the higher pleasures if their pursuit would not promote the general good.*

An Incommensurability Problem

Suppose that Mill is correct that competent judges would choose *for themselves* the mental pleasures. We have a different and far more difficult problem if judges must decide which of two states of affairs is more valuable when each state involves differing numbers of people who are enjoying different pleasures.

For example, suppose that an agent could perform either of two actions. The first (action$_1$) would result in a few people's enjoying some mental pleasures. The second (action$_2$) would result in several people's enjoying some bodily pleasures. One who argues that the mental pleasures are so superior that competent judges almost invariably choose them might be expected to argue that action$_1$ would produce an intrinsically more valuable state of affairs, no matter how many people might enjoy physical pleasures should action$_2$ be performed.[32]

Comparisons of the intrinsic worths of different states of affairs become even more complicated when we consider pains as well. Mill realizes this and again appeals to the judge criterion. "Neither pains nor pleasures are homogeneous, and pain is always heterogeneous with pleasure. What is there to decide whether a particular pleasure is worth purchasing at the cost of a particular pain, except for the feelings and judgment of the experienced?"[33]

If a competent judge is to make judgments, she must make judgments in light of something.[34] She might use a Benthamite calculus and consider the pleasure's intensity, duration, certainty, propinquity, fecundity, purity and extent.[35] All of these dimensions would be combined to form a composite score. That score would be compared to the composite scores of other pleasures. (Mill would say that such comparisons would merely involve the "circumstantial advantages" of the pleasures.) Mill rejects the Benthamite calculus, believing that it does not include all of the relevant factors. He heartily objects to Bentham's claim that playing pushpin is as good as reading poetry if all of the circumstantial advantages are the same,[36] because he believes that another consideration must be added to the calculus, viz., the (inherent) quality of the pleasure.

Critics charge that Mill has abandoned utilitarianism by introducing his qualitative distinction.[37] However, this is false, as is illustrated below.

Suppose that we want to decide who is the best tennis player. We might compare the serves, forehands, backhands, netplay, etc., and then come up with a composite score. We might then compare the composite scores and make our determination. In so doing, we would not be denying that netplaying is qualitatively different from serving, just as no one is denying that intensity is qualitatively different from duration. Rather, we would be claiming that these qualitatively different criteria can be combined to yield a quantitative assessment. So, too, Mill is claiming that we can add an additional factor of 'inherent quality' to the other (circumstantial) factors and then make an assessment.

One of the reasons that discussions of the higher and lower pleasure doctrine are so confusing is that a number of issues are conflated. One issue involves which pleasures are inherently better. Another issue involves which pleasures I, as an individual, should pursue. Yet another issue involves which pleasures society should promote.

The competent judge can indicate which pleasures are inherently superior. However, when I am trying to determine which pleasures I should pursue, I will not merely consider which pleasures are inherently better. I will also consider the consquences of my pursuing one pleasure rather than another. If I am a good utilitarian and spend much time engaging in very enjoyable contemplation which I know will benefit no one other than myself, *I will feel guilty.* (Moral considerations are not entertained when determining the *inherently* better pleasure, but they are of course entertained when determining which pleasures the individual should pursue.) "No respect is due to any employment of the intellect which does not tend to the good of mankind. *It is precisely on a level with any idle amusement* [my italics], and should be condemned as waste of time, if carried beyond the limit within which amusement is permissible."38

Here, Mill is not contradicting himself and claiming that employment of the intellect is as low a pleasure as any idle amusement. Rather, he is claiming that a pleasure's being inherently superior does not (alone) justify its being pursued.

Intellectual endeavors should be pursued, at least partly because one never knows when such endeavors might prove to be beneficial. "Nobody knows what knowledge will prove to be of use, and what is destined to be useless. The most that can be said is that some kinds are of more certain, and above all, of more present utility than others. How often the most important practical results have been the remote consequences of studies which no one would have expected to lead to them!"39 Here, Mill is justifying the pursuit of the intellectual pleasures by appealing to the good consequences which would (or might) thereby result, *not* by appealing to the intrinsic worth of the higher pleasures.

The position that the higher pleasures are intrinsically more valuable than the lower ones *might* have certain dissatisfying implications. A different theorist who held such a view might not hold, as Mill does, that each individual *herself* is the best judge of what will make her happiest.40 Such a theorist might claim that only competent judges can know which pleasures individuals would be happiest in pursuing. He could further claim that because the promotion of happiness is the test by which human actions are determined to be morally right or wrong and because the higher pleasures involve a higher or better happiness, actions which involve or promote the higher pleasures are morally preferable to those which involve or promote the lower pleasures. He might even claim that we have a moral duty to seek the higher pleasures. Indeed, he might argue that the State should only allow people to pursue whichever pleasures they desired when:

1. they were deciding which mental pleasures to pursue, or
2. they were incapable of pursuing mental pleasures.

Mill does not argue that the State should force people to pursue the higher pleasures. Nor does he argue that we always have a moral duty to pursue the higher pleasures. Nor does he argue that one's acting in ways which do not promote the higher pleasures is always morally wrong. That is because the above position (the position in which one is said to have a moral obligation to seek the higher pleasures) is *not* the *only* position which is compatible with a higher pleasure doctrine.[41]

One can recognize the intrinsic worth of the mental pleasures, but base social policy on the *intrinsic and extrinsic* worth of those pleasures.[42] When Mill recommends a particular social policy, he considers its *consequences*. He does not claim, for example, that society must force people to pursue the intrinsically more valuable higher pleasures.

We consider some of Mill's comments about education. He is a champion of compulsory education and, further, is unwilling to let the uneducated decide for themselves what they should learn. "The uncultivated cannot be competent judges of cultivation. Those who most need to be made wiser and better, usually desire it least, and if they desired it, would be incapable of finding the way to it by their own lights."[43] Yet, clearly, one need not hold a higher pleasure doctrine to believe that the uneducated will be unable to make the proper decision with respect to what they should learn.

Presumably, one would not accuse Mill of mandating that the higher pleasures always be pursued merely because he wants to assure that individuals will have a certain degree of education. Certainly, there are passages which support Mill's having been somewhat elitist. For example, he argues, "If, with equal virtue, one is superior to the other in knowledge and intelligence, or if, with equal intelligence, one excels the other in virtue, the opinion, the judgment of the higher moral or intellectual being is worth more than that of the inferior." However, there, Mill is only talking about judgments concerning public issues. He is not claiming that people should be forced by others to spend their time reading philosophy.

Mill makes quite clear that in "an affair which concerns only one of two persons, . . . one is entitled to follow his own opinion, however much wiser the other may be than himself." The more intelligent person's opinion is to be weighed more heavily than the less intelligent person's opinion when "we are speaking of things which equally concern them both; where, if the more ignorant does not yield his share of the matter to the guidance of the wiser man, the wiser man must resign his to that of the more ignorant."[44]

On Self-cultivation and Choice-making

Mill denies that the pleasures which would satisfy a brutish individual would also satisfy an individual of refined taste.

> Few human creatures would consent to be changed into any of the lower animals, for a promise of the fullest allowance of a beast's pleasures; no intelligent human being would consent to be a fool, no instructed person would be an ignoramus, no person of feeling and conscience would be selfish and base, even though they should be persuaded that the fool, the dunce, or the rascal is better satisfied with his lot than they are with theirs. They would not resign what they possess more than he, for the most complete satisfaction of all the desires which they have in common with him.[45]

Not appreciating Mill has a particular set of pleasures in mind when he talks about what would satisfy a person of refined taste, critics think that Mill's higher pleasure doctrine establishes the intrinsic worth of those pleasures which lead to one's having a sense of one's independence, self-determination, self-worth, etc. (as if people of 'unrefined' taste would not also have and value these qualities). While Mill believes that one's having a sense of these things is important, his higher pleasures doctrine *does not* establish that the higher pleasures are those which promote or are necessary for these qualities.[46] Were he to have approved of the higher pleasures for those reasons, he would have been arguing that the higher pleasures were *extrinsically* superior to the lower pleasures. When Mill argues for the intrinsic superiority of the higher pleasures, he argues that they are superior, even *excluding* their promoting independence and self-determination and even *excluding* their being necessary for the happiness of man as a creature of elevated faculties. Mill's argument is solely based on the *inherent* worths of the pleasures being compared.

Mill is not simply offering a self-actualization account in which each individual must find for herself those pleasures which she deems 'higher'.[47] He has a definite set of 'higher' pleasures in mind, even if another individual does not agree with that assessment and even if those pleasures are not peculiarly suited to that other individual's nature. "A cultivated mind ... finds sources of inexhaustible interest in all that surrounds it; in the objects of nature, the achievements of art, the imaginations of poetry, the incidents of history, the ways of mankind past and present, and their prospects in the future."[48] Here, Mill extolls the virtues of science, poetry, history, psychology, sociology, etc. He is not extolling the virtues of whichever pleasures happen to be best suited to each individual nature.

While the higher pleasures are those which are *intrinsically* superior, they are *also* extrinsically superior because they better promote both the individual's happiness and the general happiness. However, their extrinsic superiority is a contingent 'fact' and is unrelated to their being higher pleasures.

A separate argument also supporting the *extrinsic* superiority of the higher pleasures is that individuals' having the *belief* that the higher pleasures are *intrinsically* superior would *itself* promote utility, because individuals would then be more likely to pursue those pleasures. Mill makes an analogous argument with respect to virtue, suggesting that utilitarian moralists "not only place virtue at the very head of the things which are good as means to the ultimate end, but they also recognize as a *psychological fact* [my italics] the possibility of its being, to the individual, a good in itself without looking to any end beyond it." Thus, the individual might view the pursuit of virtue as an end in itself. Utilitarians would approve of this, because that state of mind is "most conducive to the general happiness."[49] So, too, individuals' looking at the mental pleasures as intrinsically valuable is acceptable to utilitarians who recognize "as a psychological fact" that individuals' doing so will most likely lead to the promotion of humankind's utility. However, that does not make the higher pleasures *intrinsically* valuable. Their worth then lies in their promoting the utility of humankind.

Mill's higher pleasure argument does not rely on these pleasures' promoting some desirable end. Nor does it rely on the benefit produced by our believing that they are intrinsically superior. His argument is that the higher pleasures are *intrinsically* superior to the lower pleasures when certain factors (e.g., intensity, duration, consequences, etc.) have been bracketed.

Mill argues persuasively that one's pursuing the mental pleasures will tend to promote the long-term interests of humankind. The pursuit of these pleasures will result in a number of improvements in a variety of technologies which will greatly improve the health and increase the happiness of humankind. Thus, the mental pleasures are better$_E$ than the physical ones in that the mental pleasures are more likely to promote long-term utility. However, one must not conflate Mill's argument that the mental pleasures are better$_E$ than the physical pleasures with his argument that the mental pleasures are better$_I$ than the physical pleasures. The arguments are distinct and only happen to pick out the same set of pleasures as superior. (It might have turned out that the better$_I$ pleasures were not the better$_E$ pleasures).

Mill's argument that utilitarianism is compatible with the existence of higher and lower pleasures has caused a great deal of controversy, at least in part, because his claims are often exaggerated or misunderstood. He does not believe that the higher pleasures are always preferable to the lower pleasures regardless of their relative intensities. He does not believe that the mental pleasures should always be pursued. Indeed, he believes that the good of humankind might require that certain intrinsically superior pleasures, e.g., contemplative pleasures, sometimes be foregone because their pursuit might contribute greatly to the individual's happiness but only negligibly to the happiness of humankind.

Mill suggests that utilitarianism is compatible with the existence (and, for that matter, the non existence) of inherently superior pleasures. The best way to determine which pleasures are higher and which lower is simply to ask (or, perhaps, to watch) those individuals who have experienced them.

The inherent qualities of pleasures will be included in utilitarian calculations, although not to the extent suggested by Mill's critics. In the next chapter, we shall see that Mill uses the long-term interests of humankind as his standard for moral evaluation (where that standard includes the quality of the pleasures). By doing so, Mill can account for both the moral and the intrinsic worth of the higher pleasures, while nonetheless avoiding some of the undesirable positions sometimes attributed to him.

NOTES

1. John Stuart Mill, *Utilitarianism*, Ch. 2, Par. 2. *Collected Works of John Stuart Mill* (henceforth referred to as *CW*), John Robson ed. (Toronto: University of Toronto Press, 1969), Vol. 10, p. 210.

2. *Ibid.*, Ch. 2, Par. 4, p. 211.

3. *Ibid.*, Ch. 2, Par. 3, p. 210.

4. *Ibid.*, Ch. 2, Par. 5, p. 211.

5. Were competent judges (whose decisions did not involve considerations of consequences or morality) to choose the bodily pleasures consistently, Mill would call the bodily pleasures intrinsically better. However, he would argue that we would have to be very different from what we in fact are for this to happen.

6. See G. E. Moore, *Ethics* (Oxford: Oxford University Press, 1971), p. 96.

7. Martin and Berger both emphasize that Mill, in talking about the pleasures which competent judges choose, is offering a *test* to determine which are the higher pleasures rather than a definition of higher pleasures. See Rex Martin, "A Defense of Mill's Qualitative Hedonism," *Philosophy* 46 (1972), p. 144; and Fred R. Berger, *Happiness Justice and Freedom: The Moral and Political Philosophy of John Stuart Mill* (Berkeley: University of California Press, 1984), p. 39.

8. The literature on this issue is voluminous. See, e.g., G. E. Moore, *Principia Ethica* (Cambridge: Cambridge University Press, 1971), p. 80; Rem B. Edwards, *Pleasures and Pains: A Theory of Qualitative Hedonism* (Ithaca: Cornell University Press, 1979); Norman O. Dahl, "Is Mill's Hedonism Inconsistent?" in *Studies in Ethics*, American Philosophical Quarterly Monograph Series, Nicholas Rescher ed. (Oxford: Basil Blackwell, 1973), pp. 37-54.

9. *Utilitarianism*, Ch. 2, Par. 6, p. 211.

10. *Ibid.*, Ch. 2, Par. 8, p. 213.

11. *Ibid.*, Ch. 2, Par. 4, p. 211.

12. *Ibid.*, Ch. 2, Par. 8, p. 213.

13. *Ibid.*, Ch. 2, Par. 4, p. 210.

14. Although Dahl assumes that intensity is a quantitative difference, he implies that a good case could be made for its being a qualitative difference. "There is a genuine question, I think, over whether intensity of pleasure is a qualitative rather than a quantitative difference of pleasure, but I shall simply assume that it is a quantitative difference." Dahl, "Is Mill's Hedonism Inconsistent?" p. 38.

For a different way to distinguish qualitatively among pleasures, see Edwards, *Pleasures and Pains: A Theory of Qualitative Hedonism*. But see my "Mill's Higher and Lower Pleasures Reexamined," *International Studies in Philosophy* 17 (1985), pp. 51-72. It will be clear from this chapter that my understanding of Mill's position has changed, although I still subscribe to my comments on Edwards's position.

Some critics mistakenly believe that, for Mill, intensity is one of the criteria by which *qualitative* distinctions can be made. Ebenstein, for example, interprets Mill to be claiming that the intensity of a pleasure is a mark of *qualitative* difference. See Larry Ebenstein, "Mill's Theory of Utility," *Philosophy* 60 (1985), pp. 539-543. However, Ebenstein does not show why differing durations would be a mark of a quantitative distinction between pleasures while differing intensities would be a mark of a qualitative distinction between pleasures. Nor does he show why the *intensity* of a pleasure is related to its intrinsic nature, whereas the *duration* of a pleasure is not.

Clearly, Mill thinks that intensity is a quantitative difference. He explicitly states that he wants to offer a different argument from the standard utilitarian claim that intellectual pleasures are longer-lasting and more intense than bodily pleasures and hence are more desirable. "When, therefore, those feelings and judgment declare the pleasure derived from the higher pleasures to be preferable *in kind, apart from the question of intensity* [my italics] ... they are entitled on this subject to the same regard." *Utilitarianism*, Ch. 2, Par. 8, p. 213.

15. *Utilitarianism*, Ch. 2, Par. 2, p. 210.

16. For a related argument, see Benjamin Gibbs, "Higher and Lower Pleasures," *Philosophy* 61 (1986), pp. 50-52.

17. *Utilitarianism*, Ch. 2, Par. 5, p. 211.

18. *Ibid.*, Ch. 2, Par. 8, p. 213.

19. *Ibid.*, Ch. 2, Par. 7, p. 212.

20. *Ibid.*, Ch. 2, Par. 8, p. 213.

21. *Ibid.*, Ch. 2, Par. 8, p. 213.

22. In a different context, Wolf talks about a desire which "is apt to have the character not just of a stronger, but of a *higher* desire [my italics], which does not merely successfully compete with one's other desires but which rather subsumes or demotes them." Susan Wolf, "Moral Saints," *Journal of Philosophy* 79 (1982), p. 424. Mill suggests that the higher pleasure sometimes not only does *not* demote the lower pleasure, but does not even successfully compete with it.

23. *Utilitarianism*, Ch. 2, Par. 10, p. 214.

24. *Ibid.*, Ch. 2, Par. 8, p. 213.

25. *Ibid.*, Ch. 2, Par. 7, p. 213.

26. *Ibid.*, Ch. 2, Par. 8, p. 213.

27. In a different context, Rawls warns against determining competence by looking at what a judge says in particular cases, precisely because Rawls wants to avoid problems of circularity. See John Rawls, "Outline of a Decision Procedure for Ethics," *Philosophical Review* 60 (1951), p. 180.

28. *Utilitarianism*, Ch. 2, Par. 7, p. 213.

29. *Ibid.*, Ch. 2, Par. 9, p. 213.

30. *Ibid.*, pp. 213-214.

31. *Ibid.*, p. 214.

32. For related comments, see F. H. Bradley, "Pleasure for Pleasure's Sake" in *Ethical Studies*, Introduction Ralph Ross (Indianapolis: Bobbs-Merrill, 1951), pp. 58 ff.

33. *Utilitarianism*, Ch. 2, Par. 8, p. 213.

34. See Wendy Donner, "John Stuart Mill's Concept of Liberty," *Dialogue* 22 (1983), p. 492.

35. See Jeremy Bentham, *An Introduction to the Principles of Morals and Legislation*, Introduction Laurence LaFleur (New York: Hafner Publishing Co., 1948), p. 30.

36. Bentham writes, "Prejudice apart, the game of push-pin is of equal value with the arts and sciences of music and poetry. If the game of push-pin furnish more pleasure, it is more valuable than either." *The Rationale of Reward*, reprinted in *The Works of Jeremy Bentham*, John Bowring ed. (New York: Russell and Russell, 1962), Vol. 2, p. 253.

37. For related comments, see Donner, "John Stuart Mill's Concept of Liberty," p. 489.

38. John Stuart Mill, "Auguste Comte and Positivism," *CW* Vol. 10, p. 353.

39. *Ibid.*

40. Riley at the very least flirts with the idea of the guardian's imposing his own decisions on non-guardians *in the name (or at least with the alleged blessing) of Mill.* See Jonathan Riley, *Liberal Utilitarianism* (Cambridge: Cambridge University Press, 1988), p. 115.

41. See John Gray, *Mill on Liberty: a Defence* (London: Routledge and Kegan Paul, 1983), p. 73.

42. For related comments, see Donner, "John Stuart Mill's Concept of Liberty," p. 489. See also James Griffin, *Well-Being* (Oxford: Oxford University Press, 1986), pp. 49 and 123.

43. John Stuart Mill, *Principles of Political Economy*, Book V, Chap. 11, Sec. 8, Par. 1, *CW* Vol. 3, p. 947.

44. John Stuart Mill, *Considerations on Representative Government*, Ch. 8, Par. 8, *CW* Vol. 19, p. 473.

45. *Utilitarianism*, Ch. 2, Par. 6, p. 211.

46. Neither Berger nor Gray seems to appreciate this. See Berger, *Happiness, Justice and Freedom*, p. 40; Gray, *Mill on Liberty: a Defence*, pp. 70 ff.

47. Gray does not seem to appreciate this. See Gray, *Mill on Liberty: a Defence*, pp. 86-87.

48. *Utilitarianism*, Ch. 2, Par. 13, p. 216.

49. *Ibid.*, Ch. 4, Par. 5, p. 235.

CHAPTER TWO

Mill's Moral View

Both the quantity and the quality of pleasures must be considered in utility calculations. However, Mill's theory needs further explication, since we must discuss *whose* happiness should be promoted. For example, Mill might claim that an individual acts rightly if her action promotes her own happiness. Or, he might claim that an individual acts rightly if her action promotes the happiness of the society in which she lives. Mill chooses neither of these, instead suggesting that the promotion of humankind's utility is paramount.

To make matters more complicated, Mill writes ambiguously when he says that actions are morally right insofar as they promote happiness. He might mean that an agent acts rightly if she performs an *action* which will promote utility. Or, he might mean that an agent acts rightly if she performs an action which is in accord with a *rule*, the general acceptance and following of which will promote utility. Most of the time, this distinction is unimportant. An action which will promote utility will also be an action which is in accord with a rule, the general following of which will promote utility. Sometimes, however, the action which will promote utility is not in accord with a rule, the general following of which will promote utility. At these times, a choice must be made.

Mill as Utilitarian: Act or Rule?

Whether one is an act-utilitarian or a rule-utilitarian, one believes that the principle of utility has a special status. It cannot be viewed as on a par with other moral rules because it is the principle upon which the whole moral system is based. The act-utilitarian believes that the principle of utility has a special status in that it is the principle by which all actions should be judged — if there is ever a conflict between the dictates of the principle of utility and any other principle or rule, the dictates of the principle of utility must be followed.

The rule-utilitarian believes that the principle of utility has a special status in that it should never be directly applied to actions. Instead, it should only be used to determine which rules people should accept and follow, i.e., those rules the general acceptance and following of which would promote the most good.[1] Once these rules are ascertained, people should always act in accord with them.

Some writers insist that Mill is an act-utilitarian (someone who believes that the rightness or wrongness of an action depends solely upon the consequences of performing that action). Act-utilitarians claim, for example, that the "rightness or wrongness of keeping a promise on a particular occasion depends only on the consequences of keeping or of breaking the promise on that particular occasion."[2] If keeping the promise would maximize utility, then the promise should be kept. If breaking the promise would maximize utility, then the promise should be broken.

Others argue that Mill is a rule-utilitarian (someone who believes that a particular action is right if it is in accord with a moral rule, wrong if it is against a moral rule). A moral rule is a rule which, if generally followed, maximizes utility.

There seems to be evidence to support both sides. Yet, most of the statements which allegedly support Mill's rule-utilitarian position either give outright support to or are consistent with an act-utilitarian position. Ultimately, this debate will be seen to have been given undue importance in the recent literature. Mill would not have ascribed to either act-utilitarianism or rule-utilitarianism as they are currently understood. Act-utilitarians are too willing to break moral rules in their quest to maximize utility.[3] Rule-utilitarians are too rigid either in not building in enough exceptions into their rules or in insisting on following those rules when doing so would clearly be disutility-producing. Mill does not want secondary rules broken readily and hence does not want to characterize them as merely 'guides' or 'rules of thumb'. He also does not want secondary rules followed if doing so would clearly be disutility-producing, which is why he is more appropriately labeled an act-utilitarian than a rule-utilitarian.

There is an even more important reason why Mill is not accurately labeled as a standard act-utilitarian, much less a standard rule-utilitarian. While he believes that the act which maximizes utility is right, *he does not believe that an action must be utility-maximizing in order to be right.* That point will be explained in future chapters. In this chapter, there will be an examination of Mill's view of the relations among acts, rules, and the principle of utility.

Mill as Act-utilitarian

In *A System of Logic*, Mill denies that we can construct a perfect moral system. Basically, he offers two points:

1. Moral rules are extremely difficult to formulate because we cannot anticipate all of the circumstances which might obtain in future situations. If we cannot thus anticipate, then we will be unable to devise rules to cover all cases and our rules will be imperfect.

2. Even if we could formulate rules to include all of the appropriate exceptions, these rules would be so complicated that most people would not be able to learn and remember them.[4]

For example, generally, one should not steal. However, stealing is sometimes permissible; indeed, "to save a life, it may not only be allowable, but a duty, to steal, or take by force, the necessary food or medicine."[5] Doubtless, there are other extenuating circumstances in which stealing would also be permissible. Thus, because of the difficulties involved (a) in formulating perfect rules, and (b) in learning and remembering them, we must view moral rules as very good guides, as very useful rules of thumb. Moral rules are not principles which must always be obeyed, they are rules which should be obeyed most of the time. However, it is the act-utilitarian rather than the rule-utilitarian who uses moral rules as (even very useful) rules of thumb.[6]

One must "know what are the practical contingencies which require a modification of the rule, or *which are altogether exceptions to it* [my italics]." Mill argues that "rules of conduct point out the manner in which it will be least perilous to act, where time or means do not exist for analyzing the actual circumstances of the case, or where we cannot trust our judgment in estimating them."[7]

When we are considering whether to follow a rule, we must consider that:

1. Rules are imperfect. There are times at which we should disobey rules in favor of following courses of action which will produce much better results.

2. Our present rules have stood the test of time — they have been proven to be effective through the ages. We must think twice (and, perhaps, twice again) before disregarding a rule.

Mill argues that rules should occasionally be disobeyed and thus he cannot be accurately labeled a rule-utilitarian. However, he gives some very helpful advice: rules can be wrong but usually are not.

When one, as an unbiassed, knowledgeable, careful deliberator, is *certain* that following the appropriate rule would produce bad results, one should definitely disobey the rule. Mill criticizes those who would insist upon following a rule despite their knowing that a different action would yield much better results. The person "who goes by rules rather than by their reasons, like the old-fashioned German tacticians who were vanquished by Napolean, or the physician who preferred that his patients should die by rule rather than recover contrary to it, is rightly judged to be a mere pedant, and the slave of his formulas."[8]

Mill is not merely arguing that improper rules should not be used; he is suggesting that the world is such a complicated place that we will be unable to devise rules which will cover all of the situations which a doctor might face. So, too, we will be unable to devise rules to cover all of the situations which a moral agent will have to face.[9] Our complicated world sometimes warrants ignoring the rules and judging the particular case according to the principle of utility. Rules of thumb are good for most cases most of the time. In those cases in which one knows that the application of the 'appropriate' rule would not promote utility, one should ignore the rule and promote utility instead.

Mill clearly favors the act-utilitarian view. In "Bentham," he writes, "Insofar as Bentham's adoption of the principle of utility induced him to fix his attention upon the consequences of actions as the consideration determining their morality, he was indisputably in the right path."[10] In a review of Taylor's *Statesman*, Mill comments, "To admit the balance of consequences as a test of right and wrong, necessarily implies the possibility of exceptions to any derivative rule of morality which may be adduced from the test."[11]

These passages explicitly show Mill's commitment to a type of act-utilitarianism. Further, when we consider that Mill is accepting the "creed which accepts as the foundation of morals, Utility, or the *Greatest Happiness Principle* [my italics],"[12] we have reason to believe that Mill's principle involves the *maximization* rather than merely the *promotion* of utility, i.e., Mill believes that action morally best which maximizes rather than merely promotes utility. He argues that the utilitarian standard involves the "*greatest* [my italics] amount of happiness altogether,"[13] and that "[a]ccording to the Greatest Happiness Principle, . . . the ultimate end . . . is an existence exempt *as far as possible* from pain and *as rich as possible* in enjoyments [my italics]."[14] Here, too, Mill is offering a maximizing condition. However, Mill does not believe that *only* those actions which maximize utility are morally right.[15]

Mill's Apparent Rule-utilitarianism

Some critics interpret Mill to be claiming that an act is right if it is in accord with a rule the general acceptance and following of which will maximize utility, i.e., they claim that Mill is a rule-utilitarian.[16] They support their interpretation by citing Mill's claim that one can accept the principle of utility as the ultimate principle and yet still accept secondary rules as the rules by which one should live.[17]

Mill offers an often-cited analogy. "To inform a traveler respecting the place of his ultimate destination is not to forbid the use of landmarks and direction-posts on the way. The proposition that happiness is the end and aim of morality does not mean that no road ought to be laid down to that goal, or that persons going thither should not be advised to take one direction than another."[18] Just as a traveler can use landmarks to reach his final destination point, one can use secondary rules to help one maximize happiness.

Yet, Mill's example is somewhat misleading, since one's always using landmarks or secondary rules might be counter-productive.[19] From a special vantage point, one might see a much better route than is indicated by the direction-post. So, too, for example, although lying is usually immoral and we are 'directed' to speak truthfully, we might realize that, because of certain extenuating circumstances, lying would be morally permissible. Our special vantage point, i.e., our knowledge of the extenuating circumstances, would allow us to ignore the rule and instead to maximize utility.

We should not 'forbid the use of landmarks and direction-posts'. However, act- and rule-utilitarians agree that such aids should not be forbidden; they disagree about whether their use should be required. Quite simply, if the traveler knows of a much better route, the act-utilitarian will suggest that he take that route, while the rule-utilitarian will suggest that the traveler follow the direction-posts.

Individuals should not "test each individual action directly by the first principle [i.e., the principle of utility]," both because such a process would be too time-consuming and because such a process would sometimes result in the individuals' acting wrongly, e.g., because they miscalculated the utilities involved. Generally, secondary rules are the ones by which individuals should live.[20] However, if there is a conflict between a secondary rule and the principle of utility, one must follow the dictates of the principle of utility.

In a different passage, Mill seems to explicitly support a rule-utilitarian position. "In the case of abstinences indeed — of things which people forbear to do from moral considerations, though the consequences in the particular case might be beneficial — it would be unworthy of an intelligent agent not to be consciously aware that the action is of a class which, if practiced generally, would be generally injurious, and that this is the ground of the obligation to abstain from it."[21]

Mill seems to be saying that an action is wrong if the class of actions to which the action belongs should not be performed. A class of actions should not be performed if, were the actions generally performed, bad consequences would result. Mill's looking at whether an action is "of a class which, if practiced generally, would be generally injurious" as "the ground of the obligation to abstain from it," is similar to one's looking at an action to see whether it is in accord with some rule and then looking at the rule to see whether its generally being followed would be harmful.[22]

This reasoning seems rather confused. He acknowledges that the ultimate goal is to promote utility and that the action in question would be beneficial. Then, he objects that the action is of a class which, if practiced generally, would be harmful. However, the agent is not wondering whether she, generally, should perform this action; she is wondering whether she should perform it this particular time. Thus, as soon as Mill raises his objection, the agent will rightly respond, "But I don't want to do it all of the time. I want to do it just once."

Mill might then explain that the agent's performing this action would increase the probability that other people would also perform it. Others might see her performing the action or they might see the results of the action. In either case, they, too, would want to perform the action in question. Mill would then point out that many people's performing the action would be harmful. Thus, for fear of promoting the performance of the action at non-beneficial times, the agent should refrain from performing the action this time. In order for anyone to be justified in performing the action this time, the benefits must outweigh the harms produced by the agent's promoting others to perform the action at non-beneficial times.

The above analysis renders Mill's reasoning more understandable. Mill is not saying that the action is forbidden merely because it belongs to a class of actions which, if generally practiced, would be harmful. Such a claim is not very convincing. If an action were acceptable only if its general performance would produce good consequences, then many noble and praiseworthy activities, e.g., dying for one's family, country, religion, etc., would not be acceptable. Indeed, the uniqueness of an action can be part of its utility. For example, in military maneuvers or card play, a ploy may be successful in part because it is so unexpected.

Mill is pointing out that actions have various subtle effects which individuals often overlook when trying to ascertain the effects of a particular action. For example, someone might not consider that:

1. Other people will see that he has broken the rule. Their respect for the rule will be lessened and they will become more likely to break the rule at non-optimal times.
2. Seeing that the rule has been broken, other people will feel less secure that the rule will be followed when it should be. Even if these people realize that the rule was broken to promote greater utility and thus they will not be tempted to break the rule when such an infraction would cause disutility, they might not be so confident in their neighbors' perspicacity. Even though they understand why this particular rule-breaking was proper and thus would not be more likely to break the rules improperly, they could not be sure that others would so understand. Insecurity would result — an obvious disutility.[23]
3. Seeing that this rule has been broken, people will be more likely to break *other* rules at inappropriate times.

Mill is not as clear about the act/rule distinction as one might like. He argues that there is a "necessity that some rule, of a nature simple enough to be easily understood and remembered, should not only be laid down for guidance, but necessarily observed, in order that the various persons concerned may know what they have to expect." Mill believes that "the inconvenience of uncertainty [which results when rules are viewed as merely providing guidance] . . . [is] a greater evil than that which may possibly arise, in a minority of cases, from the imperfect adaptation of the rule to those cases."[24]

Mill seems to be offering a rule-utilitarian account in that the rules should be "necessarily observed." However, the reason that rules should necessarily be observed is that their non-observance will cause insecurity. If Mill is afraid that a particular act of rule-breaking will cause net disutility, then he should not claim that rules must be observed, but that rules should be broken only when the various disutilites (including the increased insecurity) would be outweighed by the utility of the rule-breaking. Indeed, in the next paragraph he amends the claim that rules should necessarily be observed by arguing that "the license of deviating from [the rules], if such be ever permitted, should be confined to definite classes of cases, and of a very peculiar and extreme nature."[25]

In a different work, Mill argues that the "admission of exceptions to rules is a necessity equally felt in all ethical systems of morality. To take an obvious instance, the rule against homicide [and] the rule against deceiving . . . are suspended against enemies in the field, and partially against malefactors in private life." The particular circumstances may *require* one to do something which is normally *forbidden*. "That the moralities arising from the special circumstances of the action may be so important as to overrule those arising from the class of acts to which it belongs, perhaps to take it out of the category of virtues into that of crimes, or *vice versa*, is a liability common to all ethical systems."[26] Here, Mill seems quite clearly to be advocating an act-utilitarian line. However, on the next page, he claims, "The essential is, that the exception should be itself a general rule; so that, being of definite extent, and not leaving the expediencies to the partial judgment of the agent in the individual case, it may not shake the stability of the wider rule in the cases to which the reason of the exception does not extend."[27]

Again, Mill is afraid that the stability of the rule will be undermined and that people will disobey the rule at inappropriate times. "No one who does not thoroughly know the modes of action which common experience has sanctioned is capable of judging of the circumstances which require a departure from those ordinary modes of action."[28] Agents must not haphazardly ignore rules, especially considering that their judgment might be biassed.[29] Were secondary moral rules *simply* rules of thumb, people adopting this theory would break rules too often.

Nonetheless, Mill ultimately holds that utility must be promoted. He believes that "where time or means do . . . exist for analyzing the actual circumstances of the cases, [and] where we [can] trust our judgment in estimating them,"[30] we must ignore the rule and promote utility. We should never perform an action which we (reliably) know to be disutility-producing. A man who does so "cannot discharge himself from moral responsibility by pleading that he had the general rule in his favor."[31]

Mill explains his position in a letter. "I agree with you that the right way of testing actions by their consequences, is to test them by the natural consequences of the particular action, and not by those which would follow if everyone did the same. But, for the most part, the consideration of what would happen if every one did the same, is the only means we have of discovering the tendency of the act in the particular case."[32] In order to look at the effects of a particular action, "[w]e must look at [the action] multiplied, and in large masses."[33] Thus, the insecurity which Mill fears would be produced by rule-breakings must be attributed to particular *acts* of rule-breaking. The destabilizing of rules, i.e., the increasing of the likelihood that rules will be broken at improper times, is an effect of particular *acts* of rule-breaking. These effects must be considered whenever one proposes to break a secondary rule.

When Mill considers consequences, he *includes* the often under-appreciated considerations of character. He criticizes Bentham for not having considered whether "the act or habit in question, though not in itself necessarily pernicious, may not form part of a *character* essentially pernicious, or at least essentially deficient in some quality eminently conducive to the 'greatest happiness',"[34] and Sedgwick for not having recognized that utilitarians also believe that "an essential part of the morality or immorality of an action or a rule of action consists in its influence upon the agent's own mind: upon his susceptibilities of pleasure or pain, upon the general direction of his thoughts, feelings, and imagination, or upon some particular association."[35]

Secondary rules are important because their generally being accepted and followed will tend to promote good character. They will also promote security, which is quite important. A "change, which has always hitherto characterized, and will assuredly continue to characterize, the progress of civilized society, is a continual increase of the security of person and property."[36] Mill writes, "Security of person and property and equal justice between individuals are the first needs of society and the primary ends of government."[37]

Another important feature of secondary rules is that they give specific dictates about how to act, which is necessary because "utility, or happiness, [is] much too complex and indefinite an end to be sought except through the medium of various secondary ends."[38] Individuals "who adopt utility as a standard seldom apply it truly except through the secondary principles."[39]

Yet, one would be wrong to think that it is obvious what the secondary rules should be, *even given a particular end* (e.g., the promotion of general utilty). "The grand consideration is, not what any person regards as the ultimate end of human conduct, but through what intermediate ends he holds his ultimate end is attainable, and should be pursued; and in these there is a nearer agreement between some who differ, than between some who agree in their conception of the ultimate end."[40]

Once the secondary principles have been formulated, Mill *claims* that one can pretty readily decide which principle is appropriate in any particular case. "There is no case of moral obligation in which some secondary principle is not involved; and if only one, there can seldom be any real doubt which one it is, in the mind of any person by whom the principle itself is recognized." Indeed, he somewhat surprisingly further argues that "only in these cases of conflict between secondary principles is it requisite that first principles should be appealed to."[41]

Yet, one's having the ability to pick out the appropriate secondary rule does not imply that one has the ability to apply it correctly. The "common error of men [is] of sticking to their rules in a case whose specialties either take it out of the class to which the rules are applicable, or require a special adaptation of them."[42] Thus, it "is one thing to be master of general principles, and to be able to reason from them under assumed hypothetical circumstances: it is another thing to possess the talent of justly appreciating actual circumstances, so as to regulate the application of principles to any given case."[43]

Mill is a little misleading when he claims that the principle of utility should be appealed to only in cases involving conflicts between secondary rules, since such conflicts are easy to generate. We consider the case of lying. One secondary rule is 'Never lie'. Another secondary rule is 'Never lie unless doing so would promote utility and telling the truth would promote disutility'. In a case in which lying would promote utility and telling the truth would promote disutility, we have a conflict between rules and must appeal to the principle of utility.

"If evil will arise in any specific case from our telling truth, we are forbidden by a law of morality from doing that evil: we are forbidden by another law of morality from telling falsehood. Here then are two laws of morality in conflict, and we cannot satisfy both of them." When there is a conflict between two rules, we must "resort to the primary test of all right and wrong, and . . . make a specific calculation of the good or evil consequences, as fully and impartially as we can."[44]

Basically, Mill is suggesting that whenever one would produce net disutility by following one secondary rule, *one's act would not be in accord with a different secondary rule*, viz., 'Do not produce evil' ('Do not produce net disutility'). Whenever there are conflicts between secondary rules, one must appeal to the principle of utility. Thus, rule-utilitarians are not representing Mill's position when they argue that one may morally permissibly produce net disutility as long as one's act is in accord with a rule the general following of which would maximize utility. Mill would argue that in such a case one's act would not be in accord with the secondary rule 'Do not produce net disutility'. He would then claim that one would have to appeal to the principle of utility to settle the conflict, and that the principle of utility would not allow the individual to perform a (net) disutility-producing act.

In general, a few principles emerge from Mill's writings with respect to the issue(s) at hand:

1.   We should use secondary principles in our moral decision-making. Further, we should not be willing to break these secondary principles as readily as we would, were they merely guides to action.

2.   These secondary principles should be simple enough so that they can be readily remembered and applied.

3.   If, after including all of the relevant disutilities, we, as unbiassed, knowledgeable, careful deliberators, are certain that following the rule would promote disutility and ignoring the rule would promote utility, then we must *disobey* the rule.[45]

Co-operative Utilitarianism

Some critics believe that maximizing act-utilitarianism is untenable,[46] since agents who seek to maximize utility may be unable to do so because they lack information about what other people will do. This can easily be illustrated.

Suppose that Whiff and Poof each have to decide whether to push the buttons in front of them. The utilities can be summed up in the following diagram.[47]

		Poof	
		Push	Not-push
Whiff	Push	10	0
	Not-push	0	6

The optimal situation would involve both Whiff's and Poof's pushing the buttons. However, if one of them is not going to push a button, then neither of them should.

Suppose that neither knows what the other will do. What should Whiff do? If he pushes and Poof not-pushes, then no utiles will be produced.

As long as Whiff knows that Poof knows the possible outcomes and Poof knows that Whiff knows the possible outcomes, they will both push, since they are both seeking to maximize utility and their both pushing would produce optimal results. However, Whiff and Poof would not be helped by this solution if their situation were a little different. Suppose that as long as they both pushed or not-pushed, they each would produce ten utiles; otherwise, they each would produce minus five utiles. If neither has any idea what the other will do, neither can say what he himself ought to do.

Obviously, Whiff and Poof should talk to each other, if possible. If they cannot, then they are in a difficult position and each will simply have to make a guess about what the other will do.[48]

In discussing these issues, we must be careful to distinguish among several issues:

1. Did the agent act rightly?
2. Should the agent be blamed?
3. How much blame should he receive?

In the problem posed above, the agent does not know what to do. Should Whiff push the button? Yes, if Poof is going to push, and no, otherwise. If Whiff does not know what Poof is going to do, Whiff will have to guess, taking into account all that he knows about Poof. If Whiff guesses correctly, he will have acted rightly; otherwise, he will have acted wrongly.[49] Co-ordination problems do not prevent agents from acting rightly. They merely prevent agents from knowing what to do.

Should we blame Whiff for guessing wrongly? This is a separate issue. Whiff's lack of knowledge may affect whether or how much he should be blamed for his bad guess. It does not at all affect whether he in fact performed the right action.

Current theorists are correct that co-ordination problems may affect act-utilitarian analyses of the proper courses of action. Mill would welcome the suggestion that agents should try to be well-informed before making their decisions. However, the co-ordination utilitarians are in no better position than the act-utilitarians. Both should find out all they can about the situation at hand, *including* what other people are planning on doing, and then act accordingly.

Which Consequences Are the Effects of Particular Actions?

When Mill talks about the effects of an action, he includes many of the consequences which one might not (at first) attribute to the performance of a particular action. For example, Mill believes that one should be truthful because "the cultivation in ourselves of a sensitive feeling on the subject of veracity is one of the most useful, and the enfeeblement of that feeling one of the most hurtful, things to which our conduct can be instrumental." Thus, one's lying has a negative effect on one's character. Also, one's lying will help to "deprive mankind of the good, and inflict upon them the evil, involved in the greater or less reliance which they can place in each other's word."[50] People will feel less secure if I lie to them, both because they will trust me less and because they will tend to trust others less as well.

When Mill is trying to decide whether a particular lie would be justified, he does not merely look at the immediate effects of the lie, e.g., my being very pleased versus someone else's being slightly displeased. My lying will hurt my character, will make the other person less likely to believe people, and will make me less likely to believe people.

Mill argues that the consequences which rule-utilitarians claim should be traced back to rules can in fact be traced back to *actions*. By taking a rather broad view of which effects are correctly deemed the effects of particular actions, Mill can account for the considerations which a rule-utilitarian might cite, e.g., effects on character, security, etc., *and* Mill is able to secure an additional benefit. He can claim that lying is sometimes morally permissible,[51] for example, at those times when calamities might be averted by a little 'judicious' lying.

The Benefit of Humankind

As a type of act-utilitarian, Mill believes that an action which maximizes utility is morally right. However, his view is somewhat unusual with respect to *whose* utility should be promoted.

Mill is quite concerned about promoting the happiness of the individual. He believes that one of the reasons that individuals should pursue the higher pleasures is that, by so doing, they will be both better and happier people.[52] Mill is also quite concerned about promoting the happiness of society, arguing that even if an individual, himself, is not happier as a result of his becoming nobler, other people will thereby be happier.[53] Yet, neither the promotion of individual happiness nor the promotion of societal happiness is Mill's ultimate concern. Mill's ultimate concern is to promote the utility of humankind.

In *On Liberty*, Mill says, "I regard utility as the ultimate appeal on all ethical questions, but it must be utility in the largest sense, grounded on the permanent interests of man as a progressive being."[54] Mill's talking about "man as a progressive being" does not make each individual's interests of primary importance. Rather, the permanent interests of humankind are important. Each individual's utility is promoted as a fortunate by-product of the promotion of humankind's utility.

When talking about 'man', Mill might seem to be referring to the interests of society. Such an interpretation is incorrect.

The permanent interests of man are not simply the permanent interests of a particular society, e.g., Greek, Roman, or British. Rather, they are the interests of the Society of Man, i.e., Humankind. When Mill talks about Humankind, he is not merely talking about all of the people who happen to be living at a particular time. He is talking about "the Human Race, conceived as a continuous whole, including the past, the present and the future."[55]

Mill agrees with Comte that "reflection, guided by history, has taught us the intimacy of the connection of every age of humanity with every other."[56] We are narrow-minded if we think that we should promote the good of a particular society of a particular time period at the expense of the good of humankind. It is "the good of the human race [which] is the ultimate standard of right and wrong."[57]

Mill complains that Bentham's doctrine, which emphasizes individuals' acting out of self-interest, is very destructive of "all natural hope for good for the *human species* [my italics]." Bentham undermines "our hopes of happiness or moral perfection to the *species* [my italics]."[58]

In *A System of Logic*, Mill says that the ultimate standard is "conduciveness to the happiness of mankind."[59] In *Utilitarianism*, Mill also speaks about promoting the happiness of all humankind.[60]

Mill believes that we are able to predict what will promote the happiness of humankind, because "social phenomena conform to invariable laws."[61] We merely need to figure out what would be the ideal setting, e.g., which attitudes people should have and which actions people should perform, for happiness to be promoted. We can examine the history of humankind to see which rules and actions further that goal.[62]

When Mill talks about promoting the happiness of humankind, he does not specify whether he is talking about the average happiness or the (net) total happiness. The difference may be illustrated in the following way.

Suppose that there are four individuals in World W, each of whom is fairly happy. For the sake of illustration, we shall assign each of them a "happiness level" of 25. The question at hand is whether the world would be a better place were there an additional person, Jones, who over her lifetime would enjoy a happiness level of 10.

Were Jones to live in W, the (net) total level of happiness would be raised to 110 happiness units. However, the average happiness level would be lowered from 25 to 22. Thus, on the (net) total happiness account, W would be a better place were Jones also to live there. On the average happiness account, W would be a worse place were Jones to live there.

Family planning practices might differ, depending upon whether one adopted the former or latter account. Mill was clearly interested in promoting a decline in the population rate. "It appears to me impossible but that the increase of intelligence, of education, and of the love of independence among the working classes, must be attended with a corresponding growth of the good sense which manifests itself in provident habits of conduct, and that population, therefore, will bear a gradually diminishing ratio to capital and employment."[63] Here, he might be inferred to be promoting the average happiness. However, Mill would not be in favor of destroying all but two people (who happened to be very happy and to require no one else but themselves), even though the average happiness might thereby be increased.

Clearly, Mill wants future generations to be considered in calculations of utility. However, he does not specifically address some of the issues raised if one is indeed to consider future generations, e.g., whether one has a duty to procreate, whether future generations' interests should be discounted, if so, by how much, etc.[64]

An additional complicating factor which must be considered is that Mill does not believe that only rules and actions should be judged by the principle of utility. Attitudes should also promote utility. Mill criticizes Whewell for assuming that people's moral attitudes are above reproach. "The point in dispute is, what acts are the proper objects of those [moral] feelings; whether we ought to take the feelings as we find them, as accident or design has made them, or whether the tendency of actions to promote happiness affords a test to which the feelings of morality should conform."[65] Indeed, "intellectual progress [is] in no other way so beneficial as by creating a standard to guide the moral sentiments of mankind, and a mode of bringing those sentiments effectively to bear on conduct."[66] Thus, when Mill talks about promoting utility, he is talking about the utility of humankind. He is interested in changing both attitudes and actions in order to bring about his goal.

Merely because Mill is primarily interested in promoting the interests of humankind *does not mean* that Mill is uninterested in protecting the individual. The protection of individual liberties is extremely important, because protecting them is the best way to promote the interests of humankind. *On Liberty* is written to demonstrate *on empirical grounds* that the protection of individual liberties will ultimately be the best way of promoting the interests of humankind.[67]

The Importance of Mill's Being a Type of Act-utilitarian

It might seem unimportant to ascertain whether Mill was an act-utilitarian, since even if this controversy could be resolved the result would seem to have little bearing on any contemporary philosophical discussions. Such a view is mistaken. In understanding Mill's act-utilitarianism, we shall see how contemporary act-utilitarians can refute some of their severest critics.

Act-utilitarians are often charged with being unable to show that justice will be preserved or that promises will be kept. Mill deflects these charges by talking about the hidden disutilities caused by the performance of such actions. If justice is not preserved, insecurity will result.[68] Insecurity will also result if people habitually lie. Mill is including these results as part of the total consequences of *particular* actions.

Mill is an act-utilitarian who looks at immediate *and* eventual consequences of actions in light of how these actions will affect the utility of humankind. He thus disagrees with act-utilitarians who only look at the immediate consequences of actions or who only look at consequences in light of how they will affect a particular society or even the world at a particular time.

When theorists talk about the *remote* effects of actions, e.g., "possible effects on the agent's character, and effects on the public at large,"[69] they are talking about effects which, according to Mill, are effects of particular actions. While even Mill admits that it is difficult to determine exactly how much disutility is promoted by a particular lie, he still believes that the disutility is produced *by the action*. We may have to look at many actions of a similar type in order to ascertain all of the effects, but it is the effects of the action that concern Mill.

Mill would be confused by a critic who claimed that effects on character or on public feelings of security are reasons not to support act-utilitarianism. For Mill, these would be reasons to support *his type* of act-utilitarianism.

Since Mill's act-utilitarianism takes into account many of the factors that are taken into account by various forms of rule-utilitarianism, it might seem unimportant to make the distinction. Such a claim is false *because of the way that rule-utilitarianism tends to be formulated.*

Suppose that even after one has taken all of the hidden disutilities of a particular action into account, one still sees that one should perform what is normally called an unjust action. The act-utilitarian will claim that the unjust action should be performed. She will explain her position in one of two ways:

1.   She will claim that the performance of justice is not always morally correct, opting for a rather paradoxical view of both justice and morality.

2.   She will adopt Mill's view and claim that because the dictates of justice cannot be disutility-producing, what is normally just (i.e., what the secondary rules of justice dictate to be just) is not just in this particular case.

The rule-utilitarian would say that even if the dictates of justice do not promote utility in this particular case, the dictates generally promote utility and thus must always be followed. There is a major difference between the act- and rule-utilitarian. In a situation in which the dictates of justice do not promote utility, the act-utilitarian claims that the dictates must be ignored, while the rule-utilitarian claims that the dictates of justice must be followed.

Mill argues, "In such cases [i.e., where justice and utility conflict], as we do not call anything justice which is not a virtue [e.g., which is disutility-producing], we usually say, not that justice must give way to some other moral principle, but that what is just in ordinary cases is, by reason of that other principle, not just in this particular case." By doing this, we will avoid conceptual difficulties. "By this useful accommodation of language, the character of indefeasibility attributed to justice is kept up, and we are saved from the necessity of maintaining that there can be laudable injustice."[70]

Mill is not merely making a semantic point here. He is claiming that since justice is founded on utility, justice cannot dictate that we perform disutility-producing actions. In cases in which the apparent rule of justice dictates that we do something which is obviously disutilty-producing, we must either amend the rule or ignore it altogether.

Mill has little patience for those who would claim that not following the normal dictates of justice to promote utility would involve doing an 'evil'. He agrees with Whately's analysis of such a case. "[W]hen in a discussion, one party vindicates, on the ground of general expediency, a particular instance of resistance to government in a case of intolerable oppression, the opponent may gravely maintain that 'we ought not to do evil that good may come;' a proposition which of course has never been denied, the point in dispute being, 'whether resistance in this particular case *were* doing evil or not'."[71]

If truth-telling would be disutility-producing and lying would be utility-producing in a particular case, then lying would be morally required. Lying and acting 'unjustly', i.e., not following the normal dictates of justice, may not have (net) negative effects on one's character, on public security, or on others' lying or breaking other moral rules at inappropriate times. Lying has a bad effect on one's character only when the lie would promote one's acting in disutility-producing ways. By the same token, acting unjustly would have a bad effect on one's character only when the 'injustice' would promote one's acting in disutility-producing ways. If I lie or act unjustly because doing so would slightly benefit me and would greatly hurt others, then my so acting would be wrong — I have counted my own interests too heavily. My character will suffer in that I am promoting my own tendency to act selfishly and in that I am promoting my own and others' tendency to lie or act unjustly at inappropriate times. However, if I lie to promote utility, then my character may not suffer. I should lie when doing so would promote utility, and my character is helped rather than harmed insofar as my tendency to lie at utility-producing times is promoted. True. If I lie to promote utility, then my character might suffer in that the tendency to lie in general rather than at only utility-promoting times might be strengthened. Further, my character might suffer in that the disposition to break other moral rules might also be strengthened. Nonetheless, the disutility produced might not be sufficient to outweigh the utility of telling the lie.[72]

Suppose that Ann and I agree to meet somewhere. I go there but she fails to keep the appointment. She has broken her promise. Much disutility can result from promise-breaking, e.g., I may grow to distrust her and others.

Suppose, however, that she has very good reasons for her promise-breaking. Once I have been apprised of the facts, I might have two very different reactions:

1. I might grow to trust her as much as or more than I did before. I would realize that she has exercised good judgment. Her action would *promote* feelings of security, both in myself because I know that she has acted as she should have, and in others, especially those who directly benefited from her good use of her judgment.

2. I might still be angry and resentful, despite my knowing that her action promoted utility. Mill would condemn my resentment rather than Ann's action. He would say that "just persons [resent] a hurt to society, though not otherwise a hurt to themselves, and [do] not [resent] a hurt to themselves, however painful, unless it be of the kind which society has a common interest with them in the repression of."[73]

Mill argues persuasively for the protection of liberty and the preservation of justice on *utilitarian* grounds. We learn from him, *not* (as some rule-utilitarians and deontologists seem to imply) that the preservation of justice is usually but not always utility-producing, but that the preservation of justice is *necessarily* utility-producing. When one, as an unbiassed, knowledgeable, deliberate calculator, takes into consideration the effects of following the standard rules of justice and morality and one sees that following those rules will be disutility-producing, one will understand that those rules must be amended or ignored entirely.

It is important to understand Mill's act-utilitarianism because we can then see that some of the arguments (e.g., that insecurity and the formation of bad characters will result from performing certain actions) used by rule-utilitarians and deontologists to support their own theories, are used cogently and convincingly to support an act-utilitarian position. However, there is an important respect in which act-utilitarianism and rule-utilitarianism are not so far apart after all.

We should not conform our acts to socially useful rules when doing so would promote disutility. However, when making the appropriate calculations, we must include the remote effects of rule-breakings, e.g., effects on character, effects on general security, etc.

If we really know of a case in which following the rule would promote disutility and breaking the rule would promote utility (including all of the considerations above), then the rule-utilitarian will want to modify his rule to account for the exception, since the rule-utilitarian cannot justify a rule when the adoption of a different rule in its stead would produce more utility.[74] If we know that following a rule would be disutility-producing, then an act-utilitarian will claim that we should not *follow* that rule, i.e., he will say that we should disobey it. By the same token, if we know that our following a rule would be disutility-producing, then the rule-utilitarian will claim that we should not *have* that rule — she will say that we should instead have a different rule to follow.

Usually, agents *suspect* rather than *know* that following a particular rule would be disutility-producing. In such situations, the rule-utilitarian and the act-utilitarian face similar problems. The act-utilitarian must decide whether he should disobey the rule of thumb which is usually effective to follow. The rule-utilitarian must decide whether this rule is in need of an (or another) exception.

The claim here is *not* that act-utilitarianism and rule-utilitarianism are co-extensive. A rule-utilitarian might argue that we have to keep moral rules fairly simple if people are going to be able to accept and follow them correctly. Mill and act-utilitarians in general wholeheartedly agree with such a claim. The rule-utilitarian might further argue that these rules must be obeyed, even if on a particular occasion the rule's being obeyed would produce net disutility. At this point, Mill and act-utilitarians in general would disagree. They would argue that one must promote utility, even if one must break a secondary rule to do so.

It is important to understand Mill's act-utilitarianism because it is important to understand that he really is committed to the promotion of the utility of humankind above everything else. However, precisely because he is committed to the promotion of utility, he is justifiably worried that his calling secondary moral principles mere guides or mere rules of thumb would result in too many disutility-producing rule-breakings. As to whether Mill is better interpreted as claiming that the promotion of humankind's utility can best be achieved by ignoring disutility-producing rules or by simply amending them, this is a question which is, perhaps, neither answerable nor important to answer.

NOTES

1. Another form of indirect utilitarianism would involve motivations rather than rules. Brandt writes, "An optimific indirect theory is a *normative* theory which *roughly* holds that any *other-person-involving* act is morally permissible if it would be *best* for the moral motivations of (roughly) all agents to *permit* acts of that type in its circumstances, and that an other-person-involving act is an agent's moral duty if it would be best for the moral motivations of (roughly) all agents to *require* acts of that type in those circumstances." He explains that he means "by a person's *moral motivations* a complex consisting of a desire/aversion for some kind of action for itself, in certain circumstances, a disposition to feel guilty if one does (does not) perform an act of this sort, and a disposition to disapprove or be indignant if someone else does (does

not) perform an act of that type, in those circumstances." R. B. Brandt, "Fairness to Indirect Optimific Theories in Ethics," *Ethics* 98 (1988), pp. 342-343.

2. J. J. C. Smart, "Extreme and restricted utilitarianism" in *Mill: Utilitarianism with Critical Essays*, ed. Samuel Gorovitz (Indianapolis: Bobbs-Merrill Co., Inc, 1971), p. 195.

3. Alexander believes that act-utilitarianism's mandating that one break rules if doing so will be utility-maximizing may produce so many unwarranted rule-breakings (because agents would sometimes miscalculate and would thus break rules at inappropriate times) that one's adopting act-utilitarianism might produce less utility than would one's adopting rule-utilitarianism. See Larry Alexander, "Pursuing the Good — Indirectly," *Ethics* 95 (1985), p. 324. For an illustration of how these miscalculations might occur, see F. H. Bradley, "Pleasure for Pleasure's Sake" in *Ethical Studies* (first published 1876), Introduction by Ralph Ross (Indianapolis: Bobbs-Merrill Educational Publishing, 1951), p. 49.

4. John Stuart Mill, *A System of Logic*, Book 6, Ch. 12, Sec. 3, *CW* Vol. 8, p. 945.

5. *Utilitarianism*, Ch. 5, Par. 37, p. 259.

6. See Smart, "Extreme and restricted utilitarianism," p. 199.

7. *A System of Logic*, Book 6, Ch. 12, Sec. 3, pp. 945-946. For a similar point, see John Stuart Mill, *The Subjection of Women*, Ch. 3, Par. 10, *CW* 21, p. 307.

8. *A System of Logic*, Book 6, Ch. 12, Sec. 2, p. 944.

9. A number of theorists talk about the importance of rules' being fairly simple. See R. M. Hare, *Moral Thinking* (Oxford: University Press, 1981), p. 33; and John Rawls, "The Independence of Moral Theory," *American Philosophical Association Proceedings and Addresses* 48 (1974-1975), p. 14.

10. John Stuart Mill, "Bentham," *CW* Vol. 10, p. 111.

11. John Stuart Mill, "Taylor's Statesman," *CW* Vol. 19, p. 638.

12. *Utilitarianism*, Ch. 2, Par. 2, p. 210.

13. *Ibid.*, Ch. 2, Par. 9, p. 213.

14. *Ibid.*, Ch. 2, Par. 10, p. 214.

15. Rem Edwards claims that Mill was "neither a maximizing act nor rule utilitarian." See his "The Principle of Utility and Mill's Minimizing Utilitarianism," *Journal of Value Inquiry* 20 (1986), p. 132. See also his "J. S. Mill and Robert Veatch's Critique of Utilitarianism," *Southern Journal of Philosophy* 23 (1985), pp. 181-200. Here, it is argued that Mill agrees with standard act-utilitarians that those actions which maximize utility are right. However, he disagrees insofar as they claim that an action must be utility-maximizing in order to be right. For a related point, see Marcus Singer's "Actual Consequence Utilitarianism," *Mind* 86 (1977), p. 69.

16. See J. O. Urmson, "The Interpretation of the Moral Philosophy of J. S. Mill," *Mill: Utilitarianism with Critical Essays*, p. 170; and H. J. McCloskey, *John Stuart Mill: A Critical Study* (London: Macmillan and Co., Ltd., 1971), p. 58.

17. *Utilitarianism*, Ch. 2, Par. 24, p. 224.

18. *Ibid.*, pp. 224-225.

19. This is Mabbott's example. See J. D. Mabbott, "Interpretations of Mill's Utilitarianism" in *Mill: A Collection of Critical Essays*, ed. J. B. Schneewind (Garden City: Anchor Books, 1968), p. 194.

20. *Utilitarianism*, Ch. 2, Par. 24, p. 224.

21. *Ibid.*, Ch. 2, Par. 19, p. 220.

22. A class of actions is merely a set of actions, all of which meet one or more criteria. Or, to use a different description, a class of actions is a set of actions, all of which correspond to some rule(s). To be concerned with the consequences of performing actions of a certain class is to be concerned with the consequences of performing actions of a particular set, all of which correspond to the same rule(s). Thus, Mill seems to be espousing a rule-utilitarian position — one should not perform an action unless the rule with which it is in accord would promote the general good. The consequences which result from not following the rule seem to be of concern, not the consequences of performing the action.

23. For a similar argument, see Bernard Semmel, *John Stuart Mill and the Pursuit of Virtue* (New Haven: Yale University Press, 1984), p. 87. For related comments of Mill's, see "Whewell on Moral

Philosophy," p. 182; and *On Liberty*, Ch. 4, Par. 8, *CW* Vol. 18, p. 280.

24. *A System of Logic*, *CW* Vol. 8, Book 6, Ch. 11, Sec. 6, Par. 3, pp. 1154-55.

25. *Ibid.*, Par. 4, p. 1155. These two passages were deleted after the 1846 edition. Mill may have deleted these passages because he simply changed his mind and wanted to espouse a much more act-utilitarian line. However, passages in other works would not support this explanation. I suspect that he deleted these passages, not because his position had changed but rather because they sounded too rule-oriented and thus did not represent his position. One can easily understand Mill's difficulty. He does not want to advocate blind rule-following, but also does not want to advocate a position which would result in frequent and inappropriate violations of secondary rules. Of course, it may be that the passages were deleted because of printing costs. However, even were that true, other passages in Mill's writings support the position offered here.

26. "Whewell on Moral Philosophy," p. 182.

27. *Ibid.*, p. 183.

28. *Considerations on Representative Government*, Ch. 5, Par. 8, p. 425.

29. "Whewell on Moral Philosophy," p. 183.

30. *A System of Logic*, Book 6, Ch. 12, Sec. 3, p. 946.

31. "Taylor's Statesman," p. 640. In Chapters 4-7, there will be a discussion of how much net utility one has a duty to promote.

32. *CW* Vol. 17, p. 1881. Brown points out this letter. See D. G. Brown, "Mill's Act-utilitarianism," *Philosophical Quarterly* 27 (1974), p. 68.

33. "Whewell on Moral Philosophy," p. 181.

34. "Remarks on Bentham's Philosophy," *CW* Vol. 10, p. 8.

35. "Sedgwick's Discourse," p. 56.

36. *Principles of Political Economy*, Book 4, Ch. 1, Sec. 2, Par. 2, Vol. 3, p. 706.

37. *Considerations on Representative Government*, Ch. 15, Par. 11, p. 541. See also "De Toqueville" (1), *CW* Vol. 18, p. 80.

38. "Bentham," p. 110.

39. *Ibid.*, p. 111.

40. "Blakey's History of Moral Science," *CW* Vol. 10, p. 29.

41. *Utilitarianism*, Ch. 2, Par. 25, p. 226.

42. *The Subjection of Women*, Ch. 3, Par. 10, p. 307. Mill seems to believe that the moral judgment of individuals improves as they become more 'civilized'. See "Civilization," *CW* Vol. 18, p. 132.

43. "Taylor's Stateman," pp. 622-623.

44. *Ibid.*, pp. 638-639. See also *Utilitarianism*, Ch. 2, Par. 23, p. 223 in which Mill writes that even the rule of truth-telling, "sacred as it is, admits of possible exceptions."

45. The position described here is quite compatible with Berger's "strategy" conception of moral rules. See Berger, *Happiness, Justice and Freedom*, pp. 72 ff. The position here is also compatible with Henry West's See his "Mill's Moral Conservatism," *Midwest Studies in Philosophy* 1 (1976), pp. 71-80.

46. See Lars Bergstrom, "Utilitarianism and Future Mistakes," *Theoria* 43 (1977), pp. 84-102; Jordan Sobel, "Utilitarianism and Past and Future Mistakes," *Nous* 10 (1976), pp. 195-219; Brian Ellis, "Retrospective and Prospective Utilitarianism," *Nous* 15 (1981), pp. 325-339; Hector-Neri Castaneda, "On the Problem of Formulating a Coherent Act-Utilitarianism," *Analysis* 32 (1972), pp. 118-124. For related comments, see Fred Feldman, *Doing the Best We Can* (Dordrecht: D. Reidel Publishing Co., 1986), Ch. 1.

These theorists make interesting and important points which will not be addressed here both because these points do not directly address Mill's system and because insofar as they do indirectly address his system, they (analogously, if not directly) might be made against many, if not all, moral systems. For example, there are serious problems raised by the notion of group actions *for moral theorists in general*, at least in part, because such a notion may force theorists to reassess the basic unit of moral evaluation. There are also serious problems raised insofar as one should consider others' and one's own probable future immoral actions.

Sympathizing with some of these criticisms directed at act-utilitarianism, Holbrook argues that "an action is right if and only if it is part of that series of actions that has the greatest overall pleasure as its result." See Daniel Holbrook, *Qualitative Utilitarianism* (Lanham:

University Press of America, 1988), p. 42. He does not seem to appreciate that on this account an agent may be held morally accountable for *others'* moral misdeeds. While we should try to anticipate and consider our own and others' future actions when we deliberate about what to do currently, a theory like Holbrook's demands much more than that and seems to destroy the notions both of individual agency and of (individual) moral responsibility. In any case, the kind of analysis required to handle these problems would have to be too extensive and too foundational to be appropriately handled here.

47. This is Regan's example. See Donald Regan, *Utilitarianism and Co-operation* (Oxford: Oxford University Press, 1980), p. 18

48. Information constraints create difficulties for a variety of theories. Suppose that we adopt Regan's position and say, "What each agent ought to do is co-operate, with whoever else is co-operating in the production of the best consequences possible given the behaviors of the non-co-operators." Regan, *Utilitarianism and Co-operation,* p. 124. Or, we can adopt the proposal suggested by Postow and say, "In any given situation, any group of one or more agents ought to follow a course of action by means of which the group would produce the most good that it can produce in that situation." B. C. Postow, "Generalized Act Utilitarianism," *Analysis* 37 (1977), p. 51. (For a discussion of how agents who lack perfect knowledge should act if they wish to be rational, see David Gauthier, *Morals By Agreement* (Oxford: Oxford University Press, 1986), especially Ch. 3.) If there is no available information about what others are doing, the agent may have to flip a coin. Whether one is an act-utilitarian or a co-operative utilitarian, one will simply have to hope for the best.

49. In the next chapter, we shall see that Mill is sometimes thought to evaluate actions in terms of their foreseeable consequences. If Whiff has no reason to believe that Poof will act one way rather than the other, then neither of Whiff's alternatives is foreseeably better and he acts rightly no matter which of the two options he chooses, regardless of Poof's choice.

50. *Utilitarianism*, Ch. 2, Par. 23, p. 223.

51. *Ibid.*

52. *Ibid.*, Ch. 2, Par. 6, p. 212.

53. *Ibid.*, Ch. 2, Par. 9, p. 213.

54. John Stuart Mill, *On Liberty*, Ch. 1, Par. 11, p. 224.

55. "Auguste Comte and Positivism," p. 333.

56. *Ibid.*, p. 334.

57. *Ibid.*, p. 335. Levi argues that 'the permanent interests of man as a progressive being' are related to the actualization of certain human potentials. See Albert William Levi, "The Value of Freedom: Mill's Liberty (1859-1959)," *Ethics* 70 (1959), p. 40. That interpretation is quite compatible with this one, as long as the actualization of those potentials would indeed promote the general happiness of humankind.

By the same token, theorists are correct that Mill argues for the great importance of the promotion of autonomy and individuality, as long as they keep in mind that Mill so argues because he believes that the promotion of these qualities is necessary for the progress and well-being of humankind. See *On Liberty*, Ch. 3, Par. 1 ff, pp. 260 ff.

58. John Stuart Mill, "Remarks on Bentham's Philosophy," *CW* Vol. 10, p. 15. For related comments, see Richard Arneson, "Mill Versus Paternalism," *Ethics* 90 (1980), pp. 470-489.

59. *A System of Logic*, Book 6, Ch. 12, Sec. 7, p. 951.

60. *Utilitarianism*, Ch. 2, Par. 10, p. 214.

In the passages above, Mill is clearly interested in promoting humankind's utility. Sometimes, Mill writes as if he is interested in promoting the happiness of all sentient beings. It is not clear how the happiness of each sentient creature should be weighed, e.g., whether each counts for one and no one for more than one. See "Whewell on Moral Philosophy," pp. 186 ff. Mill writes that the maximization of the happiness of all sentient creatures would be best, "as far as the nature of things admits." *Utilitarianism*, Ch. 5, Par. 10, p. 214. It is not clear how this qualification should be treated.

In this work, it will be assumed that Mill believes that the act which maximizes humankind's (foreseeable) utility is morally best. The account can be suitably modified, depending upon how animals' interests should be weighed.

61. "Auguste Comte and Positivism," p. 290.

62. *Utilitarianism*, Ch. 2, Par. 24, p. 224.

52   The Moral Philosophy of John Stuart Mill

63. *Principles of Political Economy*, Book 4, Ch. 7, Sec. 3, Par. 1, *CW* Vol. 3, p. 765. See also "Chapters on Socialism," *CW* 5, p. 729. For a brief, related (historical) discussion of Mill's views on the dissemination of birth control information, see Michael Packe, *The Life of John Stuart Mill* (London: Secker and Warburg, 1954), pp. 56 ff. See also Gertrude Himmelfarb, *On Liberty and Liberalism* (New York: Alfred A. Knopf, Inc., 1974), p. 121.

64. A vast literature has been devoted to the topic of our obligations to future generations. See, e.g., R. I. Sikora and Brian Barry (eds.), *Obligations to Future Generations* (Philadelphia: Temple University Press, 1978).

65. "Whewell on Moral Philosophy," p. 172. Brandt seems to want to attribute his theory of indirect utility to Mill. See Brandt's "Fairness to Indirect Optimific Theories in Ethics," p. 342. As will be explained more fully in later chapters, Mill evaluates an action's rightness according to the principle of utility and he evaluates a motivation's goodness according to the principle of utility, but *not* the moral goodness of an action in terms of the goodness of the motivation which, itself, is evaluated according to the principle of utility — Mill argues that the rightness of an action and the goodness of a motivation are each *directly* evaluated according to the principle of utility. The theory which Brandt describes is more appropriately attributed to Hutcheson. See my *Francis Hutcheson's Moral Theory: Its Form and Utility*.

66. "Auguste Comte and Positivism," pp. 322 ff.

67. See my "Mill and the Utility of Liberty," *Philosophical Quarterly* 34 (1984), pp. 63-68. See also Ted Honderich's "The Worth of J. S. Mill *On Liberty*," *Political Studies* 22 (1974), pp. 463-470 and his "'On Liberty' and Morality-Dependent Harms," *Political Studies* 30 (1982), pp. 504-514.

68. *Utilitarianism*, Ch. 5, Par. 25, pp. 250-251.

69. See Williams's claim in J. J. C. Smart and Bernard Williams, *Utilitarianism For and Against* (Cambridge: Cambridge University Press, 1973), p. 100.

70. *Utilitarianism*, Ch. 5, Par. 37, p. 259. Narveson criticizes rule-utilitarianism because it might morally require that one perform

what one knows to be a non-utility-maximizing action. See his *Morality and Utility* (Baltimore: Johns Hopkins Press, 1967), p. 128.

71. *A System of Logic*, Book 5, Ch. 7, Sec. 3, Par. 4, p. 829.

72. For a related discussions, see Copp on "generic effects." David Copp, "The Iterated-Utilitarianism of J. S. Mill," *New Essays on John Stuart Mill and Utilitarianism*, p. 94.

73. *Utilitarianism*, Ch. 5, Par. 21, p. 249.

74. Goldman points out that there is insufficient appreciation of the difficulty of providing the relevant description of the appropriate moral rule within certain forms of rule-utilitarianism. See Holly Goldman, "David Lyons on Utilitarian Generalization," *Philosophical Studies* 26 (1974), pp. 78 ff. Feldman claims that Lyons uses the wrong criterion for relevance. See Fred Feldman, "On the Extensional Equivalence of Simple and General Utilitarianism," *Nous* 8 (1974), pp. 191 ff. See also Gertrude Ezorsky, "A Defense of Rule-Utilitarianism Against David Lyons Who Insists on Tieing it to Act-Utilitarianism, Plus a Brand New Way of Checking Out General Utilitarian Properties," *Journal of Philosophy* 65 (1968). For an informative discussion on this and related matters, see Gerald Gaus, "Mill's Theory of Moral Rules," *Australasian Journal of Philosophy* 58 (1980), pp. 265-279.

CHAPTER THREE

Are Utilitarian Calculations Possible?

Mill argues that actions are morally right if they are (foreseeably) utility-promoting for humankind. However, since it is very difficult, if not impossible, for an agent to know what will always promote *her own* utility, it might seem incredible for a moral system to ask, much less demand, that agents know what will promote *humankind's* utility. If Mill is really offering a moral system which is to be of any use, he must establish that considerations of the utility of humankind can actually help guide human action.

On Predicting Effects

A variety of critics of utilitarianism claim that since we cannot predict the effects of our own actions, utilitarianism cannot be a helpful moral system. Both Sedgwick and Whewell deny that one can make the necessary calculations to determine which actions will promote utility. Sedgwick suggests that "man has not foreknowledge to trace the consequences of a single action of his own; . . . utility . . . is, as a test of right and wrong, unfitted to his understanding, and therefore worthless in its application."[1] Whewell makes a similar point. "How can I tell the effects of my actions? Telling a lie or acting so as to acquire sensual pleasures leads to some unhappiness: weakens respect for Truth and Temperance. But how do I know enough of an evil to outweigh the gain?"[2]

If Mill wants his system to be taken seriously, he must respond to the objection that agents cannot predict which actions will promote utility. Mill makes two points:

1. The moral system which Whewell and Sedgwick espouse also does not yield clear dictates about which actions are right and which wrong. "They [those in the 'intuitive' school] assume the utmost

latitude of arbitrarily determining whose votes deserve to be counted. They either ignore the existence of dissentients or leave them out of the account, on the pretext that they have the feeling which they deny having, or if not, that they ought to have it."[3]

2. One can make sufficiently accurate predictions about consequences to know what one should do, since it is not "necessary to foresee all the consequences of each 'individual action' as they go down into the countless ages of coming time." Mill argues, "Some of the consequences of an action are accidental; others are its natural result, according to the known laws of the universe . . . [T]he whole course of human life is founded on the fact that the latter can [be seen] . . . The commonest person lives according to the maxims of prudence wholly founded on foresight of consequences."[4]

Mill denies that every person has moral intuitions which coincide with every other person's intuitions. He does not thereby establish that we can know what the consequences of a particular action will be, but merely implies that we must have some standard by which we can judge the correctness of an action when our intuitions about its correctness conflict. There are various possible standards — that which promotes utility, that which reason demands, that which provides the necessary goods for agency, etc. If there is no standard by which we can judge our intuitions, then if our intuitions about what is morally correct differ, there will be no way to decide which is the correct intuition.

Mill's distinction between accidental and natural results (in his second point) might *seem* to be irrelevant, since the principle of utility does not distinguish between happiness which results from natural consequences and happiness which results from accidental consequences. We are interested in promoting utility, whether it results "naturally" or "accidentally."

Yet, if Mill's distinction is formulated in somewhat different terms, not only is it *not* surprising, but it corresponds to a position favored by a variety of current theorists. When Mill talks about 'accidental' consequences, he is not talking about 'unintentional' consequences, but about consequences which could not be predicted given the *known* laws of nature. 'Known' is emphasized here because

Mill believes that all consequences could be predicted, were we cognizant of all of the causal laws. "It is certain . . . that whatever happens is the result of some law; is an effect of causes, and could have been predicted from a knowledge of the existence of those causes, and from their laws."[5]

The natural consequences are those which are foreseeable, given our current knowledge of causal laws. Insofar as Mill claims that actions should be evaluated by their *foreseeable* consequences, he is advocating what is currently known as foreseeable consequence utilitarianism.[6] However, his writings are not clear on this point — he sometimes seems to evaluate actions by their *foreseeable* consequences and sometimes by their *actual* consequences.

In *Utilitarianism*, Mill writes that "the Greatest Happiness Principle holds that actions are right in proportion as they *tend* to promote happiness, wrong as they *tend* to produce the reverse of happiness [my italics]."[7] When Mill talks about evaluating actions in terms of their tendencies, he is talking about the consequences one might reasonably expect (the consequences which are foreseeable, given present knowledge of causal laws).

Yet, in the same work, Mill admits quite approvingly that utilitarianism "regard[s] only the dry and hard consideration of the consequences of actions"[8] rather than the consequences which actions *tend* to produce. He claims that "Happiness is the sole end of human action and the promotion of it the test by which to judge of all human conduct."[9] Here, Mill does not use the *tendency* to promote happiness as the criterion by which to judge the rightness and wrongness of actions; rather, he uses the promotion of happiness as that criterion.

In "Bentham," Mill claims, "That the morality of actions depends on the consequences which they *tend* [my italics] to produce, is the doctrine of rational persons of all schools."[10] In the same work, he writes, "The morality of an action depends on its *foreseeable* [my italics] consequences."[11] However, in "Auguste Comte and Positivism," Mill argues that "the good of the human race is the ultimate standard of right and wrong,"[12] not that the *tendency* to promote the good of the human race is the ultimate standard of right and wrong.

Perhaps Mill is simply inconsistent with respect to this point. Or, perhaps Mill is not particularly interested in specifying whether he is interested in evaluating actions by their likely rather than their actual consequences, or vice versa, because his major concerns, e.g., combatting the views of the 'intuitive' school, are centered elsewhere. Nonetheless, there is some appeal to both foreseeable and actual consequence utilitarianism.

The foreseeable consequence utilitarian bases the moral worth of an action on its *probable* consequences. She is not concerned about the occasional bad result which occurs when one performs the action most likely to promote utility. So, too, even if an act might occasionally produce certain undesirable consequences because of an intervening cause, that would not change the *tendency* of that act. Insofar as Mill morally evaluates actions in terms of their tendencies, his view basically coincides with, if not is identical to, a type of foreseeable consequence utilitarian position — he would say that as long as the action is *likely* to promote the requisite amount of utility, it is right.

The above analysis is dependent upon our agreeing about how completely we should describe the relevant act. For example, the utterance of lies tends to produce disutility. However, the utterance of lies which save lives tends to promote utility. If I am trying to figure out the tendency of this act of lying-to-save-someone's-life, I will have to decide whether to look at the consequences of uttering lies in general or at the consequences of uttering lies in order to save a life.

To some extent, Mill would simply dismiss the worry alluded to above, and would claim that in such a case one should of course look at the tendency of a lie-to-save-a-life rather than at the tendency of a lie in general. "There is no difficulty in proving any ethical standard whatever to work ill, if we suppose universal idiocy to be conjoined with it."[13] Mill's comment notwithstanding, this worry cannot be dismissed so easily, since in many cases it is not clear which description (if any) is idiotic.[14]

Putting aside the difficulties associated with the completeness with which acts should be described, it should be clear that there are appealing aspects to both foreseeable and actual consequence utilitarianism. Insofar as unforeseeable consequences cannot be a part of an agent's deliberative process, it is tempting to argue that they should not be considered in the moral evaluation of actions. Insofar as the promotion of humankind's utility is morally praiseworthy (even if it happens fortuitously), it is tempting to argue that any actions which promote that end are morally praiseworthy.

Often, these temptations will not conflict, since in many cases an action which promotes foreseeable utility will also in fact promote utility. However, suppose that action A's tendency is to promote disutility. On a particular occasion, Jurgenson, who knows the tendency of A, nonetheless A-es and fortuitously promotes utility. The actual consequence utilitarian will call Jurgenson's action morally right, whereas the foreseeable consequence utilitarian will call that action morally wrong.

Or, suppose that an agent performs an action which any reasonable agent would have assumed would promote utility. Unfortunately, due to unforeseeable events, the action proves to be disastrous. The foreseeable consequence theorist will call that action morally right, whereas the actual consequence theorist will call it morally wrong.

Much of the plausibility of foreseeable consequence utilitarianism can be attributed to its allegedly not demanding the impossible of moral agents, e.g., it does not ask agents to take account of unforeseeable consequences. Yet, one must ask, 'Unforeseeable for whom?' Insofar as the consequences are unforeseeable by a reasonable agent but not for certain scientists, we are still holding the agent to an unfair standard if we determine the moral worth of an action by looking at what was "foreseeable."[15] This has lead some theorists to posit a 'reasonably foreseeable' consequence standard, since if it really is somehow unfair to consider within one's evaluation the consequences of an action which *no one* could foresee, it is also unfair to consider within one's evaluation the consequences of an action which someone, *qua* reasonable agent, could not have foreseen.

A critic might argue that agents are held to an unfair standard if they are judged according to a 'reasonably foreseeable' standard, assuming that the agent herself was unable to act as a reasonable person would have acted. However, there would seem to be ways to justify the use of the 'reasonably foreseeable consequence' standard.[16]

For example, suppose that Swanson will not choose to perform the action which a reasonable person would have chosen to perform, because he does not have all of the information which a reasonable person would need in order to make a good decision. Suppose further that Swanson had ample opportunity to get this information, but was too lazy or irresponsible to do so. We might hold him responsible (by applying the 'reasonable person' standard), because he culpably neglected to find out this relevant information.[17]

Although Mill sometimes writes as if he is offering a foreseeable consequence utilitarian system and sometimes a reasonably foreseeable consequence standard, he explains the difference between assessing actions and assessing characters in a way which helps actual consequence utilitarians to support their position. As we shall see in Chapter 6, this distinction will go a long way, although perhaps not all of the way, towards blunting the attractiveness of (reasonably) foreseeable consequence utilitarianism.

On Making Prudential Decisions

When Mill talks about the difference between natural and accidental consequences, he argues that 'the maxims of prudence are wholly founded on foresight of consequences'. If that argument is to be at all compelling, prudence and morality must be analogous in certain important respects.

When we make prudential decisions about particular actions, we tend not to ask ourselves whether the action under consideration will *maximize* our utility, but whether it will *promote* our utility. Should I jog today rather than solely work on this book? The answer is unclear. I believe that my jogging will promote but not maximize my utility. Since I believe that my jogging is a good thing (even if it is not the best thing) for me to do, I am satisfied that my jogging is prudent.

Let us suppose that had I worked on this book all day, I would have benefited more than I did by taking off some time and jogging. Jogging was a prudent action, although not the most prudent action. An imprudent action would have been one that had not promoted my interests, for example, my having gotten drunk.

If one can be more or less prudent without being imprudent, then one must wonder whether Mill's analogy is appropriate. Since Mill does not believe that actions have degrees of rightness, prudence and rightness are in this respect disanalogous. (One action cannot be more right than another without the latter action's being wrong, while one action can be more prudent than another with the latter action's being imprudent).[18]

If a prudent action is simply one which promotes one's own interests (and if there is no implicit requirement that one's interests be promoted to a certain extent), then prudent actions are disanalogous to right actions in another way. According to Mill, a right action must promote utility to a certain extent. He does not believe that an action is right merely because it promotes an infinitesimal amount of net utility.[19]

Even were Mill to claim that one acts rightly as long as one promotes utility (no matter how small the amount), and even were he to claim that actions have degrees of rightness, there would still be difficulties with his analogy between prudence and morality. If I am thoughtful, I may have a pretty good idea about which actions will promote my own long-term happiness. However, that would hardly help me to know which actions would promote the happiness of present and future generations. Thus, even if I could decide what would be a prudent action for me to perform, I might be unable to decide what would be the morally right action.[20]

Nonetheless, Mill's basic point remains. No one would claim that (in most cases in most of our daily lives) we have insufficient information about the likely effects of our actions to predict which actions would be prudent or imprudent. So, too, in most circumstances in our daily lives, we have a good enough idea about the likely effects of our actions to predict which alternatives would be morally acceptable and which not.

Preference-orderings Versus Pleasure-maximization

Many theorists today do not talk about the promotion or maximization of happiness, but instead talk about the satisfaction of desires or preferences. We can define desires or preferences in terms of an agent's tendency to perform in certain ways, given certain conditions (i.e., in terms of observed behaviors), whereas happiness can only be measured through introspection — it can only be measured by the agent herself.

Critics argue that if utility is defined in terms of happiness, interpersonal comparisons of utility are not possible (since an agent cannot, through introspection, measure someone else's happiness). However, if utility is defined in terms of the satisfaction of desires (in terms of external behaviors), then we can make interpersonal comparisons of utility, since desires can be measured by someone other than the agent herself. Thus, defining utility in terms of the satisfaction of desires seems to be more useful than defining it in terms of pleasure.

If the promotion of utility is our moral standard, then we must define utility in a way which makes its promotion at least theoretically possible. If desire-satisfaction would allow for interpersonal comparisons of utility whereas pleasure-promotion would not, then (*ceteris paribus*) there is good reason to choose the former.[21]

Although the move from 'pleasure-promotion' to 'preference-ordering' is initially attractive, its attraction soon disappears. Theorists are fooling themselves if they believe that looking at non-mentalistic desires will help them make meaningful interpersonal utility calculations. To see why, we need only try to define 'desire'.

For example, we might define 'desire' by suggesting that if an individual has a desire to bring about a certain state of affairs (S), he will *tend* to do those things which are likely to bring about S; he will *tend* to be pleased if S unexpectedly occurs and displeased if S unexpectedly does not occur.[22] If we adopt this definition, then wherever we see a term which has mentalistic connotations, e.g., 'being pleased', 'being displeased', etc., we must define it in non-mentalistic terms, e.g., by talking about tendencies to act in certain ways. Otherwise, we will be no better off than we were when talking about the mentalistic terms 'happiness' or 'pleasure'.

Let us look at 'desire' defined in terms of tendencies which do not make use of internal states. A being has a desire to do or receive something if she acts in particular ways almost every time that certain circumstances obtain. For example, if I go and eat something almost every time that I have not eaten for ten hours, I have a desire to eat whenever I have not eaten for ten hours.

Such a definition is not as helpful as it might first appear. When I push the 'p' key on my word processor, a 'p' appears on the screen. While my word processor does not smile every time that the 'p' key is pushed and a 'p' appears and thus we do not know that my processor's 'desires' are being satisfied, I also do not smile when the 'p' appears. We tell that I, as a writer, am pleased that a 'p' appears when I push a particular key, because I do not try to erase the letter which is printed. I continue to press the 'p' key and continue not to erase the letter which appears when the key is pushed.

If we look at tendencies for a course of action to be repeated and no accompanying tendencies to counteract the effects of the first action, e.g., my hitting the 'delete' key, then my word processor desires certain characters to appear when the keys are pushed. Yet, it seems absurd to talk about my word processor as having desires satisfied unless we are speaking in some metaphorical sense.[23]

Utilitarianism is a system which seeks to maximize the utility of sentient beings. The reason that we talk about satisfying my but not my word processor's desires is that we assume that I have internal conative states and that my processor does not. The desire theory is plausible only to the extent that it, too, is laden with mentalistic connotations. While theorists are correct that desires are easier to measure when stripped of all mentalistic connotations, theorists are incorrect if they think that they are measuring anything useful.[24]

When we look at how people act in order to determine what makes them happy, we are using a method by which we hope to approximate the internal states — we look at behaviors which, we hope, will fairly accurately reflect the happiness and unhappiness which people feel. However, if 'desires' and 'happiness' are both based on internal states, a critic might claim that utilitarianism has a measurement problem which, even theoretically, is impossible to solve.

Such a criticism proves too much. If valid, it would not only impugn utilitarianism, but also any system which postulated that humans (excluding conscious agents themselves) had mental states at all.[25]

Even if one rejects that our making interpersonal comparisons is fundamentally incoherent, one still must face other difficulties. It might seem, for example, that one would have to learn about *each* person's tastes in order to aggregate them.[26] However, we *can* make interpersonal comparisons which, although not completely capturing individual preferences, are nonetheless good enough to yield informative judgments.[27]

Many (if not most) ethical and social systems require that we make interpersonal comparisons.[28] Even if we do not have the sort of justification which we would like for our interpersonal utility comparisons, we must and do make these comparisons anyway.

Cardinal Versus Ordinal Comparisons

There is a more important reason why theorists have preferred preference-ordering to pleasure-maximization, which can be explained if we consider the allusion to the Benthamite calculus in Chapter 1. Bentham suggests that we can calculate the value of a pleasure by considering its intensity, duration, propinquity, fecundity, purity, and extent. If we could simply multiply these factors together to yield some numerical value which accurately reflected the value of a pleasure, both intrapersonal and interpersonal utility comparisons might not seem very difficult to make. Yet, theorists have rightly suggested that the Benthamite proposal is unworkable — it is too difficult to get fixed values of pleasures for *one* individual, much less for a group of individuals.[29]

Theorists plausibly argue that it would be much easier to get a rank-ordering of pleasures (i.e., an ordinal ranking) for an individual than it would be to get the exact values of various pleasures for an individual, since we can get some idea of a person's preference-ranking by simply watching how she spends her money. However, neither cardinal theories (i.e., where one assigns a numerical value) nor ordinal theories (where one 'simply' assigns a rank-ordering) are without fault.[30]

To make matters worse, insofar as we are trying to make utilitarian calculations, we have to concern ourselves with *inter*personal rather than *intra*personal utility calculations. If we simply cannot make cardinal assignments (notwithstanding what some theorists seem to have thought), then our ability to make exact interpersonal utility comparisons will be non-existent.[31] Were ordinal intrapersonal comparisons completely unproblematic, they would still often be difficult to aggregate.[32] However, given that they are not entirely unproblematic even on the intrapersonal level, it might seem that utilitarianism is a system which, in Sedgwick's words, 'is unfitted to man's understanding and therefore worthless in its application'.

Yet, we can make very *rough* comparisons of aggregate welfare.[33] If we could not do so, then both utilitarian theorists and public policy makers would be in a great deal of trouble. "It is truly a whimsical supposition that if mankind were agreed in considering utility to be the test of morality, they would remain without any agreement as to what *is* useful." People cannot sincerely argue that the principle of utility gives no dictates about which actions will indeed promote human welfare. "Men really ought to leave off talking a kind of nonsense on this subject, which they would neither talk nor listen to on other matters of practical concernment."[34]

Thus, one might say (following Aristotle) that one cannot demand a greater precision in a subject than is appropriate for that subject.[35] We have a good enough idea about which actions will promote aggregate utility and about which actions will promote aggregate disutility to give us moral guidance, even if in fact we cannot make exact interpersonal utility comparisons. However, a different (although related) problem is suggested when we try to get even a rough idea about what would indeed promote aggregate welfare, *viz.*, whether we should take people's attitudes and opinions as we find them or whether we should subject them to some kind of 'correction'.

Pleasures as They Are Versus Pleasures as They Should Be

Whether we look at desire-satisfaction or pleasure-maximization, we must decide whether *all* desires or pleasures should be considered in our utility calculations. For example, someone might desire that a particular event (E_1) occur because she *mistakenly* believes that its obtaining would lead to the occurrence of some other event (E_2) which she greatly desires. Since she does not really want E_1 to occur (if its obtaining would make E_2 less likely to occur), we might exclude from our calculus her desire for E_1. Generally, we might exclude desires based on factual or logical errors.

Yet, we will not resolve all of our difficulties by merely excluding these kinds of factual or logical errors. Suppose, for example, that Jones knows that he will produce a great deal of unhappiness for others by performing a particular action, *which is one of his reasons for performing that action.* Jones has not made a factual or logical error; on the contrary, he has carefully deliberated about how best to satisfy his malicious desires. An individual may promote his own utility in a logical manner, taking into account all of the relevant information, and nonetheless produce much disutility because of his malevolent attitudes.[36]

Mill provides an answer to this problem. Preferences based on counter-productive attitudes are not reinforced because humankind's utility is not advanced by reinforcing them. Whether we talk about desire-satisfaction or pleasure-production, we must have some criteria by which to judge which desires and attitudes we should have. Mill provides a criterion by which to judge these attitudes, *viz.,* whether the attitudes themselves will promote the utility of humankind.

Suppose that there is a sadistic society or world. Many people derive much enjoyment from torturing a small minority. The enjoyment produced by that torturing more than outweighs the pain which is thereby produced.

Mill would say that the sadistic attitudes are not proper. Their impropriety can be demonstrated if we compare two worlds, S and B. S is the world which is composed of sadists. B is a world composed of benevolent people.

In S, the inhabitants greatly enjoy torturing, so much so that much net utility is produced by their inflicting severe pain on a small minority. In B, the inhabitants greatly enjoy helping each other, so much so that there is much net utility in their aiding their fellow beings.

In B, there is no disutility which must be produced in order for utility to be produced. No one has to inflict pain on someone else in order to be happy. If the benevolent people enjoy being benevolent as much as the sadistic people enjoy being sadistic, then B will be a happier world than S, since B would not have a small number of people who were tortured.

In both worlds, there will be some unhappiness due to disease, natural disasters, etc., but we shall assume that such unhappiness will be roughly equal in both worlds. Indeed, we shall assume that the two worlds are exactly similar, except that S is composed of sadists and B is composed of benevolent people.

In order for S to have more aggregate happiness than B has, humans would have to enjoy hurting each other much more than they enjoy helping each other. Perhaps such a claim is not difficult to believe. However, a much stronger claim must be made in order for Mill to approve of, or even condone, humans' being sadistic, *viz.*, that humans, by their very nature, enjoy hurting each other more than helping each other.

Mill would never assent to such a claim. He would say of the person who thought that humans were evil by nature that she was mistaking the "temporary or local phases of human character for human character itself." Mill believes "in the wonderful pliability of the human mind."[37] Further, he claims that, fortunately, humans are not evil by nature, but instead have a natural desire to be in unity with other human beings.[38]

Mill does not make his theory of human psychology sufficiently clear.[39] It is quite clear, however, that Mill believes that most human's attitudes can be molded as long as one uses good methods of positive and negative reinforcement, e.g., societal and family opinion, role models, etc.

We might distinguish between two types of molding or education:

a.   Through education, the person is made aware of capabilities and attitudes that she already has. "Human beings have faculties more elevated than the animal appetites, and, when once made conscious of them, do not regard anything as happiness which does not include their gratification." This type of molding does not change attitudes; it merely brings them to light. For example, Mill believes that if a person were able to experience the mental pleasures, then she would choose them, just because humans are the sort of creatures who enjoy mental pleasures more than physical ones. So, too, Mill believes that the human natural tendency to be a social animal who cares about other sentient creatures only needs to be brought to light and, possibly, nurtured.[40]

b. Through education, the person's attitudes are changed. Mill believes that through the use of external sanctions and of proper training at an early age, people can be made to acquire almost any attitude. Even if humans did not have a natural inclination to be benevolent, they could acquire such an attitude through this molding process.[41]

Mill believes that society should use both sorts of molding processes. He hopes and rather optimistically expects that humans will someday become sufficiently benevolent that they will value their own interests no more than they value the interests of others.

According to Mill, when I am attempting to figure out the consequences of my action, I must consider whether my action will lead to others' having inappropriate (disutility-producing) attitudes. Insofar as they would, my action is (ceteris paribus) wrong. Sadistic pleasures, per se, are not discounted in the utility calculation.[42] However, because they lead to others' displeasures currently and because their being promoted will lead to others' future displeasures, the satisfaction of sadistic desires will be morally wrong.

The above is not meant to suggest that when we correct people's attitudes, we should merely try to develop within them the kind of attitudes which a "competent" judge would have. For example, insofar as a judge believed that certain kinds of abstract contemplation which could not even indirectly lead to the promotion of humankind's utility might nonetheless be intrinsically superior to all other pleasures, her values might be counterproductive to inculcate (or promote) generally. Such a judge should not be prevented from engaging in this sort of contemplation, but that is a different matter requiring independent justification. The kinds of attitudes the inculcation of which would lead to the promotion of the utility of present and future generations need not coincide with the attitudes of someone who is capable of appreciating the higher pleasures.

Prudence Versus Morality

Mill attempts to refute critics' claims that consequences of actions are not ascertainable by pointing out that people frequently make prudential decisions based on foresight of future consequences. Mill then claims that just as one can base one's prudential decisions on one's ability to foresee consequences, one can base one's moral decisions on that same ability. As long as one has, or can be made to have, the proper benevolent attitudes, one should have no difficulty in knowing which actions are morally correct.

Mill has two problems when he compares calculations of prudence with calculations of morality:

1.   His comparison of morality with prudence is a little suspect. Morality seems to have a "sacred" aura surrounding it. Prudence does not. By comparing morality with prudence, we lose the sacred aspect associated with morality.

By comparing morality with prudence, Mill suggests that we have sufficient foresight of future consequences to judge how we morally should act. However, by making this comparison, Mill blurs an important difference between the two. The degree of certainty which we have in predicting future consequences may warrant our taking a risk and acting, even if it does not warrant our being blamed for having failed to promote utility.

If I act imprudently, I suffer the consequences — I do not promote my own utility. However, I suffer no further punishment. I am not morally blamed for my imprudence. I can shrug my shoulders, hold my head up high, and continue on with my everyday affairs. My only 'punishment' is that I do not enjoy the utiles that I might otherwise have enjoyed.

Yet, we do not want the person who acts immorally to shrug his shoulders, hold his head up high, and continue on with his everyday affairs. Nor do we wish the person to escape all punishment. By talking about morality as prudence generalized,[43] we risk blurring the difference between:

a. the reactions which are appropriate for an agent to have who has just realized that he has acted *imprudently*, and

b. the reactions which are appropriate for an agent to have who has just realized that he has acted *immorally*.[44]

2. Mill's analogy between prudence and morality is problematic because agents do not always know which action is prudent. For example, when I try to figure out what would be prudent for me to do, I make educated guesses. I do not know which action(s) would be prudent. I look at all of the relevant information which I have at hand and try to make a prediction.

In response to the criticism that "there is not time, previous to action, for calculating and weighing the effects of any line of conduct on the general happiness," Mill argues that for "the whole past duration of the species," "mankind have been learning by experience the tendencies of human actions."[45] Thus, Mill claims that we do know in many instances which action will promote utility.[46]

Yet, the problem still remains, since one often does not know which action would be prudent to perform. For example, suppose that a particular individual is trying to decide whether she should go to college and, if she should, which college she should attend. She does not know how long she is going to live. Were she only to live another year, the prudent course of action might be very different from what it would be, were she to live to be one hundred and twenty-five. This woman will choose a college, if she decides that she should attend one, if only because her not choosing one seems less likely to promote her own utility than would her choosing one. However, she does not *know* what will promote her own interests. She just has to guess.

She will not be guessing blindly. She will have some information to help her make a decision. She simply will not have enough information to *know* what the correct decision is. Mill would not be bothered by this individual's not knowing which course of action will be best, since "an amount of knowledge quite insufficient for prediction may be most valuable for guidance."[47]

By comparing morality with prudence, Mill countenances an element of guesswork in our moral decision-making. Just as an individual cannot always tell which action will promote his own utility, an individual will not always be able to tell which action will promote the utility of humankind.

Mill must face a further difficulty which is involved in predicting what will promote humankind's utility. Even if the woman who had to make a decision about college could predict which action would promote her own utility, she probably would not be able to predict which actions would promote the utility of humankind. At least when an individual is trying to promote her own utility, she has some knowledge of many of the relevant circumstances. If she is trying to promote humankind's utility, she is unlikely to have enough of the relevant information to make an informed judgment.

Her having the proper benevolent attitude might not enable her to know which actions would make others happy. For example, my benevolent attitude would not help me in determining whether my writing a book on Mill would promote utility or disutility.

To some extent, Mill can solve this problem by talking about competent judges. However, merely because I am a competent judge with respect to the higher and lower pleasures does not establish that I am a competent judge with respect to knowing what indeed will promote the long-term interests of humankind. Insofar as "competent" judges are more capable of making moral judgments, that capability is based upon their understanding what will promote humankind's utility, not on their appreciating the intrinsic superiority of the higher pleasures.

Are Effects in Principle Knowable?

Mill probably shifts between foreseeable consequence and actual consequence utilitarianism because of his ambivalence about the predictability of human action. He believes that human actions are more easily predicted than some of the occurrences which the physical sciences predict and are less easily predicted than some of the others. Physiology "is embarrassed by greater natural difficulties, and is probably susceptible of a less degree of ultimate perfection, than the social science; inasmuch as it is possible to study the laws of one man's mind and actions apart from other men, much less imperfectly than we can study the laws of one organ or tissue of the human body apart from the other organs or tissues."[48] Yet, there "are reasons enough why the moral sciences must remain inferior to the more perfect of the physical; why the laws of their more complicated phenomena cannot be so completely deciphered, nor the phenomena predicted with the same degree of assurance."[49]

Were the human character completely known and were the totality of influences on the human character considered, Mill believes that total prediction of human action would be possible.[50] However, it is quite difficult, if not impossible, to take account of all of the influences on individuals and hence quite difficult, if not impossible, to make infallible predictions. "[E]ven if our science of human nature were theoretically perfect, that is, if we could calculate any character as we can calculate the orbit of any planet, *from given data*; still as the data are never all given, nor ever precisely alike in different cases, we would neither make infallible predictions, nor lay down universal propositions."[51]

The Relative Unimportance of the Possibility of Prediction

Mill argues that even if we cannot be certain about the consequences of our actions, we have enough information to know how to act. Nonetheless, different utilitarian moral systems might be constructed, given the difficulty of predicting consequences. For example, we might evaluate actions by their reasonably foreseen consequences, by their foreseeable consequences, or, retrospectively, by their actual consequences.

Critics have claimed that utilitarianism cannot be a valid system unless agents can know the consequences of their actions beforehand. Mill disagrees. Were these critics correct, they would be providing a formidable attack on *most moral systems*. Certainly, any theory which held that individuals had a duty to be beneficent would also be subject to that same attack.

Yet, this kind of attack also applies to theories which do not require beneficence. Any theory which is achievement-oriented (i.e., holds that a particular end should be *promoted* or *attained* rather than merely *attempted*) will be open to an analogous criticism.

Suppose that a theory mandates that agents promote others' autonomy. Insofar as consequences are unpredictable, one cannot know that one's action will indeed accomplish that end. One's action might, because of unforeseeable or unforeseen events, promote another's lack of autonomy rather than promote her autonomy. While we have a good idea about which actions will promote others' autonomy, we do not know which actions will do so. Mill's point is that we do not need to *know* what will indeed promote an end in order to have a good enough idea about how to promote that end. Just as we do not need to *know* which action will promote our own interests in order to act prudently, we do not need to *know* which action will promote humankind's interests in order to act morally rightly.[52]

Since Mill is not a maximizing act-utilitarian, agents will have some leeway when trying to perform morally right actions. As long as agents can figure out what is likely to promote (the requisite amount of) utility rather than what is likely to maximize utility, they can act rightly. They may not be able to figure out the *best* action, but that is not what they are morally required to do. The same point can be made about attitudes. One is blameworthy if one does not have utility-promoting attitudes. One does not need to have utility-maximizing ones in order to be free from justified blame.

Mill's comparing calculations of prudence with calculations of morality may be problematic because:

1.   the realm of morality seems more sacred than does the realm of prudence,
2.   decisions of prudence are easier to make than are decisions of morality, i.e., than are decisions about what would be prudent for humankind, and
3.   we do not always know which actions would be prudent.

Nonetheless, we often have a pretty good idea about which actions and attitudes promote utility. Further, we do not need *knowledge* of future consequences in order to have a very useful guide to help us figure out how we should act. Finally, insofar as we must *know* beforehand which action is right in order for a moral assessment of our actions to be appropriate, very few (if any) currently favored moral systems offer a way in which actions may appropriately be morally evaluated.

NOTES

1. Adam Sedgwick, *A Discourse on the Studies of the University* (New York: Humanities Press, 1969), p. 55.
2. William Whewell, *Elements of Morality Including Polity* (New York: Harper and Brothers, 1845), Sec. 548, p. 389.
3. "Whewell on Moral Philosophy," p. 179.
4. "Sedgwick's Discourse," p. 63.
5. *A System of Logic*, Book 3, Ch. 17, Sec. 2, Par. 1, p. 526.
6. Some theorists believe that Mill is a foreseeable consequence utilitarian. See Marcus Singer, "Actual Consequence Utilitarianism," *Mind* 86 (1977), pp. 67 ff; and, Bart Gruzalski, "Foreseeable Consequence Utilitarianism," *Australasian Journal of Philosophy* 59 (1981), p. 164. See also Packe, *The Life of John Stuart Mill*, p. 198.
7. *Utilitarianism*, Ch. 2, Par. 2, p. 210.
8. *Ibid.*, Ch. 2, Par. 20, p. 220.

In the passage from which this is taken, Mill is distinguishing between assessments of actions and assessments of characters. Had he had a foreseeable consequence position in mind, he could have easily said that utilitarianism makes people 'regard only the dry and hard consideration of the *tendencies* of actions'. Further, when he offers his response here, he does *not* say that people are in error in thinking that utilitarians evaluate actions in terms of their *consequences* rather than their *tendencies*. He instead invokes his action/character distinction.

9. *Ibid.*, Ch. 4, Par. 9, p. 237.
10. "Bentham," *CW* Vol. 10, p. 111.
11. *Ibid.*, p. 112.
12. "Auguste Comte and Positivism," *CW* Vol. 10, p. 335.

The claim here is *not* that either foreseeable consequence or actual consequence utilitarians are unable to offer a coherent, systematic account of Mill's moral philosophy in light of the above citations. On the contrary, both kinds of theorists can consistently account for these comments and neither theory can simply be dismissed out of hand.

Thus, it is denied here that probable consequence utilitarianism "confuses the effects of an action with the motives or epistemic state of the agent." See Holbrook, *Qualitiative Utilitarianism*, p. 5. While actual consequence utilitarians *can* account for the epistemic state of the agent by including it within *character* assessment, probable consequences utilitarians are *not* guilty of a conceptual mistake by including it within *action* assessment.

13. *Utilitarianism*, Ch. 2, Par. 24, p. 224.

14. This problem is not peculiar to utilitarianism. Kant, for example, has an analogous problem when deciding how to formulate maxims. The question would be whether in the case described a rational being could will as a universal law that (1) all people lie, or (2) all people lie-to-in-order-to-save-a-life. There is some controversy among Kant commentators about which is the proper formulation and about what Kant would say is the morally appropriate course of action in the case suggested.

15. See my "Actual Versus Foreseeable Consequence Utilitarianism," *Southern Journal of Philosophy* 27 (1989), pp. 585-598.

16. Hutcheson distinguishes between *foreseeable* consequences and *foreseen* consequences and argues that the former may be used in the evaluation of characters while the latter may be used in the evaluation of actions. Francis Hutcheson, *A Short Introduction to Moral Philosophy* 2nd ed. (Glasgow: Robert and Andrew Foulis, 1755), pp. 119 ff. This point will be developed more fully in Chapter 6.

17. For a related argument, see my "Frankfurt, Aristotle and PAP," *Southern Journal of Philosophy* 23 (1988), pp. 238 ff.

18. M. Singer suggests that on Mill's account one can act more or less rightly. See his "Actual Consequence Utilitarianism," p. 69. Holbrook also believes that actions can have degrees of rightness. See *Qualitiative Utilitarianism*, p. 110. Here, it is argued that Mill uses 'right' to mean 'morally permissible'. Acts would not vary in degrees of rightness, although some right acts would be better than others.

19. Since Mill does not argue that *only* utility-maximizing actions are morally right, he is not open to the charge that the analogy is inapt because there is only one act (the utility-maximizing one) which is morally right, while there are many acts which are prudent.

20. Hardin argues that "there are at least three in-principle cognitive obstacles to our calculating the overall good of the consequences of our actions: (1) we lack the information required to carry out such calculations ... (2) we lack relevant causal theories of the implications of our actions, and (3) we could not do the necessary calculations in any case because our minds have limited capacity." Russell Hardin, *Morality Within the Limits of Reason* (Chicago: University of Chicago Press, 1988). For a related discussion, see also David Gauthier, *Morals By Agreement*, pp. 123 ff. We shall see that Mill can avoid, at least to some extent, some of the moral difficulties to which these limitations give rise. See Chapter 6.

21. See Rolf Sartorius, *Individual Conduct and Social Norms* (Encino: Dickenson Publishing Co., Inc., 1975), p. 27.

22. This is Brandt's definition of a desire. See Richard Brandt, "Two Concepts of Utility" in *The Limits of Utilitarianism*, Harlan Miller and William Williams eds. (Minneapolis: University of Minnesota Press, 1982), p. 170.

23. If one claims that word processors cannot act but can only behave and thus should not be included within this discussion, then one is basing one's analysis upon one's ability to detect the presence or absence of internal states. One's analysis would still be laden with mentalistic connotations. If one claims that word processors seem unable to self-initiate, one ignores that processors can perform many functions without being 'told to' each time via the keyboard.

Suppose, for example, that my word processor has a built-in dictionary, and every time that a word is typed which is not included within the dictionary the word is highlighted *without any prompting from the keyboard*. Were one to claim that the word processor is merely following a program, one would have to find a good, non-question-begging way to distinguish between the processor's program and a human's character.

The claim here is *not* that our treating word processors *as if* they had desires would be absurd. Nor is the claim that our doing so would necessarily be unhelpful. See Daniel Dennett, "Intentional Systems" in his *Brainstorms* (Montgomery: Bradford Books, 1978), p. 7. The claim here is merely that our claiming that word processors literally have desires seems absurd.

24. It should by no means be thought that theorists are unanimous in believing that desire-satisfaction is superior to happiness-maximization. See Amartya Sen, *Choice, Welfare and Measurement* (Oxford: Basil Blackwell, 1982), p. 72; and Richard Brandt, *A Theory of the Good and the Right* (Oxford: Clarendon Press, 1979), p. 24.

Griffin proposes an "informed" desire theory. However, his theory has certain difficulties. Since he seems to believe that desires of the dead should be included in determinations of well-being, his system would seem to make our figuring out what would indeed promote well-being even more difficult than would other kinds of theories. (See Chapters 1 and 2 of *Well-Being*.) Insofar as he only allows "informed" desires to count, where he wants to "appeal not to person's actual desires but to what really would increase or decrease the quality of their lives" (p. 47), he may not only *not* be solving the calculation problem (since he needs to say much more than he does if he is going to show why this would no longer be a problem for him), but he also may be risking radically separating "well-being" from the pleasure/happiness/contentment which people actually do or even can feel in their own lives.

25. See Sartorius, *Individual Conduct and Social Norms*, p. 29.

26. See Griffin, *Well-Being*, p. 119.

27. See Sen, *Choice, Welfare and Measurement*.

28. See Sartorius, *Individual Conduct and Social Norms,* p. 29; Hare, *Moral Thinking*, p. 118; and Griffin, *Well-Being*, pp. 80 ff.

29. For criticism of the Benthamite calculation, see Riley, *Liberal Utilitarianism*, pp. 57 ff.

Of course, if we cannot get exact measurements for intensity, duration, etc., then theorists will have much more difficulty in arguing that Mill makes utilitarian calculations too vague by adding an 'inherent quality' factor.

30. See Hardin, *Morality Within the Limits of Reason*, pp. 172-173. For some of his reasons, see note 25.

31. Even if we could add up utilities across persons, we might not want to do so. See Hardin, *Morality Within the Limits of Reason*, pp. 173 ff; Gauthier, *Morals By Agreement*, p. 125.

32. Hardin, *Morality Within the Limits of Reason*, p. 172.

33. See Hardin, *Morality Within the Limits of Reason*, pp. 55 ff and 176.

34. *Utilitarianism*, Ch. 2, Par. 24, pp. 224-225.

35. Aristotle, *Nicomachean Ethics*, Book 1, Chap. 3, 1094b 25 ff.

36. See John Harsanyi, "Rule Utilitarianism and Decision Theory," *Erkenntnis* 11 (1977), pp. 29-30.

37. "Auguste Comte and Positivism," p. 306.

38. *Utilitarianism*, Ch. 3, Par. 10, p. 231.

39. For a discussion of Mill's theory of human psychology, see Berger, *Happiness, Justice and Freedom*, Ch. 1.

40. *Utilitarianism*, Ch. 2, Par. 4 ff., p. 210.

41. *Ibid.*, Ch. 3, Par. 8, p. 230.

42. Griffin argues that, ultimately, no satisfactions of desires (with the possible exception of the satisfaction of uninformed desires) can be excluded from utility calculations. See his "Modern Utilitarianism," *Revue International de Philosophie* 36, pp. 339 ff.

His attempt to show why sadistic desires will not appropriately be fulfilled is different from, although in some ways analogous to, the analysis offered here. See his *Well-Being*, p. 26.

43. A prudent action involves the promotion of an individual's utility. A moral action involves the promotion of humankind's (all individuals') utility.

44. Kant criticizes moral theories of enlightened self-interest because they put "the motives to virtue and those to vice in the same class, teaching us only to make a better calculation while obliterating the specific difference between them." Immanuel Kant, *Foundations of the Metaphysics of Morals* (1785), Lewis White Beck trans. (Indianapolis: Bobbs-Merrill Co., Inc., 1959), p. 61 (B. 442). So, too, utilitarians can (and should) argue that one may lose the specific difference between the moral and the prudent if one simply thinks of morality as prudence generalized. The prudentialist who acts wrongly may not only be miscalculating but may be trying to figure out the

wrong thing, since he is trying to figure out what would promote his own interest rather that what would promote the general interest. The promotion of the latter (the general interest), but not the former (the individual's own interest), has this sacred aura around it.

Various Mill commentators (mistakenly) argue that since (according to Mill) prudent actions are never required by duty, one should never be punished by conscience for failing to perform them; whereas since morally right actions are required by duty, one should be punished by conscience for failing to perform them. Mill's views on the moral status of prudence and prudent actions will be discussed in later chapters.

45. *Utilitarianism*, Ch. 2, Par. 24, p. 224.

46. Sartorius makes a similar claim when he says that "we know very well what the consequences of our acts will be in many significant instances." Sartorius, *Individual Conduct and Social Norms*, p. 19.

47. *A System of Logic*, Book 6, Ch. 6, Sec. 2, Par. 2, p. 878.

48. *Ibid.*, Book 3, Ch. 11, Sec. 1, Par. 7, p. 456.

49. *Ibid.*, Book 3, Ch. 23, Sec. 7, Par. 4, p. 603.

50. *Ibid.*, Book 6, Ch. 2, Sec. 2, Par. 1, pp. 836 ff.

51. *Ibid.*, Book 6, Ch. 3, Sec. 2, Par. 2, p. 847.

Mill's believing that all actions are *determined* helps explain why he spells out 'probable' consequences in terms of *epistemic* considerations. He does not distinguish between probable and foreseeable consequences by talking about the former as 'objective' and the latter as 'subjective', but instead uses the terms interchangeably. "Objectively" (i.e., were there no epistemic constraints), the most probable consequences *will be* the actual consequences if all relevant factors have been considered in the appropriate ways.

52. For further discussion of achievement-oriented systems, see my "Actual Verus Probable Consequence Utilitarianism."

CHAPTER FOUR

On the Difference Between Morality and Expediency

Mill's claim that our studying human history will provide us with sufficient guidance about which actions will promote the utility of humankind is rather straightforward. Unfortunately, his writings are not always so clear. Some aspects of his theory are quite obscure and confusing. For example, Mill believes that actions which produce (foreseeable) utility are both expedient and morally right. Yet, he clearly wants to differentiate between morality and expediency.

Various critics offer interpretations to help elucidate Mill's theory. They argue that according to Mill an action is morally praiseworthy or blameworthy only if the praising or blaming of that action would itself promote utility. These interpretations are not particularly palatable and do not account well for Mill's writings. A better interpretation of Mill's theory is that *external* sanctions are appropriately imposed only if the imposition itself would promote utility, but that *internal* sanctions are appropriately imposed whenever an action does not promote utility. In this chapter, we shall examine why these commentators' interpretations are in error and why the interpretation offered here is a better and more plausible account of Mill's position.

The Ultimate Principle

Part of the confusion stems from a comment Mill makes in *A System of Logic*. He talks about "the Art of Life, in its three departments, Morality, Prudence or Policy, and Aesthetics: the Right, the Expedient, and the Beautiful or Noble, in human conduct and works."[1]

Each area might seem to have its own principle of regulation. The moral would be judged according to one principle, the expedient would be judged by another, and the beautiful or noble would be judged by yet another. However, Mill believes that "if that principle be rightly chosen [i.e., the principle by which to judge the non-moral], it will ... serve quite as well for the ultimate principle of Morality, as for that of Prudence, Policy or Taste." If Mill is correct, then all three areas will be guided by the same principle.

Such a universal principle might be rather difficult to discover. Nonetheless, Mill believes that he has found this all-encompassing principle, claiming that the "general principle to which all rules of practice ought to conform, and the test by which they should be tried, is that of conduciveness to the happiness of mankind ... in other words, that the promotion of happiness is the ultimate principle of Teleology."[2]

If Mill has indeed discovered the ultimate principle by which all aspects of life should be judged, then a few problems are suggested. For example, how can one distinguish between the prudential and the moral if they are both to be judged by the principle of utility?

Ryan's View

Ryan quite plausibly maintains that 'prudential' refers to self-regarding actions and 'moral' refers to other-regarding actions.[3] (Actually, he should say that 'moral' refers to both self- and other-regarding actions, or all-regarding actions.) Indeed, one might expect to find such a distinction within a utilitarian framework, viz., that prudent actions are those which promote the individual's happiness and that moral actions are those which promote the general happiness.

Yet, such an interpretation cannot account for the aesthetic aspect of life.[4] We can come to understand the aesthetic by examining two other passages in Mill's writings:[5]

1. In *A System of Logic*, the aesthetic corresponds to the "Beautiful or Noble."[6]

2. In "Bentham," Mill talks about an action's "aesthetic aspect, or that of its beauty." The aesthetic quality is something which "we admire or despise." An action's "beauty ... or the reverse, depend[s] on the qualities which it is evidence of. Thus, a lie is ... *mean*, because it is cowardly — because it proceeds from not daring to face the consequences of telling the truth — or at best is evidence of want of that *power* to compass our ends by straightforward means, which is

conceived as properly belonging to every person not deficient in energy or understanding."[7]

3. In *Utilitarianism*, Mill talks about a characteristic which distinguishes "morality in general from the remaining provinces of expediency and worthiness."[8]

These passages suggest that the aesthetic quality is concerned with the noble or the beautiful. It is determined by looking not at the action, *per se*, but at the agent's character. We look to see if the action is something which we "admire or despise," a judgment which "depends on the qualities which it [the action] is evidence of," e.g., whether it is motivated by benevolence or malice.

We can explain "the Art of Life, in its three departments, Morality, Prudence or Policy, Aesthetics: the Right, the Expedient, and the Beautiful or Noble, in human conduct and works" in the following way, insofar as we are talking about the "Art of Life" *for the individual herself*: The right or moral is concerned with all-regarding actions. The expedient is concerned with self-regarding actions. The aesthetic is concerned with both types of actions — it is concerned with the character or nobility of the man or woman who performs the actions.

Mill says that all three aspects of life should be judged by the *same* principle. Were it 'one should perform those actions which will promote happiness', there would be no difficulties in applying the principle. Expedient actions would be those which would promote the happiness *of the agent*, while right actions would be those which would promote the happpiness *of humankind*. The aesthetic aspect of an action would reflect the agent's character. Traits that promoted humankind's utility would be aesthetically pleasing; traits that promoted humankind's disutility would be aesthetically displeasing.

The common principle for all the Aspects of Life, however, is 'one should promote the general happiness'. Prudence (or self-happiness) is judged in light of the principle of (general) utility. Mill seems to be claiming that what is good for everyone is also good for the self. The two categories seem to collapse into one. Indeed, since the aesthetic is also judged in light of the same principle, all three aspects of life might seem to collapse into one.

Mill does not wish to collapse all areas of life into one big area. He claims that "happiness is the sole end of human action, and the promotion of it the test by which to judge all of human conduct; from whence it necessarily follows that it must be the criterion of morality, *since a part is included in the whole* [my italics]."[9] Morality is only a part of human life. Yet, Mill claims that the same principle is appropriately used to judge all aspects of human conduct, obviously believing that the principle of utility plays several roles.[10]

Scholars have expended much time, energy, and thought in trying to understand how the principle of utility can have such versatility. They offer ingenious formulations of how Mill differentiates between an expedient action and a right one, which, unfortunately, are neither accurate nor particularly palatable.

Certainly, Mill is responsible for some of the confusion. He uses terms in a variety of ways and, unless one is careful, one may misunderstand what he is arguing. For example, we consider a term like 'right'. When people call an action right, they sometimes mean that the action is *best* and sometimes that it is *permissible*.[11]

When Mill uses the principle of utility as the moral "standard" or "criterion," he is using it to determine which actions are *permissible*. Mill thus believes that a utility-maximizing action would be right (using either sense of the term 'right'). However, he does not believe that only utility-maximizing actions are right (where 'right' means 'permissible'), and instead suggests that a much weaker standard be used to determine moral permissibility.

Mill also uses 'expedient' ambiguously. The "department" of life involving the Expedient is the department of Prudence *or* Policy. It is not difficult to understand why he offers a *disjunction* here. Insofar as 'expedient' does not have a pejorative connotation, the expedient refers to that which promotes long-term happiness. However, one must ask, 'Whose long-term happiness is to be promoted?' Insofar as we talk about the individual's long-term happiness, the expedient is concerned with the prudent. Insofar as we talk about the long term happiness of Society (whether that be an individual society or the Society of Humankind), expedience refers to "*Policy*," i.e., it is concerned with the acts, rules, etc. which promote the *general* happiness.

Rightness need not involve maximal good. So, too, expedience need not involve maximization of good; it need only involve the promotion of good. Thus, there is another potentially confusing point which must be remembered when one considers Mill's comparison of the moral and the expedient (whether 'expedient' refers to 'that which promotes the individual's good' or 'that which promotes the general good'), *viz.*, that neither need involve maximization.

The expedient and the moral are two distinct categories. However, an entirely different question is whether any or all morally right actions are also expedient. Morally right actions produce a certain degree of utility. Actions which promote that degree of utility are also expedient. Merely because the Right and the Expedient are two distinct categories does not imply that an action cannot be placed in both of them. According to Mill, *a morally right action is also an expedient action.*

In part, Mill's theory is confusing because, in a much-discussed passage, he implies that matters of expediency do not involve duties and are not within the moral realm. Critics have developed whole interpretations of Mill relying on the crucial passage which contains this claim. For example, some argue that one can show how Mill's theory of value and his theory of obligation diverge if one carefully examines the passage. Yet, it is misleading to talk about this divergence. Mill's theory of moral value determines what is morally best and what is morally worst. Mill's theory of obligation determines which acts are permissible and which are impermissible, i.e., Mill's theory of obligation determines how much utility one is required to promote. *That determination is made along the scale of what is morally best and what is morally worst.* Both his theory of moral value and his theory of moral obligation are normative — the former tells us which acts, dispositions, etc. are best, while the latter tells us which are morally acceptable.

Precisely because this passage plays such a central role in current Mill scholarship, it and the various interpretations of it will be examined here quite closely. This painstaking examination is justified because of the pivotal importance of the passage which is quoted below.

> We do not call anything wrong unless we mean to imply
> that a person ought to be punished in some way or other
> for doing it — if not by law, by the opinion of his fellow
> creatures, if not by opinion, by the reproaches of his own
> conscience. This seems the real turning point of the

distinction between morality and simple expediency. It is a part of the notion of duty in every one of its forms that a person may rightfully be compelled to fulfill it. Duty is a thing which may be exacted from a person, as one exacts a debt. Unless we think that it may be exacted from him, we do not call it his duty. Reasons of prudence, or the interest of other people, may militate against actually exacting it, but the person himself, it is clearly understood, would not be entitled to complain. There are other things, on the contrary, which we wish that people should do, which we like or admire them for doing, perhaps dislike or despise them for not doing, but yet admit that they are not bound to do; it is not a case of moral obligation; we do not blame them, that is, we do not think that they are proper objects of punishment.[12]

Dryer's View

D. P. Dryer offers one interpretation. The inexpedient, he says, is that which does not maximize general utility. However, merely because something is inexpedient does not mean that it is wrong. "Mill maintains that it would in fact be wrong for a man to do a certain action if and only if three conditions are fulfilled:

(1)   some alternative would have more desirable effects,
(2)   it would be contrary to a rule the observance of which would in general have more desirable consequences than would failure to observe it, and
(3)   it is an action of a kind the condemnation of which would in general have more desirable consequences than the absence of such general condemnation."[13]

Suppose there are two actions open to an agent. The first is utility-maximizing in this particular case. The second would be utility-maximizing in most cases. According to Dryer's formulation, neither action would be wrong. The first action would not be wrong because condition (1) is not met — there is no alternative which would have more desirable effects. The other would not be wrong because condition (2) would not be met — the second action is not contrary to a rule the observance of which would in general have more desirable consequences than would the failure to observe it.

Mill writes, "To admit the balance of consequences as a test of right and wrong, necessarily implies the possibility of exceptions to any derivative rule of morality which may be deduced from that test." He makes clear that in "any particular case, the whole of the circumstances should be taken into view." Further, "if a man willfully overlooks the latter [i.e., the special circumstances of the case], when they are pregnant with mischievous consequences, he cannot discharge himself from moral responsibility by pleading that he had the general rule in his favor."[14]

Suppose that Jones performs what he knows to be a disutility-producing action. Jones points out that the action is in accord with a rule the general observance of which would be utility-maximizing. According to Dryer's interpreation, Jones could claim that he had done nothing wrong because 'he had had the general rule in his favor', e.g., Jones could claim that he should have told the truth in this case, despite the foreseeably horrible consequences, because one generally should tell the truth. Mill would say that Jones "could not discharge himself from moral responsibility." Mill would condemn Jones, saying that the person "who goes by rules rather than by their reasons, like the old-fashioned tacticians who were vanquished by Napolean, or the physician who preferred that his patients should die by rule rather than recover contrary to it, is rightly judged to be a mere pedant, and the slave of his formulas."[15] Dryer's view must be rejected.

Copp's View

Copp looks at the passage and offers the following version of Mill's account of wrongfulness. "S's doing A would be wrong if, and only if,

(a) there is a maximal alternative to S's doing A, and
(b) it would be maximally expedient that if S did A, S would feel regret for this to some degree."[16]

Copp explains that "one who acts wrongly ought to be punished by his own conscience, and perhaps also by public opinion or by law. Punishment by law or opinion might be appropriate in some cases of wrongful behavior, but *punishment by conscience is appropriate in all cases of wrongful behavior* [my italics]."[17]

Copp is suggesting that an action, A, is wrong if there is some alternative action which would promote more utility than A would, and if utility would be maximized by the agent's feeling regret for his action. Initially, Copp's formulation is very appealing, since it seems to exclude from the moral sphere exactly the sorts of actions that a rule-utilitarian would want excluded. For example, choosing the inferior of two comedies for an evening's entertainment would not be immoral, since punishing the agent for such a mistake would seem not to maximize utility.

Unfortunately, the initial appeal soon disappears, since the results of Copp's formulation are not particularly appealing. While he has managed to exclude some of the actions which do not seem to belong within the immoral category, e.g., choosing some musicals, he has also managed to exclude some actions which definitely do belong within that domain, e.g., some murders, thefts, etc.

If Copp is correct that a non-utility-maximizing action is morally wrong if and only if its punishment by conscience would be utility-maximizing, then actions which deontologists *and utilitarians* would call 'wrong' may not be wrong in Copp's system. For example, suppose that Jones wants to kill Smith because Jones is named in Smith's will and Jones wants the money. Jones knows that Smith is planning on changing his will. Fortunately for Jones, she is the only one who knows that Smith is going to change his will and name Anderson as his beneficiary. (Anderson would use the money much more wisely than Jones would.)

Jones decides to murder Smith. She knows that if anyone even suspects that Smith has been murdered, Jones will be one of the prime suspects. She swears by all that is holy that she will never again perform such an odious deed. (She will have no need to kill again — she will already have Smith's money.) She decides to put some fast-acting, painless, traceless poison in Smith's tea. Smith will die quickly and easily. Everyone will assume that Smith (that compulsive overworker) has had a heart attack.

If Copp is correct that a non-utility-maximizing action is wrong if and only if its punishment by conscience would be utility-maximizing, then Jones's action is not wrong. The imposition of pangs of conscience will not be utility-maximizing in this case.

As far as Smith is concerned, it would not be utility-maximizing for Jones to feel guilty. Smith cannot be brought back to life by Jones's feeling conscience-stricken. Unless one wants to talk about the pain which Smith's ghost feels, one must say that Smith will feel no more pleasure by Jones's feeling conscience-stricken than by Jones's feeling guilt-free.

As far as the public is concerned, it would not be utility-maximizing for Jones to feel guilty. We must consider the following four points:

1.   Jones will never commit another crime. Now that she has all of Smith's money, she has no need to be a criminal. Guilt would not serve as an effective deterrent in this case because no future actions need be deterred.

2.   The public's knowing that Jones felt guilty might not make them feel any more secure. They would have no way of knowing that her currently feeling guilty would in any way dissuade her from committing a similar crime, were she so inclined sometime in the future.

3.   The public's knowing that Jones feels guilty must be differentiated from Jones's feeling guilty. Jones can feel guilty without anyone else's knowing about it. The effects of one's feeling guilty need not be the same as the effects of the public's believing that one feels guilty. To show that guilt feelings are warranted, one may have to show that they are warranted even if the public does not know that they exist.

4.   The public does not even know that a crime has been committed. They think that Smith died of a heart attack. The public would be better off, if Jones's feeling guilty is warranted, for Jones to feel guilty in secret. Jones will not commit another crime in any case. Their feelings of security need not be diminished by the knowledge that Smith was murdered, as long as they are in no more danger than they were before he was murdered. If Jones will hurt no one else in any case, then their feelings of security need not be diminished.

If society is not going to benefit by Jones's feeling guilty and if Smith is not going to benefit by Jones's feeling guilty, then we shall have to figure out a way in which Jones will be happier by feeling guilty. Her happiness must more than offset the pain that she will feel from her conscience. Copp makes very clear that warranted feelings of guilt are not pleasant.[18]

Copp might claim that Jones's feeling guilty would improve her character. However, her character will not be improved in the sense that she will be deterred from committing future murders, since she will never repeat her crime whether she feels guilty or not. (Jones no longer needs the money. The risks involved in committing any future crime would more than outweigh the possible benefits.)

Perhaps Jones's character will be improved in the sense that she will realize that she cannot perform wrongful acts without suffering. However, according to Copp's interpretation, we do not yet know whether Jones's action was wrong.

According to Copp's reading of Mill, the moral quality of an action is based upon the efficacy of the sanction. If a man's feeling guilty for having committed a non-utility-maximizing action would produce more good in the world than would have been produced had he not felt guilty, then the man's action was morally wrong. The man who has effective guilt feelings (feelings which in some way cause more good to exist in the world) should feel guilty. The action which he committed was morally wrong because his feeling guilty maximized utility.

Yet, this account involves a fundamental confusion. If we adopt it, we must judge the moral quality of an action by looking at whether utility is maximized by the agent's feeling guilty. Yet, according to Mill's type of act-utilitarianism, an action is morally wrong if it does not, or is not likely to, promote the good of humankind.

Copp has not properly distinguished between the action and the sanction. The action is morally wrong because unhappiness resulted from its performance. Given that the state of the world already involves the immoral action's having taken place, the sanction would produce utility if its imposition would produce more good than would its non-imposition.

Suppose, however, that condition (b) is not met. A man has ineffective guilt feelings, i.e., guilt feelings which promote no utility.

Then, the action which he committed was not immoral, since the sanction was not warranted. Thus, once-in-a-lifetime, secret actions like Jones's may not be wrong, since the agent's feeling guilty may not promote utility. Indeed, even if the actions are neither secret nor once-in-a-lifetime, Copp's theory implies that non-utility-maximizing actions are wrong if and only if the guilt feelings produced by the actions are efficacious — any action which resulted in counter-productive feelings of guilt could not be classified as immoral.

To justify Jones's feeling guilty for killing Smith, we must justify the existence of an essentially internal phenomenon, i.e., feelings of guilt. We must show that the existence of guilt feelings will promote utility. Copp does not even discuss the notion of an inefficacious feeling of guilt, i.e., a painful feeling which does not produce positive results, e.g., guilt feelings which do not prevent future occurrences of similar actions, do not improve the character of the agent, do not lead to generous donations to charities, etc.

Copp's formulation of Mill's argument assumes that guilt feel-ings necessarily promote utility. Often, guilt feelings produce disutility, e.g., one vents one's anger and pain by treating others unkindly. Yet, one of the implications of Copp's view is that inefficacious guilt feelings can affect the moral quality of an action.

Mill and most utilitarians would call most rapes, thefts, and murders immoral. However, according to Copp's view, *if the guilt feelings arising from the performance of these actions produce net disutility,* because not enough utility is produced to compensate for the pain felt by the agent, *then the actions cannot be classified as immoral.*[19]

Our partially determining the moral worth of actions by looking at whether the agent's feeling guilty would in fact be efficacious might yield other dissatisfying results as well (from the rule-utilitarian's point of view), e.g., we might then have to label my choice of the inferior comedy as immoral. Suppose that I chose the lesser of two comedies and felt guilty about it. The guilt might turn out to be efficacious, since I in the future might do more research before buying tickets. Theoretically, my doing research would cause me to support those shows which merited my support. If my guilt feelings maximized utility, then they would be warranted. If my guilt feelings were warranted and my action was non-utility-maximizing, then I would have committed an immoral act. However, even if I had performed a non-utility-maximizing action and even if I would maximize utility in the future because I had had those guilt feelings for having performed a non-utility-maximizing action, most rule-utilitarians would still not want to say that I had acted immorally by going to the inferior show.

Act-utilitarians are sometimes charged with morally evaluating actions which are not appropriately morally evaluated — they are charged with being moral fanatics because they morally evaluate even trivial actions.[20] Copp's version may not escape this charge. For example, one might argue that one's choosing the inferior of two comedies is a trival concern and hence should not be morally evaluated. However, as shown above, *both* Copp *and* the standard act-utilitarian may have to argue that one's choosing the inferior of two comedies is sometimes appropriately morally evaluated. If one's feeling guilty about having chosen the inferior comedy is efficacious because one would thereby be caused to be more careful in the future, then (even according to Copp) one's action would be appropriately morally evaluated, since:

1.   one would have performed a non-utility-maximizing action, and

2.   one's feeling guilty (or regretful) for having done so would be utility-maximizing.

The claim here *is not* that Copp would be charged with moral fanaticism as *often* as the standard act-utilitarian would be so charged — the latter would morally evaluate certain actions which Copp would not. The claim here *is* that both Copp and the standard act-utilitarian will sometimes be open to the charge of being too morally fanatical.

Copp's formulation might exclude from the moral realm some actions which are clearly immoral and might include within the moral realm some actions which, at least arguably, are not immoral, e.g., choosing inferior comedies. Further, his formulation might yield different moral evaluations of similar crimes.

Suppose that there are two people who have committed a robbery. Sally feels guilty. She returns her share of the loot. In addition, she donates a large sum of money to charity. Further, because of her guilt, she never again commits such an action. Sally's stealing was immoral because the sanction was warranted — its imposition was utility-maximizing.

Bill also feels guilty. His guilt causes him to make life miserable for everyone around him. Further, he continues to steal. Bill's stealing is not immoral because the imposition of guilt feelings is not warranted. The feelings of guilt only promote more disutility. A system which calls Sally's action 'immoral' and Bill's action 'not immoral', when Sally and Bill are both willing partners in the same crime, is not a particularly appealing system.

Copp does not seem to realize that he is implying that an agent whose conscience overcompensates by inflicting too much pain (enough pain to outweigh any good resulting from the agent's feeling guilty) can never act immorally. This agent's feeling pangs of conscience would never be utility-maximizing.

Although Copp does not seem to realize that people with inefficacious guilt feelings never act immorally on his account, he does realize that he has a problem with once-in-a-lifetime actions. He tries to get around it by talking about "generic spillover."[21]

'Generic spillover' is based upon the assumption that human consciences cannot make fine distinctions. It might be non-utility-maximizing for a conscience to punish a particular type of action. However, if:

1. that particular type of action is a subset of a larger set of actions,
2. the conscience cannot distinguish between the particular subset and the larger set,
3. the conscience should punish the larger set of actions, and
4. more utility would be produced by punishing the larger set (including the subset) than would be produced by not punishing the larger set,

then the conscience should punish the larger set of actions *including the subset of actions which would be non-utility-maximizing to punish.*

For example, it is utility-maximizing for people to feel guilty about committing murders in general, even if it is not utility-maximizing for people to feel guilty about committing once-in-a-lifetime murders. Copp is claiming that human consciences may not be able to distinguish between once-in-a-lifetime murders and murders in general. If a conscience would not punish someone for committing a once-in-a-lifetime murder, then it would also not punish someone for committing some or all other kinds of murder. Yet, people who commit these other kinds of murder should be punished. It would produce more utility if consciences punished people who committed once-in-a-lifetime murders, despite their being non-utility-maximizing to punish, in addition to people who committed other kinds of murder, than if consciences failed to punish people who committed once-in-a-lifetime murders as well as people who committed other kinds of murder.

Copp's generic spillover argument argument is heavily dependent upon the way that our fallible consciences *do* behave rather than on how they *should* behave. Yet, Mill would hardly agree with someone whose moral system relied so heavily on which actions consciences do or do not *in fact* punish. That was one of the views of the intuitive school which he was trying to combat. Mill insists that the dictates of conscience are themselves appropriately judged in light of the principle of utility. Were an evil genius to change us so that our consciences only punished utility-promoting actions rather than disutility-promoting ones, we would *not* say that no disutility-promoting actions were morally wrong. Rather, we would say that the consciences *should* punish the disutility-producing actions even if in fact they would not, and that the disutility-producing actions were morally wrong even if our consciences would not in fact punish them.

Mill criticizes Blakey for arguing that "God does not [merely] *declare* what is good, and *command* us to do it, but ... God actually *makes* it good," because that view has some unwelcome implications. "If we had the misfortune to believe that the world is ruled by an evil principle, that there is no God, but only a devil, or that the devil has more power over us than God, we ought by this rule to obey the devil. Mr. Blakey is evidently quite unconscious of these consequences of his theory. But, that they are legitimate consequences who can doubt?"[22] So, too, Mill would argue, were our consciences to approve of disutility-producing actions, disutility-producing actions would nonetheless not be morally right.

Yet, Mill's refusal to accept that "we ought to take the feelings [of morality] as we find them as accident or design has made them" and his claim that "the tendency of actions to promote happiness affords a test to which the feelings of morality should conform"[23] should *not* be understood to mean that we should completely ignore our existing moral intuitions. However, Copp's claims notwithstanding, Mill is not arguing that only those of our inexpedient actions which would be utility-maximizing to punish are wrong.

Copp would say that Raskolnikov (in Dostoyevsky's *Crime and Punishment*) behaved immorally because:

1.   Raskolnikov's killing the old woman was non-utility-maximizing, and
2.   Raskolnikov's feeling regret for his action was utility-maximizing.

Suppose that we could be sure that Raskolnikov would never again commit murder (for whatever reason). The pangs of conscience would not be utility-maximizing. They would not be preventing anything — Raskolnikov would never commit another murder, anyway. Copp would argue that Raskolnikov had still acted wrongly. It would be utility-maximizing for him to feel the pangs of conscience for this particular murder because it would be utility-maximizing for him to feel the pangs of conscience for committing murders in general.

Suppose that Raskolnikov$_2$ could distinguish between the once-in-a-lifetime murder of a niggardly, malicious, old woman and the murder of a more worthy human being. Would Copp say that Raskolnikov committed a wrong action because his conscience could not distinguish between this once-in-a-lifetime murder and other types of murders, but that Raskolnikov$_2$ did not commit a wrong action because his conscience could make such a distinction?

Copp's interpretation looks even more peculiar if we consider that consciences might *develop* the capacity to differentiate between somewhat similar actions. For example, suppose that *today* Raskolnikov's conscience cannot distinguish between once-in-a-lifetime murders and murders in general. It would be utility-maximizing for him to feel guilty for murdering the old woman because it would be utility-maximizing for him to feel guilty about committing murders in general. However, suppose that *tomorrow* or *next week* or *next year* Raskolnikov's conscience will acquire the ability to differentiate between once-in-a-lifetime murders and murders in general. His killing the woman at that time would not be wrong.[24]

Copp criticizes those who interpret Mill as an act-utilitarian by saying, "On no act-utilitarian reading would the distinction between morality and simple expediency turn on the appropriateness of a sanction in the case of moral failures."[25] Yet, we are not yet sure that Mill is saying this — that is one of the points at issue. Further, very few moral theorists of any persuasion would determine the morality of an action by looking at the effectiveness of the sanction. Copp's moral theory would hold that my X-ing could be wrong because my conscience could not distinguish it from Y-ing, whereas Smith's X-ing would be morally acceptable because her conscience could distinguish it from Y-ing. Yet, in both situations, the action is the same. The only difference lies in the differing qualities of discernment of our consciences.

Copp understands that according to his theory "it might be wrong for one person to do a given kind of thing in given circumstances which would not be wrong for another person in the same circumstances." Copp offers the consolation that "it may be quite unlikely that a case would actually occur which was of this sort and which conflicted with our reflective judgments."[26] He seems to forget that our reflective judgments would not allow identical actions performed by different people or by the same person at different times to have different moral descriptions.

One might try to amend Copp's position and say that a non-utility-maximizing action is wrong if the experiencing of guilt feelings *should be* utility-maximizing rather than *is* utility-maximizing. Inefficacious guilt feelings would not be a problem if we were concerned with how one's conscience should behave rather than with how in fact it does behave.

Unfortunately, this amended version will also be unacceptable (or, at the very least, unhelpful). Our talking about when a sanction *should be* utility-maximizing implies that we have some *independent* standard by which to judge the appropriateness of the sanction's being utility-maximizing. It would be as if we already knew which actions were immoral and we were trying to juggle the numbers to make the sanctions against such actions utility-maximizing.

If we talk about sanctions which should be utility-maximizing, then we cannot talk about measuring the actual costs of the sanctions versus their actual benefits. Copp's interpretation, where he talks about the actual effects of the sanction, might be represented by the following equations:

C = Cost $\qquad\qquad$ A = Action Committed
B = Benefit $\qquad\qquad$ A_1 = Some Other Action
S = Sanction $\qquad\qquad\qquad$ Open to the
U = Action Utility Sum $\qquad\quad$ Agent to Perform
U_1 = Sanction Utility Sum

$$[B(A_1) - C(A_1)] - [B(A) - C(A)] = U;$$
$$B(S) - C(S) = U_1$$

The first equation is to determine whether the net benefit of performing an alternative to A would outweigh the net benefit produced by the performance of A. The second equation is to determine whether the benefits of imposing a sanction against the agent for having A-ed would outweigh the costs of that imposition. If there is ever a set of values such that U is positive and U_1 is not negative, then the action committed was morally wrong. If there is no A_1 which would make U positive, then the action which the agent committed was utility-maximizing. If U_1 is negative, then the costs of the imposition of the sanction outweigh the benefits of the imposition of that sanction.

If we talk about what $B(S)$ and $C(S)$ should be, i.e., if we already have in mind that the benefits of the sanction should be equal to or greater than the costs of the sanction, then we already have some U_1 in mind such that U_1 would not be negative. If we already have some U_1 in mind which we consider appropriate, then one must wonder how we arrived at that conclusion. It could not be from our own theory, because we are trying to change $C(S)$ and $B(S)$ in order to yield the 'correct' result. If we want to talk about what $C(S)$ and $B(S)$ should be in order to get the 'correct' U_1, then we must be using a different moral theory to establish what the correct U_1 is. Thus, whether Copp talks about warranted sanctions as only involving those guilt feelings which are efficacious or he talks about those guilt feelings which should be efficacious, his formulation of Mill's writings must be rejected.

Lyons' View

Lyons looks at the passage in which Mill talks about the difference between morality and simple expediency and comes up with a somewhat different formulation. "To show that an act is wrong, is to show that a coercive rule against it would be justified."[27] Lyons explains that "from the fact that an act is inexpedient . . . it does not follow that sanctions against it would be justified. For sanctions have costs . . . of the sort that a utilitarian always counts, *and these costs attach to the distinct acts connected with sanctions* [my italics]."[28]

Lyons' formulation has one of the advantages that Copp's formulation has — certain actions which do not seem to belong to the moral realm would not be included within it, e.g., choosing inferior entertainments. Coercive rules against choosing inferior comedies would probably not be justified.

Indeed, in Copp's version, if my guilt feelings (due to my having seen an inferior comedy) maximized utility, then my having chosen the inferior comedy was morally wrong. However, merely because my guilt feelings maximized utility does not mean that a coercive rule against choosing inferior comedies would be justified. As long as *most* people would not have utility-maximizing guilt feelings as a result of having seen the inferior comedy, no coercive rule labeling the choice of inferior comedies as immoral would be justified.

One drawback in Lyons' theory is that he makes Copp's mistake that an action is wrong if and only if the experiencing of guilt feelings would be utility-maximizing.[29] Lyons has failed to take into account that while the experiencing of guilt feelings tends to produce fewer disutilities than does the experiencing of other types of sanctions, the experiencing of guilt feelings also tends to produce fewer utilities than does the experiencing of other sorts of sanctions. Indeed, one's experiencing guilt feelings does not always promote any utility at all. People are not thereby always prevented from committing other crimes, they are not thereby always forced to look more kindly upon their neighbors, etc. The experiencing of guilt feelings does not always serve any utility-producing functions at all. To rest a theory of morality on the *efficacy* of guilt feelings is to misunderstand the effects of guilt and the appropriate bases for morality.

Suppose, however, that Lyons amends his version — he does not need to say that an action is wrong only if the imposition of guilt feelings would be utility-maximizing. Lyons maintains that "sanctions have costs of the sort that a utilitarian always counts."[30] In his amended version, Lyons might also take into account the sorts of benefits which one might expect to be produced by the different sorts of sanctions.

According to Lyons' interpretation, an action's being immoral is not based solely upon the action's being non-utility-maximizing. To call something immoral is to say that sanctions against the action would be justified. Sanctions have costs. For a sanction to be justified, its being used must produce more utility than would its not being used.

Basically, Lyons is presenting the following argument:

If the imposition of a sanction would only add to unhappiness, then the sanction is not justified and 'we do not mean to imply that a person ought to be punished in that way'. If no sanction is justifiable, then we do not think that the person should be punished. If we do not think that the agent should be punished, then we do not think that the action was immoral.

Lyons' explanation is an ingenious method of differentiating the expedient from the moral. Unfortunately, it is open to the same criticisms which were directed at Dryer and Copp.

The implications of such a position are not particularly appealing. Even if Lyons no longer maintains that it is always utility-maximizing for consciences to punish immoral actions, his system still yields rather implausible results.

Suppose that a very powerful woman murders her husband. Using Lyons' criteria, the murderer may not have acted immorally.

In order for an action to be immoral, a coercive rule mandating either internal or external sanctions must be justified. If no such rule can be justified, then the action is not immoral.

Internal sanctions would only be warranted if the sanctions were efficacious. If the murderer feels guilty but the only result of her feeling that way is that she vents her guilt in a disutility-producing way, then the guilt is not warranted. Lyons cannot justify a coercive rule which mandates the imposition of inefficacious guilt feelings.

In order for external sanctions to be warranted, they must be productive of utility. In the example of the husband-killer, the murderer has let it be known that any external sanctions imposed against her would be most unwelcome. Indeed, any external sanctions, either a court trial or the expression of public disapproval, would result in the immediate closing of the factory. The bank in which she has a controlling interest would immediately begin foreclosure procedures against the properties of various townspeople. In short, much disutility would be caused by any external sanctions.

In addition, the murderer promises her most solemn oath that she will never commit such a crime again. (She will never remarry.) In fact, she says, not only will she never kill again, she is quite prepared to make a deal. If no external sanctions are imposed, she will donate a large sum of money to the local hospital. The word 'deal' should be emphasized. She is not donating out of guilt, but is donating as part of a package deal securing her freedom.

Various utilities and disutilities must be considered. On the one hand, no one likes the idea of being blackmailed and the factory owner should not be encouraged to feel that she can commit crimes with impunity.

On the other hand, not many people know that the factory owner was the murderer. Further, she has never lied before and is quite possibly telling the truth now. The town leaders feel quite sure that:

1. the murderer will never kill again, and
2. if they keep their part of the bargain, the owner will donate a huge sum of sorely-needed money to the local hospital.

Much hardship would result from the imposition of sanctions. If one could be reasonably sure that the owner would never again commit such a crime, much more utility would result from ignoring the crime than from accusing the murderer. Many lives could be saved, both financially and medically. According to the system proposed by Lyons, the murder in the above example was not immoral, since the murderer's guilt feelings were inefficacious (she was the sort who would vent her guilt feelings by treating others unkindly) and the external sanctions would result in much disutility.

Or, let us consider another example. White is the only doctor in a small town. She has committed a small theft. Internal sanctions would not be warranted because she has a very strong sense of guilt. Were she to realize that she had done something morally wrong, her guilt feelings would totally incapacitate her and she would be unable to perform her medical duties.

To put the doctor in jail for her 'crime' would rob the town of its only doctor. To express public disapproval would cause her and her family to move, if only out of shame. Again, the town would lose its only doctor. The doctor is unlikely to perform the action again for whatever reasons. The imposition of external sanctions against the doctor would produce much more disutility than would ignoring the 'crime'. Again, the sanctions' not producing sufficient utility would mean that the 'crime' in question was not immoral.

Lyons' system has some very unusual implications. The immorality of an action depends upon the power or position of the agent, and whether the agent is willing to use her power. The factory owner might not have threatened to close down the town. She might have been willing to have endured the sanctions just as if she had been a powerless person. Ironically, had the factory owner been willing not to have been vengeful, her action would have been immoral, since the costs of the external sanctions would then have been much lower. If the doctor had been able to suffer the pangs of conscience without going to pieces, then her action would also have been immoral.

Lyons does not avoid these problems by talking about coercive rules. Just as the costs of imposing sanctions might vary depending upon the particular person against whom the sanction was to be imposed, the costs of imposing sanctions might vary depending upon the particular *type* of person against whom the sanction was to be imposed. For example, it might be very costly to impose sanctions against malicious tycoons, whereas it might not be particularly costly to impose sanctions against benevolent paupers.

Lyons claims that an action is wrong if a coercive rule against it can be justified. When we are trying to determine whether a particular coercive rule is justified, we are given two choices:

    a.   Suppose that coercive rule R obtains, a rule which prohibits all people from A-ing.

    b.   Suppose that no coercive rule R obtains. All people are allowed to A.

Yet, there is another possibility which Lyons fails to consider.

    c.   Suppose that coercive rule R obtains, a rule which prohibits some people from A-ing but allows other people to A.

Those people whom it would be utility-maximizing to prohibit from A-ing will be prohibited from A-ing. Those people whom it would not be utility-maximizing to prohibit from A-ing will not be prohibited from A-ing.

Lyons cannot justify a coercive rule preventing all A-ing if there is another rule which produces even more utility, e.g., a rule which only prohibits A-ing by people whom it would be utility-maximizing to prohibit from A-ing. For example, powerful, malevolent people should not be prohibited from A-ing if prohibiting them from so acting would be non-utility-maximizing.

Powerful, malevolent people might lash out if any sanctions were imposed against them. Powerless, benevolent people would not lash out if they had sanctions imposed against them. Using the rationale which Lyons suggests, we should adopt moral rules which would punish benevolent, powerless people who performed in certain ways, but which would not punish malicious, powerful people who performed in those same ways.[31]

Even a sophisticated rule-utilitarian would have trouble justifying a whole class of inefficacious external sanctions, e.g., imposing sanctions against those people both willing and able to cause a great deal of disutility. Lyons' rule would have to be 'One can impose external sanctions only against those who cannot or will not make the sanctions disutility-producing'. Any other coercive rule which Lyons proposed would be difficult to justify, since he would be able to devise another rule (which proscribed the imposition of external sanctions against very powerful and vengeful people) which would yield more utility.

Lyons might claim that rules which only allowed the rich/powerful to act in certain ways might cause a great deal of resentment. Perhaps so. We then merely need to postulate that the rich/powerful would become *very* nasty if sanctions were imposed against them, more than nasty enough to outweigh the resentment of the inequality.

Mill would disagree with Lyons' interpretation. In the passage from *Utilitarianism* quoted by Lyons, Mill says that people who have acted immorally deserve punishment. However, Mill argues, "*Reasons of prudence, or the interest of other people, may militate against actually exacting it* [my italics]."[32] Such a comment suggests that the costs of the sanction have not already been figured into the punishment. If an action's being wrong implied that the punishment's imposition would be utility-maximizing, then other people's interests would hardly be a reason not to impose sanctions. (The importance of Mill's comment regarding whether punishment should actually be exacted is generally overlooked.)

Lyons' theory suggests that Mill is guilty of double-counting. Mill would allegedly be including the cost of the sanction when figuring out whether an action was required by duty. He would be counting the cost of the sanction again when he says that reasons of prudence or the interests of other people may militate against actually imposing the sanctions.

Mill believes that people with improperly developed natures will not have consciences which indicate the correct course of action. That Mill admits that one's conscience can yield incorrect dictates has several implications which Lyons must take into account. For example, if one has a 'faulty' conscience, one can have inefficacious guilt feelings. One might feel too guilty or not guilty enough after performing various actions. If the guilt feelings are either too strong or too weak, our moral calculations will be thrown off, assuming that our moral evaluations are based upon the amount of guilt that one feels. Lyons will have much difficulty in justifying a coercive rule which mandates the imposition of inefficacious guilt feelings.

Mill's talking about moral feelings which do not dictate correctly implies that there are 'correct' moral feelings. However, this implies that Mill is using a moral standard, *which is neither based upon when pangs of guilt actually occur nor upon the actual severity of the pangs of guilt when they do occur.*

Mill agrees with his father that "conscience itself, the very desire to act right, often lead[s] people to act wrong," e.g., inquisitors who "sincerely believed burning heretics to be an obligation of conscience."[33]   Mill speaks approvingly of Bentham who "passed judgment on the common modes of reasoning in morals and legislation, deduced from phrases like 'laws of nature', 'right reason', 'the moral sense', 'natural rectitude', and the like, and characterized them as dogmatism in disguise imposing its sentiments upon others under cover of sounding expressions which convey no reason for the sentiment, but set up the sentiment as its own reason."[34]   Mill criticizes Blakey for confounding "two distinct, though nearly connected, questions: the *standard* or *test* of moral obligation, and the *origin* of our moral *sentiments*. It is one question what rule we *ought* to obey, and why; another question how our feelings of approbation and disapprobation *actually* originate. The former is the fundamental question of practical morals; the latter is a problem in mental philosophy."[35]   Mill clearly believes that the dictates of a particular person's conscience need not be correct and that they too must be subject to the ultimate standard, i.e., the principle of utility.

Sometimes, Mill explains, external sanctions are not warranted.

> There are good reasons for not holding [the agent] to the responsibility but these good reasons must arise from the special expediencies of the case: either because it is a kind of case in which he is on the whole likely to act better when left to his own discretion, than when controlled in any way in which [the members of] society have it in their power to control him; or because the attempt to exercise control would produce other evils, greater than those which it would prevent. When such reasons as these preclude the enforcement of the responsibility, the conscience of the agent himself should step into the vacant seat, and protect those interests of others which have no external protection; judging himself all the more rigidly, because the case does not admit of his being made accountable to the judgment of his fellow creatures.[36]

Thus, Lyons' theory about the costs of sanctions does represent Mill, *but only insofar as the sanctions are external.* Indeed, Mill says that when the external sanctions are too costly, "the conscience of the agent himself should step into the vacant seat, and protect those interests of others which have no external protection." (Mill uses 'should' instead of 'will' because not every agent has true moral feelings.)

One's having correct moral feelings is especially important in those cases in which the imposition of external sanctions is not warranted. These are precisely the times when Lyons' interpretation is the most dangerous. If external sanctions are not warranted and one does not have true moral feelings, then Lyons would say that if one's guilt feelings did not maximize utility, then the action in question was not immoral. Mill would say that in these instances it is especially important that the agent feel guilty, precisely because he is not subject to punishment from others. Even if the agent has a 'defective conscience', he still should feel guilty, because someone with true moral feelings would have felt guilty. The agent has acted immorally, even if his pangs of conscience do not maximize utility.

If Lyons' interpretation is correct, then Mill is confused when he distinguishes between those who have true moral feelings and those who do not. Mill says that if one has true moral feelings, one's conscience will step into the vacant seat. If one does not have true moral feelings, then one's conscience will not step in or will step in incorrectly.

Suppose that there are two people, Rob and Roberta. *Rob has true moral feelings, while Roberta does not.*

Roberta performs an action. Rob would have felt guilty had he performed it. Roberta does not feel guilty, despite her having performed it.

Suppose that more utility is produced by Roberta's not feeling guilty (she has inefficacious guilt feelings) as would have been produced by her having felt guilty. Suppose further that the imposition of external sanctions would not be utility-maximizing. According to Lyons, Roberta's action was not immoral, because her feeling guilty would not have been utility-maximizing. Thus, Roberta has true moral feelings, since her conscience did not punish her when punishing her would not have maximized utility.

If Lyons objects that he is talking about coercive *rules*, then we can simply generalize Roberta's case. People like Roberta who perform actions like Roberta's should not feel guilty, since their feeling guilty would be non-utility-maximizing.

Yet, a person with true moral feelings, e.g., Rob, would have felt guilty for having performed such an action. Even if Roberta did not feel guilty, Mill would have said that she should have felt guilty. Even if imposing external sanctions against her would not have been utility-maximizing and even if her conscience' imposing sanctions against her would not have been utility-maximizing, Roberta would still not be relieved of the responsibility for her actions. She still has acted immorally.

Mill says, "Reasons of prudence, or the interest of other people, may militate against actually exacting [the duty], but the person himself, it is clearly understood, would not be entitled to complain." Thus, even if the costs of punishing Roberta outweigh the expected benefits of punishing her, she is still culpable. She is not entitled to complain about her treatment. Lyons' interpretation of Mill would imply that Roberta had not acted immorally, because sanctions against her would not have been utility-maximizing. Lyons' interpretation must be rejected.

Brown's View

Brown adopts a somewhat different tack. He agrees with Lyons and Copp that "the prima facie expediency of punishing a kind of conduct is a necessary condition for its being wrong."[37] However, he disagrees with them about the function of conscience within Mill's moral system.

Brown suggests that Mill's saying that all immoral actions should be punished by the agent's conscience, if not by law or public opinion, is "an afterthought, and a rhetorical flourish."[38] Brown discounts Mill's reliance on conscience as a punisher for moral wrongdoing, despite Mill's claim in *Utilitarianism* that conscience is the "ultimate sanction . . . of all morality,"[39] despite Mill's criticizing Bentham for having omitted considerations of conscience,[40] and despite Mill's claim in *On Liberty* that there are cases in which the agent's conscience must be active, precisely because the imposition of external sanctions would not be warranted.

Brown cites two passages to support his interpretation of Mill. Brown writes, "When Mill says that one element of the concept of a right is a demand for punishment, he elaborates the point by speaking of 'a valid claim on society to protect him in the possession of it, either by the force of law, or by that of education and opinion'."[41] But Mill, in this quotation, is talking about the protection of rights, not about what makes an action right or wrong. Of course, the protection of rights involves the force of law, or education and opinion. But that simply does not address the issue at hand.

Brown also cites a passage from Mill's notes to his father's *Analysis of the Human Mind* (1869 vol. 2:325).

> No case can be pointed out in which we consider anything as a duty, and any act or omission as immoral or wrong, without regarding the person who commits the wrong and violates the duty as a fit object of punishment. We think that the general good requires that he should be punished, if not by law, by the displeasure and ill offices of his fellow-creatures: we at any rate feel indignant with him, that is, it would give us pleasure that he should suffer for his misconduct, even if there are preponderant reasons of another kind against inflicting the suffering.[42]

Mill is saying that if we consider something to be a duty, then we consider the person who fails to perform the duty as a fit object for punishment. What sort of punishment? Usually, the offender should be punished either by law or by the displeasure and ill offices of his fellow creatures. Sometimes, however, a person is a fit object of punishment, even though he should suffer *neither through the law nor through society*.

If Brown is correct that law and society are the only relevant punishers, then we must ask ourselves in what sense a person could be a "fit object of punishment" if neither law nor society should punish him. Brown interprets Mill as if he were claiming that a person can be a 'fit object of punishment', even if (because of prevailing societal conditions) that person should not be made to suffer. Were Brown correct, Mill would not have said, "We do not call anything wrong unless . . . a person ought to be punished in some way or other for it." Instead, Mill would have said, "We do not call anything wrong unless . . . *prima facie* a person ought to be punished in some way or other for it."

According to the passage which Brown cites, an agent guilty of misconduct should be punished by law or by his fellow creatures, unless there are preponderant reasons not to impose the sanction. If these preponderant reasons obtain, then Mill says that *we* should not inflict the suffering. *He does not say that the agent should not suffer.* Indeed, we would be pleased if the agent's conscience were to inflict some pangs.

The cited text is quite compatible with Mill's comment in *On Liberty* in which he says that all violations of duty do not necessarily warrant the imposition of an *external* sanction, although they would warrant that the agent's conscience 'step in'. In the passage which Brown cites, Mill says that we would be pleased should the agent suffer, even though we should not inflict the suffering. Thus, Mill leaves open the possibility that the agent's conscience will inflict the suffering. Indeed, later in the same paragraph, Mill says, "We endeavor, as far as possible, that our social institutions shall render us this service [i.e., punishing the wrongdoer]. We are gratified when, *by that or other means* [my italics], the pain is inflicted . . . " The "other means" presumably refers to, or at least includes, the agent's conscience.

Brown is mistaken in wanting to discount the role of conscience. His mistake is due to his interpretation of *On Liberty*. Brown is correct that Mill believes that "conduct must be harmful to other people, before any occasion can arise for defence, retaliation or the control of these." However, Brown goes too far when he says that "conduct is wrong only if it is harmful to others."[43]

On Liberty is a tract about those areas of life which should be free from societal interference. Neither the State nor society should interfere with my actions unless I harm others. However, merely because no external interference would be warranted does not imply that my action is morally permissible. Mill makes quite clear that some

immoral actions should neither be prevented nor punished by either the
State or society.

Brown's interpretation of Mill is open to some of the same objections which were aimed at Lyons. It also suggests that Mill is
guilty of double-counting. Mill says that external sanctions need not
be imposed if such an imposition would be non-utility-maximizing.
Were Brown's interpretation correct, Mill would include the costs of
the sanction when figuring out whether an action was morally right
and would count the costs again when trying to figure out whether the
sanction should be imposed.

According to Brown's reading of Mill, malicious, powerful tycoons
rarely act immorally, since they can make the imposition of external
sanctions non-utility-maximizing. Indeed, even *prima facie*, there
would not be utility in punishing most immoral actions performed by
powerful and malicious agents.

Mill admits that public policy might require that certain sanctions
not be imposed against powerful, malicious people. Yet, he would
never claim that these people have not acted immorally merely because
the imposition of external sanctions against them would be disutility-
producing. Indeed, Mill makes very clear that when the "attempts to
exercise control would produce other evils, greater than those it would
prevent . . . , the conscience of the agent himself should step into the
vacant seat." Brown's interpretation of Mill must also be rejected.[44]

Mill believes that an action is immoral if a disinterested, properly
functioning conscience would punish it.[45] Dryer, Copp, and Lyons all
believe that a properly functioning conscience will punish only when
the punishment itself would be utility-maximizing. This view is not
particularly attractive. Too many clearly immoral actions might not
be immoral if we subscribed to this view. Mill believes that a
disinterested, *properly functioning* conscience will punish an action,
even if the imposition of such an internal sanction would be disutility-
producing. For example, some of the secret, once-in-a-lifetime actions
discussed in this book would be punished by conscience, even if such
guilt feelings were not efficacious.

The philosophers discussed above have grasped the essential question, *viz.*, when would a properly developed conscience impose a
sanction. However, they have misunderstood Mill's answer to that
question.

According to Mill, external sanctions are rightly imposed when:

a.   a wrong action has been committed, and
b.   the imposition itself would promote (net) utility.

However, Mill does not use that same standard for internal sanctions. Were he to have done so, then he would have risked eliminating condition (a).

Mill calls an action wrong when it should be punished by law, public opinion, or conscience. If an action should be punished whenever the imposition of sanctions would produce utility, then he would be arguing that sanctions are rightly imposed when:

a.   a wrong action, i.e., *an action against which the imposition of sanctions would produce net utility,* has been committed, and
b.   the imposition itself would promote (net) utility.

Basically, this formulation would then reduce to 'An action is wrong when the imposition of sanctions against it would promote (net) utility'. On that view, even a utility-maximizing action might be wrong, i.e., might be an action against which the imposition of sanctions would promote (net) utility.

Theorists might rightly object that the two conditions specified above do not capture their arguments.[46] Basically, they argue that condition (a) should read:

a.   "A non-utility-maximizing action has been committed."

Were these theorists' interpretations correct, then anytime that one performed an action which produced slightly less utility than the utility-maximizing action would have produced, one would have acted wrongly as long as one's feeling slightly guilty for a short period of time would have promoted utility. (An analogous criticism can be made of rule-based interpretations.) Certainly, that is a coherent system. However, it simply is not Mill's.

The greater difficulty with that interpretation occurs when individuals have very counter-productive consciences. Those kinds of individuals (at least if very powerful and malicious) may not be acting wrongly even when they perform *disutility*-producing actions. As long as neither the imposition of internal sanctions nor the imposition of external sanctions would promote utility, an agent's *disutility*-producing action would be at most inexpedient. If Mill believes that all disutility-producing actions are wrong, then none of the above theories can be an accurate interpretation of Mill's system.

Many theorists believe that according to Mill the efficacy of the sanction must be considered when one morally evaluates actions. Two different kinds of reasons are offered above to cast doubt on that interpretation:

1. There is an *external* difficulty with such a position, viz., if we try to apply this system we will end up with rather counter-intuitive results. Whether we consider the act-utility or the rule-utility of the imposition of the sanction(s) when we morally evaluate actions, we will claim that certain actions are wrong which most people believe are not wrong and that certain actions are not wrong which most people believe are wrong.

2. There is an *internal* difficulty to this interpretation, viz., it is contradicted by some of Mill's writings. Insofar as Mill claims that "actions are right in proportion as they tend to promote happiness, wrong as they tend to produce the reverse of happiness,"[47] he is not incorporating the costs of the sanction in the moral evaluation of the action. On his view, (net) disutility-producing actions are morally wrong even if the imposition of sanctions against those actions would also produce (net) disutility.

Certainly, Mill is partially to blame for these misinterpretations. His confusing comments about the difference between morality and expediency have misled his interpreters. In the next chapter, we shall see how Mill distinguishes between morality and expediency. We shall also see that Mill offers a moral standard to determine the rightness/wrongness of an action which does not at all depend on the utility/disutility of the imposition of a sanction against that action. Instead, that standard will be linked to (some of) the attitudes of the society in which the agent lives.

NOTES

1. *A System of Logic*, Book. 6, Ch. 12, Sec 6, Par. 2, p. 949.
2. *Ibid.*, Bk. 6, Ch. 12, Sec. 7, Par. 3-4, p. 951.
3. Alan Ryan, *John Stuart Mill* (New York: Pantheon Books, 1970), p. 215.
4. Ryan realizes this difficulty. *Ibid.*, p. 216.
5. These passages are pointed out by D. G. Brown in his "Mill on Liberty and Morality," *Philosophical Review* 81 (1972), p. 154.
6. *A System of Logic*, Book. 6, Ch. 12, Sec. 6, Par. 2, p. 949.
7. "Bentham," p. 112.
8. *Utilitarianism*, Ch. 5, Par. 15, p. 247.
9. *Ibid.*, Ch. 4, Par. 9, p. 237.
10. As Brown points out, "But the most pressing question for this interpretation is ... : in what terms can the Principle of Utility possibly be stated, if it is to have this conclusiveness and versatility of role?" Brown, "Mill on Liberty and Morality," p. 154.
11. J. N. Findlay makes this point. See his *Values and Intentions* (London: George Allen and Unwin, Ltd., 1961), p. 339.
12. *Utilitarianism*, Ch. 5, Par. 14, p. 246.
13. D. P. Dryer, "Mill's Utilitarianism," *CW* Vol. 10, p. cv.
14. *CW* Vol. 19, pp. 638 ff.
15. *A System of Logic*, Book. 6, Ch. 12, Sec. 2, Par. 2, p. 944.
16. Copp, "The Iterated-Utilitarianism of J. S. Mill," p. 84.
17. *Ibid.*, p. 86.
18. *Ibid.*, p. 85.
19. Admittedly, this account assumes that guilt feelings might be intense enough that they, if of sufficient duration, could more than offset the pain caused by a rape, theft, or murder. Yet, certainly, there is no theoretical reason why this could not be so.
20. See Marcus Singer, "Consequences, Desirability and the Moral Fanaticism Argument," *Philosophical Studies* 46 (1984), pp. 227-237.
21. Copp, "The Iterated-Utilitarianism of J. S. Mill," p. 94.
22. "Blakey's History of Moral Philosophy," p. 27.
23. "Whewell on Moral Philosophy," p. 172.

24. The point here is *not* that utilitarianism cannot handle the Raskolnikov case, although act-utilitarians cannot claim that the murder of the old woman is in principle objectionable (the act-utilitarian cannot claim that no set of utilities could justify such an action). The point here is that Mill's utilitarianism as outlined in this book handles the problems posed by this type of case better than Copp's interpretation of Mill's utilitarianism does.

Thus, all of the counter-examples in this chapter involve *disutility*-producing actions which would be *disutility*-producing to punish. Mill and most utilitarians would call these actions immoral. However, theorists who adopt any of the interpretations of Mill's theory offered in this chapter will not be able to call these (or suitably modified) actions immoral.

25. Copp, "The Iterated-Utilitarianism of J. S. Mill," p. 80.

26. *Ibid.*, p. 97.

27. David Lyons, "Mill's Theory of Morality," *Nous* 10 (1976), p. 109.

28. David Lyons, "Human Rights and the General Welfare" in *Rights*, ed. David Lyons (Belmont: Wadsworth Publishing Co., Inc., 1979), p. 181.

29. *Ibid.*, p. 180.

30. *Ibid.*, p. 179.

31. Rawls rejects a view which holds "to each according to their threat advantage." See his "The Independence of Moral Theory," p. 11. The question here is whether Lyons would be able to provide a non *ad hoc* rationale to reject such a view.

32. *Utilitarianism*, Ch. 5, Par. 14, p. 246.

33. John Stuart Mill, *Autobiography*, *CW* Vol. 1, p. 51.

34. *Ibid.*, p. 67.

35. "Blakey's History of Moral Science," p. 26.

36. *On Liberty*, Ch. 1, Par. 11, p. 225.

37. D. G. Brown, "Mill's Criterion of Wrong Conduct," *Dialogue* 21 (1982), p. 32.

38. *Ibid.*, p. 36.

39. *Utilitarianism*, Ch. 3, Par. 5, p. 229. Semmel correctly recognizes the importance of conscience. See Semmel, *John Stuart Mill and the Pursuit of Virtue*, pp. 176, 195. See also Albert William

Levi, *A Study in the Social Philosophy of John Stuart Mill,*
University of Chicago doctoral dissertation, 1938, p. 30.
  40. "Remarks on Bentham's Philosophy," p. 13.
  41. Brown, "Mill's Criterion of Wrong Conduct," pp. 35 ff.
  42. *Ibid.,* p. 39.
  43. *Ibid.* Edwards also subscribes to this interpretation. See his
"J. S. Mill and Robert Veatch's Critique of Utilitarianism" *Southern
Journal of Philosophy* 23 (1985), pp. 181-200. So does John Gray.
See his "Indirect Utility and Fundamental Rights" in *Human Rights,*
Ellen Paul, Jeffrey Paul and Fred Miller, Jr. (eds.) (London: Basil
Blackwell, 1984), p. 79. Kilcullen believes that this interpretation is
correctly ascribed to Mill, but that the position is unconvincing. See
John Kilcullen, "Mill on Duty and Liberty," *Australasian Journal of
Philosophy* 59 (1981), especially p. 298.
  44. One might argue that basically each theorist is claiming that
an action is a 'candidate' for being classified as immoral if the
difference between its expected utility and the expected utility of the
utility-maximizing action is no less than the cost of any of the
appropriate sanctions. However, since the pangs of conscience can
vary in degrees of pain, one could simply say that the intensity-
duration combination of the pangs of conscience should be equal to the
difference between the happiness produced by the action in question and
the happiness which would have been produced by the utility-
maximizing action.
  I am not claiming that the 'candidate' interpretation
corresponds to any of the theories mentioned above. Nonetheless,
such a theory might classify (virtually) all non-utility-maximizing
actions as deserving some degree, however small, of punishment and
hence (virtually) all non-utility-maximizing actions would be
immoral, assuming that the only relevant costs of the pangs would be
felt by the agent.
  Of course, another question is raised here. What about the
costs involved in developing appropriate consciences within
individuals? Edwards argues that these costs should be taken into
account when determining the wrongness of actions. See his "J. S.
Mill and Robert Veatch's Critique of Utilitarianism," p. 183. I do not
believe that we should include the costs of developing/educating

consciences when considering whether the imposition of the pangs of conscience would be utility-maximizing.

1. When Mill talks about the internal sanction, he talks about a "more or less intense" pain. See *Utilitarianism*, Ch. 3, Par. 4, p. 228. Insofar as we talk about whether the imposition of the internal sanction would be warranted *this* time, we seem to be assuming that a properly developed conscience has already been instilled.

2. Were we to include the costs of developing/educating conscience in our calculations, we might have disutility-producing actions the punishment of which would be disutility-producing. Insofar as disutility-producing actions are wrong (which Mill clearly says), this interpretation cannot be accurate.

3. We will have difficulty in determining how to distribute the costs of developing consciences. Should we figure out the costs and divide them up equally among each of the agent's actions? Or should we divide them up among each of the agent's non-utility-maximizing actions? Etc.

4. When we want to determine the costs of imposing sanctions, we can look at how much pain is caused in the agent and, possibly, how much pain she causes others as a result of her feeling pangs of conscience. Since we usually do not act specifically to develop/educate consciences, we would have difficulty in determining which costs are appropriately deemed the costs of developing proper consciences.

45. Mill defines wrong actions in terms of those actions which *would* be punished by a properly developed conscience. He does not define 'wrong' in terms of those actions which a conscience would *tend* to punish, i.e., Mill does not define wrong actions in terms of those actions which conscience would have a *disposition* to punish.

46. Condition (a), as specified above, appeals to wrongness because that would allow for an independent standard of obligatoriness which is totally unrelated to the efficacy of the sanction. It will be argued in the following chapters that internal sanctions are appropriately imposed whenever condition (a) is true, and external

sanctions are appropriately imposed whenever conditions (a) and (b) are true.

47. *Utilitarianism*, Ch. 2, Par. 2, p. 210.

CHAPTER FIVE

A New Interpretation of Mill's Theory

Mill's distinction betweeen morality and expediency does not involve a calculation of when the imposition of sanctions would maximize (or even promote) utility. Such a theory would call certain actions wrong which he does not believe are wrong and would not call certain actions wrong which he clearly believes are wrong. We shall see in this chapter how Mill distinguishes between the two by making use of his distinction between that which is morally best and that which is morally obligatory.

Morality Versus Expediency

Morality and simple expediency are distinguishable in that the former involves duty whereas the latter does not. An agent can appropriately be punished for failing to fulfill her duty; however, as long as she is not ignoring one of her obligations she can at most be exhorted to act differently. Whether a person who has failed to perform an act can appropriately be "compelled" or, instead, "only persuaded and exhorted" is "the characteristic difference which marks off . . . morality in general from the remaining provinces of Expediency and Worthiness."[1]

This "characteristic difference" is easily misunderstood. For example, when Mill talks about what *marks off* morality from expediency, he is *not* claiming that Expediency begins where Morality ends. He writes, "It has always been evident that *all cases of justice are also cases of expediency* [my italics]."[2] Those who interpret Mill to be claiming that morality and expediency are nonoverlapping categories do not represent Mill's position.

Indeed, since all cases of Justice are also cases of Expediency, the just (in one sense) may be viewed as a subset of the expedient. Mill distinguishes between the two by talking about the intense feelings which are associated with justice but not with expediency. It is the "intensity of sentiment which places the Just . . . above the simply Expedient."[3] Those intense feelings are associated with those actions which people are morally obligated to produce. We can exhort people to do more or try to persuade them to do more, but we cannot rightfully demand of them that they do more. Of course, if they do more than morality requires, they are performing very good deeds. This is in the realm of Expediency, because that 'province' includes all actions which produce the acceptable level of utility, all actions which maximize utility, and all actions which produce a level of utility which is between the two.[4]

On Prudence

Mill sometimes uses 'expedience' to refer to the interests of the individual and sometimes "to the common interest of mankind."[5] If one concentrates on the meaning of expedience which involves self-interest, one might mistakenly read the passage which distinguishes between Duty and Expediency as somehow suggesting that questions of prudence are not moral questions. Yet, we cannot talk about my own happiness as if it were not a part of everyone's happiness.[6] If I could act in either of two ways, one of which would promote my long-term unhappiness and the other of which would promote my long-term happiness, and I would not affect anyone else's happiness by my choice, I would have the moral duty to perform the latter, not because I have a duty to act prudently (Mill denies that we have that duty, *per se*), but because I have a duty to promote general utility. Insofar as an agent is human, her own happiness must be included within the utility calculation. If an agent has two choices and she can only promote utility by benefiting herself, Mill cannot consistently claim that she acts rightly if, in this case, she fails to benefit herself. Mill is quite clear on this point. "As between his own happiness and that of others, utilitarianism requires [the agent] to be as strictly impartial as a disinterested and benevolent spectator."[7]

Mill concentrates on the agent's duty to promote others' good because he believes that people do not need encouragement to pursue their own good. He chides a view "according to which virtue consists in a correct calculation of our own personal interests, either in this world only, or also in another [i.e., in the 'world to come'],"[8] precisely because he believes that the promotion of one's own interests is virtuous *only* insofar as it benefits society.[9]

Society need not merely sit back and passively hope that people will act in ways which will promote both their own and the general good. Instead, society can take positive steps to make those interests coincide by setting up a good system of external rewards and punishments and by instilling the appropriate attitudes in its members. "That nothing which is a cause of evil on the whole to other people can be really good for the agent himself, is indeed a possible tenet, and always a favorite one with moralists, although in the present age the question has rather been, not whether the proposition is true, but *how society and education can be so ordered as to make it true* [my italics]."[10]   Mill argues, "Penal laws exist . . . because even an unanimous opinion that a certain line of conduct is for the general interest does not always make it people's individual interest to adhere to that line of conduct."[11] By passing these laws, society can make certain lines of conduct in the individual's own interest because she will be punished by fine or imprisonment unless she so acts.

Yet, penal laws are not always effective. For example, if a person has good reason to believe that she will not be caught, she might not worry about the law or about the penalties for failing to follow that law. For this reason, society must inculcate within its members the proper benevolent attitude. "No man's individual share of any public good which he can hope to realize by his efforts, is an equivalent for the sacrifice of his ease, and of the personal objects which he might attain by another course of conduct. The balance can be turned in favor of virtuous exertion, only by the interest of *feeling* or by that of *conscience*."[12]

Mill suggests that "education and opinion, which have so vast a power over human character, should . . . establish in the mind of every individual an indissoluble association between his own happiness and the good of the whole."[13] Thus, society should make sure to incul-cate within individuals the appropriate attitudes. If individuals have these attitudes, then they will believe that their acting rightly will be in their own interest. Further, their consciences will provide the proper reinforcement by imposing pangs of guilt for the performance of wrong actions.

These reinforcements might be imposed prospectively or retro-spectively. Mill neither believes that conscience is only active after a wrong action has been committed nor that conscience' only role in dissuading us from committing wrong actions is in forcing us to anticipate the pangs which will be imposed, should we perform the action. He denies that "all our acts are determined by pains and pleasures *in prospect*, pains and pleasures to which we look forward as the *consequences* of our acts."[14] Instead, it may be that the agent "recoils from the very thought of committing the act . . . [in question]. His conduct is determined by pain; but by a pain which precludes the act, not by one which is expected to follow it."[15]

If the agent has proper attitudes, the agent's prudent action will also be the action which promotes general utility. Mill would of course call the performance of such an action morally right, although *not* merely because it was the most prudent action to perform.

One point cannot be overemphasized, especially since its nonappreciation has led to fundamental misinterpretations of Mill's moral view. Mill can differentiate among the aesthetic, the prudent, the moral, and the (generally) expedient without claiming that an expedient action cannot also be morally right.

Suppose that Jones performs self-regarding action, *A'*. *A'* would be *prudent*, if it promoted *Jones's* utility,[16] *morally right* and *expedient* if it promoted *humankind's* utility (to the relevant degree), and *aesthetically* pleasing if it reflected *good character* traits. Merely because *A'* fits into one of these categories does not preclude its fitting into other categories as well.[17]

The claim here is *not* that 'prudent' means 'morally right', but merely that for the person who has the right attitudes the prudent action will correspond to the morally right action. Philosophers at least as far back as Socrates have tried to establish that agents promote their own interest when acting morally rightly. Mill agrees, although he makes a further suggestion, *viz.*, that we arrange rewards and punishments to make it even clearer that agents will promote their own interests by promoting the common interest.

The most expedient action maximizes both the agent's and society's utility. Critics who interpret Mill's comment about what *marks off* morality from expediency to imply that there are two separate, non-overlapping categories do not seem to appreciate the implications of such a position, since they would either have to deny that the action which maximized both the agent's and society's utility was expedient or deny that it was in the moral realm. On Mill's view, no such choice need be made, since such an action is *both* expedient and morally right.

Mill talks about "an unlimited range of moral worth, up to the most exalted heroism, which should be fostered by every positive encouragement, *though not converted into an obligation* [my italics]."[18] One does not have a *duty* to perform the utility-maximizing action and, *in that sense*, the utility-maximizing action is in the realm of the expedient but not in the realm of the moral.

However, the utility-maximizing action is in the moral realm in the sense that it has moral worth and deserves much praise.

Mill's distinction between the expedient and the moral is more easily understood if one thinks in terms of a distinction between that which is expedient and that which is required by duty. The expedient action might be utility-maximizing, whereas the action required by duty promotes the requisite amount of utility. The requisite amount is determined by general societal standards. *It is not determined by looking at the efficacy of any of the sanctions.*

Even if one understands that the same action may be aesthetically pleasing, expedient, and morally right, Mill's position is still potentially confusing. For example, very expedient actions are right insofar as 'right' means morally permissible, but are not right insofar as 'right' means morally required.

Mill's differentiation among the categories is also confusing, at least in part, because of the large amount of overlap among the categories. A prudent action is one which promotes the utility of the individual. Both expedient actions and morally right actions promote the utility of humankind. An aesthetically pleasing action is one which manifests utility-promoting attributes of the agent. Since each individual is a member of humankind, any action which affects his utility must also affect the utility of humankind. Since aesthetically pleasing actions manifest utility-promoting characteristics, many aesthetically pleasing actions will also be utility-promoting actions.

Mill claims that expedient actions, when we are using the 'true' meaning of 'expedient', promote utility. Sometimes, however, we use 'expedient' to imply that the agent is promoting his own interests at everyone else's expense. The "expedient, in the sense in which it is opposed to the right generally means that which is expedient for the particular interests of the agent himself; as when a minister sacrifices the interests of his country to keep himself in place." Or, it may mean "that which is expedient for some immediate object, some temporary purpose, but which violates a rule whose observance is expedient in a much higher degree. The expedient, in this sense, instead of being the same thing with the useful, is a branch of the hurtful."[19]

We can understand Mill's distinctions among the prudent, the expedient, the moral, and the aesthetic, even when a particular action is prudent, expedient, right, and aesthetically pleasing. Indeed, since prudence involves the utility of the agent and since both morality and expediency involve the utility of humankind, we are much less surprised by the overlap among prudence, expediency, and morality than by Mill's apparent claim that some areas of prudence do not fall within the realm of morality.

Let us reconsider the passage of central concern in the last chapter. Mill says that "we call any conduct wrong, or instead, some other term of dislike or disparagement, according as we think that the person ought, or ought not, to be punished for it; and we say it would be right to do so and so, or merely that it would be desirable or laudable, according as we would wish to see the person whom it concerns compelled, or only persuaded and exhorted, to act in that manner."

We do say that people have various duties to themselves. One owes oneself certain sorts of treatment — getting an education, taking care of oneself physically, etc. Further, many people *rightly* punish others for not treating themselves properly. "You should be ashamed for not taking better care of yourself" is a kind of condemnation. That expression of disapproval is a punishment, albeit a mild one.

These same people might not believe that any stronger sanctions (than the expression of disapproval) would be appropriate. For example, many people feel that one should finish high school for prudential reasons. They might say that it is a shame not to finish it. However, once one has reached a certain age, one is no longer compelled to go. Those people still think that one should finish high school, that one has a duty to oneself to acquire (at least) that level of education. However, they believe that forcing one to go to school against one's will is not warranted.[20]

We consider whether people should be allowed to smoke tobacco in public places. When people argue in favor of laws prohibiting such activities, they argue that smokers, if they smoke in areas also populated by non-smokers, also harm the non-smokers. Thus, if one wants to discuss this issue within the context of an examination of Mill's writings, anti-smokers are claiming that smoking should not be viewed as being solely within the self-regarding sphere. Since non-smokers can be harmed by someone's smoking in their presence, smoking must be viewed as falling within the other-regarding realm.

Mill provides a rationale to support the claim that smokers' smoking tobacco is morally wrong, *ignoring the harmful passive effects of smoking*. He talks about the duty to take care of one's health as a duty to *others*, claiming that "the principal hygienic precepts should be inculcated, not solely or principally as maxims of prudence, but as a duty to others, since by squandering our health we disable ourselves from rendering to our fellow-creatures the services to which they are entitled." He agrees with Comte that "the prudential motive is by no means fully sufficient for the purpose, even physicians often disregarding their own precepts." The "personal penalties of neglect of health are commonly distant, as well as more or less uncertain, and require the additional and more immediate sanction of moral responsibility."[21] Insofar as maintaining one's health involves a duty to *others*, others might be justified in imposing sanctions against one for failing to perform that duty.[22]

Some duties which we owe to ourselves are not owed to others. "What are called duties to ourselves are not socially obligatory unless circumstances render them at the same time duties to others. The term duty to oneself, when it means anything more than prudence, means self-respect or self-development, and for none of these is anyone accountable to his fellow creatures, because for none of them is it for the good of mankind that he be held accountable to them."[23]

Thus, we have a duty (to ourselves and *not* to others) to perform certain self-regarding actions. An agent who fails to fulfill such a duty is blameworthy. However, such an agent is not blameworthy by others, "because for none of these is anyone *accountable to his fellow creatures*." Only the agent's conscience should punish him for failing to perform one of his duties to himself. Indeed, if one wishes to understand Mill's moral and political views, it is crucially important to remember that there are a variety of blameworthy acts which *are only appropriately punished by conscience and are not appropriately punished by anyone other than the agent herself.*

In *On Liberty*, Mill writes that the "distinction between the loss of consideration which a person may rightly incur by defect of prudence or of personal dignity, and the reprobation which is due to him for an offence against the rights of others, is not a merely nominal distinction." For example, if someone merely acts imprudently, "we may express our distaste, and we may stand aloof from [that] person as well as from [the] thing that displeases us; but we shall not therefore feel called on to make his life uncomfortable." Indeed, "instead of wishing to punish him, we shall rather endeavor to alleviate his punishments, by showing him how he may avoid or cure the evils his conduct tends to bring upon him. He may be to us an object of pity, perhaps of dislike, but not of anger or resentment"[24]

Here, Mill is distinguishing between the appropriate kinds of treatment which the agent will receive from others. However, one would be mistaken to interpret this passage as simply an attempt by Mill to protect the individual from societal pressure to conform,[25] since both expressions of dislike and expressions of resentment may strongly influence individuals to act 'properly'. While Mill is trying to limit what society may appropriately say or do *even about wrongful behavior*, he is not trying to shield the individual's self-regarding behavior from all societal influence.

In *On Liberty*, Mill distinguishes between our compelling and our only persuading or exhorting agents to act in a certain manner. There, he is talking about the appropriate courses of action which may be taken with respect to the self-regarding virtues *by people other than the agent herself*. "[E]ven education works by conviction and persuasion as well as by compulsion, and it is by the former only that, when the period of education is passed, the self-regarding virtues should be inculcated." This does not mean that people must remain silent when they see others hurting themselves. "Human beings owe to each other help to distinguish the better from the worse, and encouragement to choose the former and not the latter. . . . But neither one person, nor any number of persons, is warranted in saying to another human creature of ripe years that he shall not do with his life for his own benefit what he chooses to do with it."[26]

Mill is talking about the range of appropriate measures that society or individuals other than the agent can take. Mill is not including the role of conscience in his discussion. So, too, in the passage from *Utilitarianism* where Mill talks about which sanctions would be appropriate to impose against particular actions, his examples only involve a discussion of which sanctions would be appropriate for *others* to use. Again, he does not include the role of conscience.

Mill fears that society will overstep its bounds in its attempts to assure that individuals will perform the correct self-regarding actions. Society might decide not only to educate individuals about the proper courses of action to take, but also to *force* people to act 'properly'. However, Mill can be very severe in his limitation of the appropriate societal measures which may be taken to assure the performance of the correct self-regarding actions *and still claim that one acts immorally in not promoting one's own utility*. Merely because neither the State nor society should do anything to make an individual perform or refrain from performing certain self-regarding actions does not imply that the agent's conscience should not punish the agent for acting in self-destructive ways. The agent's self-destructive, self-regarding actions can be immoral without being appropriately subjected to punishment from others.

In general, Mill would prefer that society not compel individuals to act rightly, but instead that individuals act rightly of their own accord. He would also prefer that people perform *other-regarding* actions because of the pleasures involved in doing so rather than because of the pains involved in omitting to do so. The "object should be to stimulate services to humanity by their natural rewards; not to render the pursuit of our own good in any other manner impossible, by visiting it with the reproaches of others and our own conscience."27

Since Mill claims that the general utility (*including* the agent's own utility) should be promoted, he cannot claim that self-regarding, destructive actions are not within the moral realm. Indeed, since he claims that there are at least some *duties to self* and since he claims that agents are not accountable to others for failing to fulfill these duties, the only consistent interpretation of Mill's position involves:

a. his distinguishing among the external sanctions, i.e., saying that some actions deserve certain kinds of punishments while other actions only deserve different, milder punishments, and

b. his distinguishing between those actions which deserve external sanctions (which we as observers could impose) and those actions which deserve only internal sanctions (which only the agent's conscience could rightfully impose).

Mill writes,

> Utilitarian morality fully recognises the distinction between the province of duty and that of virtue, but maintains that the standard and rule of both is the general interest. From the utilitarian point of view, the distinction between them is the following — There are many acts, and a still greater number of forbearances, the perpetual practice of which by all is so necessary to the general well-being that people must be held to it compulsorily, either by law, or by social pressure. These acts and forbearances constitute duty. Outside these bounds, there is the innumerable variety of modes in which the acts of human beings are either a cause, or a hindrance, of good to their fellow-creatures, but in regard to which it is, on the whole, for the general interest they they should be left free; being merely encouraged, by praise and honor, to the performance

of such beneficial actions as are not sufficiently stimulated
by benefits flowing from them to the agent himself. This
larger sphere is that of Merit or Virtue.[28]

It is important to see what point Mill is making. He is criticizing Thornton, who "seems to admit the general happiness as the
criterion of social virtue, but not of positive duty — not of justice and
injustice in the strict sense; and he imagines that it is in making a
distinction between these two ideas that his doctrine differs from that
of utilitarian moralists."[29]

Mill is arguing that the principle of utility should be used as the
standard both for virtue and for duty. (Thus, theorists who argue that
the principle of utility is not a normative principle are not
representing Mill's position.) However, when Mill discusses duty
here, he is discussing those acts the performance or non-performance
of which would merit the imposition of *external* sanctions, not those
acts the performance or non-performance of which would deserve
internal but not external sanctions.

Mill cannot (consistently) argue that self-regarding acts are outside
of the moral realm, since actions which only involve my utility still
involve *some* utility. However, Mill can (and does) consistently argue
that society should not interfere with self-regarding actions, *even
though they are within the moral realm.* "The interference of society
to overrule his [the agent's] judgment and purposes in what only
regards himself must be grounded on general presumptions which may
be altogether wrong." Even if those presumptions are right, they "are
as likely as not to be misapplied to individual cases." Thus, society
should not concern itself with self-regarding actions. "All errors
which [the individual] is likely to commit against advice and warning
are far outweighed by the evil of allowing others to constrain him to
what they deem his good."[30]

Thus, Mill is suggesting that society should not interfere in
matters which only concern the agent. The agent may act wrongly.
However, attempts by the government or society to regulate self-
regarding actions would be bungled more often than not, and thus they
should not concern themselves with those kinds of actions. On this
account, the agent may be acting immorally by performing or not
performing certain self-regarding actions. However, he is not subject
to blame from others for doing so.

According to Mill, we have a duty to ourselves to perform certain
self-regarding actions. However, we do not call anything a duty unless

its non-performance is blameworthy. Thus, Mill seems to be claiming that the non-performance of at least some self-regarding actions is blameworthy. If Mill had believed that some self-regarding actions were outside the moral sphere and were not blameworthy even by conscience, then he would have had to have provided a rationale to distinguish between those self-regarding actions which we have a duty to perform and those which we do not have a duty to perform.

By saying that self-regarding actions are not blameworthy *by others*, Mill can accomplish his goal of preventing the State and society from interfering with self-regarding actions. He will thus be able to maintain that there is a self-regarding sphere and that the promotion of general utility (and not merely the promotion of *others'* utility) is morally correct.

When we consider how Mill distinguishes between actions which are blameworthy and actions which instead deserve a different form of disparagement, we see that he is talking about the kinds of sanctions that *others* can impose against the agent. Mill is precluding others from punishing agents for their non-performance of certain expedient actions. He is not suggesting that agents who act self-destructively should not feel guilty. Indeed, he criticizes Bentham for not realizing that "Morality consists of two parts. One of these is self-education; the training, by the human being himself, of his affections and will."[31] The person who trains himself poorly should (all else equal) condemn himself.

Critics discuss Mill's claim in *On Liberty* that just as "there should be different opinions, so it is that there should be different experiments in living,"[32] as if he were claiming that because others should not interfere with these experiments in living, any experiment in living is perfectly acceptable. Yet, Mill makes quite clear that some modes of living are not acceptable (although nonetheless not deserving interference from others), arguing that "it would be absurd to pretend that people ought to live as if nothing whatever had been known in the world before they came into it; as if experience had as yet done nothing towards showing that one mode of existence, or of conduct, is preferable to another."[33]

Mill's Usage of 'Ought'

One might wonder why other Mill commentators have not adopted this interpretation of his writings. Some of the reasons have already been suggested, e.g., the ambiguity of terms like 'right' and 'expedient'. There is yet another ambiguous term which has caused much confusion, *viz.*, 'ought'.

'We do not call anything wrong unless we mean to imply that a person *ought* to be punished in some way'. The 'ought' here is ambiguous — it could be a moral ought or a logical/definitional ought. Mill helps clarify his meaning in a letter. "It appears to me that to [those with true moral feelings] the word *ought* means that if they shall act otherwise they shall be punished by this internal and perfectly disinterested feeling [i.e., conscience]."[34]

Let us replace 'ought' with the meaning of 'ought':

'We do not call anything wrong unless we mean to imply that a person with true moral feelings who so acts shall be punished by this internal and perfectly disinterested feeling'.

Mill is offering a definition.

wrong = blameworthy by conscience

However, he realizes that if the conscience is acting improperly, then it will not punish, even when it should punish, which is why he qualifies his definition by saying that

wrong = blameworthy by conscience
if the person has true moral feelings

'Ought' is used here to help provide a definition. Indeed, Mill is talking about what 'ought' *means*.[35] Basically, he is describing what will happen to a person with 'true moral feelings'. True. We must figure out when the conscience of a person with true moral feelings would impose pangs of guilt. However, we cannot simply define "true moral feelings" in terms of "when consciences do punish." We must find a different definition — one which tells us when consciences *"ought"* to punish.

We could say that the person with true moral feelings will be punished by his conscience whenever such a punishment would be utility-maximizing. That position has a variety of drawbacks which have already been discussed.

It has an additional drawback. When Mill says 'we do not call anything wrong . . . ', he is appealing to common usage. Today, we do not mean that an action is wrong only if its punishment by conscience would be utility-maximizing. Nor did people mean that then. Rather, we mean and they meant that there is a necessary connection between saying that something is morally wrong and saying that it should be punished by conscience, i.e., that it would be punished by a properly functioning conscience. That connection is a conceptual one, where a properly functioning conscience punishes all wrongs. *We must provide an independent criterion for determining wrongness.* That standard will be discussed below. But the 'ought' here is referring to a conceptual connection between conscience' punishing an action and that action's wrongness, not to those times when the experiencing of guilt pangs would be utility-maximizing.

Perhaps an example would serve to illustrate the point. Suppose we were to say, "We do not call anything in bad taste unless we mean that it ought to offend the audience." We believe that something in bad taste would probably offend the audience. However, merely because no one present happened to be offended (because they all had bad taste) does not imply that no one should have been offended. If a person with good taste would have been offended, then the comment was in bad taste, even if in fact no one was offended.

The 'ought' here is used just in case no one present has good taste. We cannot say that someone *will be* offended by the remark, because we do not know the composition of the audience. We can only say that even if no one was offended they should have been offended, because a person with good taste would have been offended. So, too, Mill guards against the possibility that the agent does not have true moral feelings by saying that nothing is wrong unless it *ought* to be punished by conscience. Even if an agent was not punished by his conscience for his immoral action, he should have been, because a person with a properly functioning conscience would have been.

Mill's Minimizing Utilitarianism?

Even if the claims made above are correct, *viz.,*

    a.   that Mill claims that self-harming actions are (all else equal) morally wrong, although possibly not blameworthy by others, and
    b.   that when Mill is talking about right actions, he is talking about *permissible* actions rather than the *best* action,

Mill's position might seem neither difficult to understand nor the one suggested here. One might believe that, quite simply, Mill is a minimizing utilitarian, i.e., someone who believes that one is merely obligated to promote (net) happiness. Mill suggests that the "Greatest Happiness Principle holds that actions are right in proportion as they tend to promote happiness, wrong as they tend to produce the reverse of happiness."[36] He does *not* suggest that actions are (only) right if they tend to *maximize* happiness.

Those theorists who attribute to Mill a minimizing-utilitarian position tend to cite numerous passages from "Auguste Comte and Positivism" for support. Although they are correct that Mill is not a maximizing utilitarian, they are incorrect that he is merely a minimizing utilitarian.

Mill writes in the passage which was of concern in the last chapter, "There are other things, on the contrary, which we wish that people should do, which we like or admire them for doing, perhaps dislike or despise them for not doing, but yet admit that they are not bound to do, it is not a case of moral obligation." We need a way to determine which things are matters of obligation and which are not.

When Mill talks about those actions which deserve punishment in this passage, *he is including the sanction of conscience.* Often, in other works when he is talking about when sanctions may appropriately be imposed, he is only talking about *external* sanctions. He clearly does not believe that external sanctions are appropriate whenever internal sanctions are appropriate, as is indicated by his claiming, "When such reasons as these [i.e., reasons of expediency] preclude the enforcement of the responsibility, the conscience of the agent himself should step into the vacant seat . . . , because the case does not admit of his being made accountable to the judgment of his fellow creatures."[37] Since Mill believes that conscience may appropriately impose sanctions even when individuals external to the agent may not, one's establishing that the imposition of external sanctions would not be appropriate in a particular case would *not* establish that the agent had acted morally permissibly. As long as the agent's conscience would appropriately impose sanctions, her action would have been immoral, even if not appropriately punished by others.

Mill makes clear that some actions which are non-utility-maximizing deserve no sanctions, *not even from conscience.* This is clear both in the passage of central concern in Chapter 4 and in various passages in "Auguste Comte and Positivism."[38]

Indeed, critics have not paid sufficient attention to Mill's comments in "Auguste Comte and Positivism." As is sometimes noted,

o

Mill writes, "The proper office of those sanctions [i.e., *both* external and internal sanctions] is to enforce upon every one, the conduct necesary to give all other persons their fair chance: conduct which chiefly consists in not doing them harm, and not impeding them in anything which without harming others does good to themselves." Here, Mill appears to be offering a minimizing utilitarian position. However, *lest one think that he is offering a minimizing position*, he adds that "inasmuch as every one who avails himself of the advantages of society, leads others to expect from him all such positive offices and disinterested services *as the moral improvement attained by mankind has rendered customary* [my italics], he deserves moral blame if, without just cause, he disappoints that expectation."[39] If a society were able to establish "in the mind of every individual an indissoluble association between his own happiness and the good of the whole,"[40] altruistic behavior might become quite common.

Mill is aware that his position implies a sliding scale of obligatoriness — what is not obligatory during one century might be obligatory in the next if humankind has progressed in the meantime. "Through this principle the domain of moral duty in an improving society is ever widening. When what once was uncommon virtue becomes common virtue, it comes to be numbered among obligations, while a degree exceeding what has grown common, remains simply meritorious."[41]

Insofar as Mill is linking obligation to what people in society *do* think blameworthy, he cannot simply ignore the customary morality. However, Mill is not thereby giving up his belief in the importance of the promotion of utility, since the customary morality is (at least partially) determined by what experience has shown to promote the interests of humankind. "[M]ankind must by this time have acquired positive beliefs as to the effects of some actions on their happiness; and the beliefs which have thus come down are the rules of morality for the multitude, and for the philosopher until he has succeeded in finding better."[42]

The binding force of conscience "consists in the existence of a mass of feeling which must be broken through to violate our standard of right, and which, if we do nevertheless violate that standard, will probably have to be encountered in the form of remorse."[43] Insofar as conscience will impose sanctions when we violate our "standard of right" and insofar as our standard of right involves existent attitudes, conscience is relying at least to some extent on the existing morality when it imposes pangs.

Mill believes that the moral feelings are acquired rather than innate. They are "susceptible of being brought by cultivation to a high degree of development."[44] Insofar as he is recommending that society constantly try to develop and improve the sentiments of its members so that individuals will weigh other people's interests as heavily as they weigh they own, we would expect "common virtue" to expand more and more as time passes and society progresses.

"In the comparatively early stage of human advancement in which we now live, a person cannot indeed feel that entireness of sympathy with all others, which would make any real discordance in the general direction of their conduct in life impossible."[45] Thus, humans have not developed sufficiently to have these feelings of disinterested benevolence, which is why our standard of obligatoriness is relatively low. However, Mill implies that there is reason for hope. "In an improving state of the human mind, the influences are constantly on the increase, which tend to generate in each individual a feeling of unity with all the rest; which feeling, if perfect, would make him never think of, or desire, any beneficial condition for himself, in the benefits of which they are not included."[46] Once humankind reaches that stage, the standard of obligatoriness will be rather high.

Mill's Relativism

If indeed the position offered here is correct, then Mill is open to the charge of relativism. He recognizes and accepts that charge. However, one must be careful when explaining in what ways Mill is relativistic.

Mill accepts that actions which would be meritorious in one century might be required by duty in the next, since he believes that the contents of one's duties are in part determined by *when* one lives. Indeed, Mill presumably should admit that what would be meritorious in one society might be required in a different society, *even in cotemporaneous societies*, since what individuals might think is required by duty in one society might not be identical to what individuals think is required by duty in another society.[47]

Nonetheless, the principle of utility is the basic principle of morality. The action which maximizes humankind's utility is morally best, no matter which country one inhabits. By the same token, the action which maximizes humankind's disutility is morally worst, no matter which country one inhabits. Further, no matter which country one inhabits, disutility-producing actions are wrong. The only respect in which Mill is a relativist is that he is willing to link duty (how much utility one is morally required to produce) to the society in which one lives.

Mill is *not* willing to take the views of each society as he finds them. He denies that "we ought to take the [moral] feelings as we find them, as accident or design has made them," and instead argues that "the tendency of actions to promote happiness affords a test to which the feelings of morality should conform."[48] The important point for Mill is that he does not believe that the standard of morality (i.e., of *obligation*) is the same throughout the centuries. "The contest between the morality which appeals to an external standard [e.g., the principle of utility], and that which grounds itself on internal conviction [when that conviction is not itself to be judged in light of the principle of utility], is the contest of *progressive morality against stationary* [my italics] — of reason and argument against the deification of mere opinion and habit."[49]

Thus, in one sense Mill is not willing to take moral feelings as design or accident has made them — he does not believe that a practice is morally worthy merely because we happen to (morally) approve of it. "The feeling of justice might be a peculiar instinct, and might yet require, like our other instincts, to be controlled and enlightened by a higher reason." Mill compares our intellectual instincts to our animal instincts. "If we have intellectual instincts, leading us to judge in a particular way, as well as animal instincts that prompt us to act in a particular way, there is no necessity that the former should be more infallible in their sphere than the latter in theirs; it may as well happen that wrong judgments are occasionally suggested by those, as wrong actions by these."[50] Were we to approve as just the promoting of one person's happiness at the expense of many individuals' happiness, we would be wrong — that sentiment would need correction.

Yet, there is a different sense in which Mill is willing to take feelings as he finds them. He is not willing to hold people to a standard which is above what the general feelings of society dictate is appropriate, as long as those attitudes are indeed productive of utility. "It is not good that persons should be bound, by other people's opinion, to do everything that they would deserve praise for doing."[51] Indeed, Mill denies that people should by bound *by their own consciences* to do everything that they would deserve praise for doing.[52]

One should not be surprised by Mill's claim that what is required at one time might not be required at an earlier time. Mill talks about the improvement of morality in a variety of works. For example, in *On Liberty* he talks about the improvement of the moral powers of individuals.[53] In "Sedgwick's Discourse," he calls the theory of utility "a theory of right and wrong"[54] which is subject to change, arguing that "changes . . . are anticipated in our opinions on that subject [i.e., morality], as on every other, both from the progress of intelligence, from more authentic and enlarged experience, and from alterations in the condition of the human race, requiring altered rules of conduct."[55] Mill criticizes Whewell for making "assaults on the only methods of philosophizing from which any *improvement in ethical opinions* [my italics] can be looked for."[56]

Mill realizes that people might mistakenly believe that his system is not utilitarian. He criticizes Whewell for believing that if "any one who believes that the moral sentiments should be guided by the happiness of mankind proposes that moral sentiments, so guided, should be cultivated and fostered, Dr. Whewell treats this as a deserting of moral principles, and borrowing or stealing from his."[57]

To understand Mill's position, one must appreciate that the moral feelings play numerous roles, making their cultivation especially important. Obviously, if one has the appropriate moral feelings, one is more likely to choose to do the right thing, since the moral feelings will motivate one to act rightly. However, Mill is not merely concerned with their role in promoting us to act rightly. He is further concerned with their role in *determining* rightness.[58]

Mill argues that questions of rightness and wrongness are addressed "to our reason and conscience."[59] Reason will tell us, among other things, whether the action in question is likely to promote utility. Conscience will approve or disapprove accordingly. Of course, we cannot take the feelings of conscience as we find them. Those feelings arise from association, but must be "guided" in light of the principle of utility.[60]

Those moral feelings which we have (which do indeed promote utility) will be the feelings in light of which we decide whether the person has produced enough utility for his action to be considered 'right'. Insofar as Mill's theory of obligation is linked to what we *do* think blameworthy (even after we have excluded all non-utility-producing attitudes), Mill is linking that standard to the general (utility-producing) attitudes of the society in which the individual lives.

Mill clearly gives some weight to existing opinions. "I consent that established custom, and the general feeling, should be deemed conclusive against me [where he is recommending something contrary to it, *viz.*, that women be treated as equals] *unless that custom and feeling from age to age can be showed to have owed their existence to other causes than their soundness* [my italics],"[61] i.e., to causes which are not in accord with the principle of utility. Were the general practices, in this case the unequal treatment of women, to have promoted utility, he would have countenanced them.[62]   However, since they did not (and do not), they are morally unacceptable.

There are a number of reasons why one might want to take existing attitudes (perhaps modified in light of the principle of utility) as a determinant of obligation rather than simply imposing a whole new set of attitudes in light of which obligatoriness should be established. Practically, it is much easier to achieve compliance if the requirements are not totally foreign. In a related comment, Mill discusses how legislators should view historical circumstances.

> The 'national views' may regard slavery as a legitimate condition of human beings, and Mr. Livingston, in legislating for Louisiana, may have been obliged to recognise slavery as a fact, and to make provision for it, and for its consequences, in his code of laws; but he was bound to regard the equality of human beings as the foundation of his legislation, and the concession to the 'historical element' as a matter of temporary expediency; and while yielding to the necessity, to endeavor, by all the means in his power, to educate the nation into better things. And so of the other subjects mentioned by Dr. Whewell — property, contracts, family, government. The fact that, in any of these matters, a people prefer some particular mode of legislation, on historical grounds — that is, because they have been long used to it, — is not proof of any original adaptation in it to their nature or circumstances, and goes a very little way in recommendation of it as for their benefit now. But it may be a very important element in determining what the legislator can do, and still more, the manner in which he should do it: and in both these respects Bentham allowed it full weight. What he is at issue with Dr. Whewell upon, is in deeming it right for the legislator to keep before his

mind an ideal of what he would do if the people for whom
he made laws were entirely devoid of prejudice or accidental
prepossessions: while Dr. Whewell, by placing their
prejudices and accidental prepossessions 'at the basis of the
system' [Lectures, p. 255], enjoins legislation not in
simple recognition of existing popular feelings, but in
obedience to them.[63]

Here, Mill is recommending that existing attitudes be considered in
what legal and, presumably, *moral* requirements one makes. (This is
written in "Whewell on *Moral* Philosophy.") Mill is suggesting,
however, that such attitudes do not *validate* the practices, i.e., we
should not simply be 'obedient' to them. Rather, the common attitudes
and practices must be considered when one is trying to figure out how
to develop within people the proper (utility-promoting) feelings.

Mill believes that his comments about the legislator are appropriately applied to moral questions. He claims (on the very next page)
that "Bentham recognises the most important but most neglected
function of the legislator, the office of an instructor, both *moral* [my
italics] and intellectual."[64]   Instructors consider what level of
achievement their students have already attained and try to improve
them in light of those existing levels. Instructors do not and should
not ignore the levels of progress of their students if they are interested
in making or allowing their students to progress.

When we consider the analogy, however, we must keep in mind
what it is that the 'instructors' are trying to improve, *viz.*, the moral
feelings. It is not as if the moral feelings are not used until they reach
the most progressive state. On the contrary, they are being used to
determine blameworthiness all during the education process. Further,
this improvement process occurs during many millennia rather than
during a semester. Mill makes quite clear that the improvement of the
moral feelings is a very slow process.[65]

Mill argues that the "ultimate sanction . . . of all morality . . .
[is] a subjective feeling in our own minds."[66]   It will impose
sanctions if we "violate our standard of right" or, if someone else is
performing the act, it will cause us to have feelings of moral
disapprobation towards the act and, possibly, the agent. However,
these 'subjective feelings' are linked to the level of progress of the
society in which one lives.

Mill claims that "we call any conduct wrong, or employ, instead,
some other term of dislike or disparagement, according as we think

that the person ought, or ought not, to be punished for it."[67]   He
must be envisioning something like the following:
    We see an act. We react negatively. We consider whether our
reaction is "conformable to the general good, [since] just persons
[resent] a hurt to society, though not otherwise a hurt to themselves,
and [do] not [resent] a hurt to themselves, however painful, unless it
be the kind which society has a common interest with them in the
repression of."[68] If indeed our reaction is in accord with the general
good, then the act is wrong; otherwise, the act would merely be
'undesirable'.
    When we consider whether our reaction is conformable to the gen-
eral good, we consider (in this case) whether the action we are viewing
is harmful generally (as opposed to being merely harmful to
ourselves). If it is, then the act is wrong. Insofar as we are
determining the wrongness of the act, the relevant question is *not*
whether the imposition of the sanction would promote utility. That
issue is relevant when determining whether the wrongful act should be
punished through the imposition of *external* sanctions. It is not
relevant in the determination of wrongness.
    In order for this process to work in the way that Mill envisions,
we must in general have attitudes which are in accord with the
principle of utility. Otherwise, our initial reactions would be so
skewed that this system would never work. In that case, 'actions
would be right insofar as they promoted utility and wrong insofar as
they promoted the reverse'.
    Mill acknowledges that our moral feelings are corruptible. Con-
science "is quite susceptible, by a sufficient use of the external
sanctions and of the force of early impressions, of being cultivated in
almost any direction: so that there is hardly anything so absurd or so
mischievous that it may not, by means of these influences, be made to
act on the human mind with all the authority of conscience."[69]
    Yet, Mill believes that our moral reactions are, generally, in ac-
cord with the principle of utility — they need improvement rather than
complete revision. Of course, attitudes can be in accord with the
principle of utility whether they are (merely) utility-promoting or,
instead, are actually utility-maximizing. Mill is hopeful that
humankind will (continue to) progress; he hopes that attitudes will
become more and more utility-promoting as time passes.

Moral Fanaticism

The charge of moral fanaticism which is often made against act-utilitarianism sometimes means that the system requires too much (is fanatical in *how much* it demands), because it requires agents to maximize rather than merely to promote (even large amounts of net) utility. Mill's system is not open to this charge. By linking obligatoriness to the (modified) standards of society, Mill can avoid the charge that his system makes demands which are too strict. However, his system may be open to the charge of fanaticism, nonetheless.

Sometimes, when critics charge act-utilitarianism with moral fanaticism, they mean that the system considers every act to be morally "momentous" — that no acts are outside of the moral realm.[70] To that charge, Mill must make a response.

Mill might claim that:

a.   there are no acts outside of the moral realm (the charge is true). However, the criticism is no longer particularly damning because acts merely have to promote the requisite amount of utility rather than maximize it. Or,

b.   just as the amount of utility which one is required to produce is linked to the level of progress of one's society, so, too, the number of (types of) actions included within the moral realm is linked to the level of progress in one's society. For example, Mill might claim that the more progressive the society, the greater the number of types of actions which would be included in the moral realm.

When Mill maintains that the level of utility which one must produce is linked to the level of progress of one's society, he is *not* arguing that one satisfies one's obligation as long as one produces X utiles, *regardless of the circumstances in which one finds oneself.* One should save someone who is drowning in a pool rather than go back inside to get the sunscreen which someone else had inadvertently left behind, and one would be wrong to do the latter. Were no one drowning, one's doing the latter might not only be sufficient to fulfill an obligation, but might actually be meritorious.

Were we always required to produce the level of utility which is equivalent to what is involved in saving a life, there would often be cases in which we *could not* meet our obligation. In many cases, we simply cannot produce a great deal of net utility.

To some extent, Mill is arguing that we only have an obligation to perform those acts which a reasonable, benevolent individual would think us morally blameworthy for not performing. Yet, the reasonable, benevolent individual is shaped, at least partly, by the society in which she lives. It is because societies continue to progress and thus might reasonably differ with respect to how much utility individuals might be required to produce that Mill does not give one standard for obligatoriness which would be applicable cross-temporally and cross-culturally.

If one wishes to explain Mill's system, one cannot define 'morally wrong' in terms of when punishment by conscience is utility-maximizing. Such a definition would imply that the same action performed by different people, who are similar in all relevant respects except that one person's conscience is a more severe taskmaster than the other person's, might have different moral descriptions. If Sam's conscience punishes him 'too severely' for his non-utility-maximizing actions but Sue's conscience punishes her 'justly' for her non-utility-maximizing actions, then an action performed by Sam might not be immoral even though the same action would be immoral if performed by Sue.

In the example above, had Sam and Sue lived in different societies or in different time periods, Mill would have been willing to have accepted differing standards of obligatoriness for Sue and Sam. Mill never would have accepted differing standards for people in the same society (during the same time period).

Mill's position as outlined in this book allows him to claim that:

1. actions are wrong insofar as they are (foreseeably) not sufficiently utility-producing,
2. conscience is an additional moral regulator, and
3. some actions deserve blame from conscience but not from law or society.

Merely because an agent should not have external sanctions imposed against him for one of his actions *does not imply that the agent has not acted wrongly.* If the agent should experience pangs of conscience, then the action is wrong.

This interpretation does not preclude agents from living unconventional lives. Neither the State nor society would be justified in interfering with such lives. Further, even conscience would not be justified in punishing the nonconformist in many cases.

Insofar as conscience is only justified in punishing insufficiently utility-producing actions, conscience would not be justified in punishing the non-conformist who has indeed found a better way for himself to live. Indeed, a non-conformist who felt uncomfortable living according to the standard dictates of society might feel guilty for *not* experimenting. Conscience would probably punish the person who was living in ways which not even a reasonable person would believe would be productive of utility, since there would be little chance that his unconventional ways would be beneficial. Thus, insofar as someone chooses to live in self-destructive ways, he would be subject to the pangs of conscience, even if his actions are strictly self-regarding. However, the account presented here does not preclude agents from experimenting in order to find the most conducive environment for their developing into flourishing beings who can help both themselves and humankind.[71]

Conscience is extremely important for Mill. It can impose sanctions, even when society should not impose them. Indeed, the current interpretations of Mill are inaccurate in a *crucial* way by ignoring this aspect of conscience. Either these interpretations involve a complicated calculus which includes whether the experiencing of guilt feelings would be utility-maximizing and thus preclude heinous, once-in-a-lifetime actions from being immoral, or they ignore conscience entirely. Merely because society's imposition of sanctions against a particular agent is even *prima facie* unwarranted does not give that agent a moral *carte blanche*. Conscience fills the gap which society leaves open. Mill utilizes conscience as an additional moral regulator, precisely because of its ability to impose internal sanctions.

Virtually all commentators on Mill agree that self-regarding actions are not liable to punishment *from the State or from society*. However, many wrongly infer that Mill therefore believes that self-regarding actions are outside of the moral realm.[72] If these commentators understood Mill's distinction between internal and external sanctions and his reliance on conscience to punish all moral wrongs, they would not have confused the appropriateness of society's or the State's imposing sanctions against a self-regarding action and that action's not being morally wrong. Even if an action is not liable to punishment from others, it may still be liable to punishment from conscience. Those critics who deny that Mill believes that self-regarding actions are within the scope of morality will have some difficulty in explaining how they can read Mill as a utilitarian. In the next chapter, the role of conscience will be examined in light of the crucial part that it plays in Mill's moral theory and in utilitarian theory in general.

NOTES

1. *Utilitarianism*, Ch. 5, Par. 14-15, pp. 246-247.
2. *Ibid.*, Ch. 5, Par. 38, p. 259.
3. *Ibid.*, Par. 34, p. 256. See also Ch. 5, Par. 25, p. 251 and Ch. 5, Par. 2, p. 241.
4. Mill does not make clear whether the expedient is anything which tends to the good, i.e., promotes net utility, or whether it must promote a certain amount of good. Sometimes, he implies the former. See, e.g., *Utilitarianism*, Ch. 5, Par. 6, p. 242. However, insofar as he says that *intensity* constitutes the only difference between the "feeling of right and wrong and that of ordinary expediency and inexpediency" (*Utilitarianism*, Ch. 5, Par. 25, p. 251), it would seem that expediency is tied to one's producing a certain level of good.

To make matters more complicated, in backward societies anything which promotes utility will be deemed right and expedient. However, in more developed societies, one will have to promote a certain amount of utility in order for one's act to be deemed right. Of course, this is only a semantic difficulty. Mill could easily say that in a relatively developed society not all expedient acts are right, i.e., claim that in a well-developed society one must perform acts which are sufficiently expedient in order for them to be right. Or, he could simply define expedient as that which promotes the requisite amount of good.

5. *Utilitarianism*, Ch. 5, Par. 6, p. 242.
6. Kilcullen makes this point. See Kilcullen, "Mill on Duty and Liberty," p. 298.

Precisely because Mill believes that the agent herself should be counted no more or less heavily than others in moral calculations, theorists (who want to talk about an action's being wrong only if its punishment by conscience would be utility-maximizing) must avoid the temptation to argue that *only* other-harming actions would be immoral. There is no reason to believe that an action which has great adverse effects on the agent herself would be less utility-producing for conscience to punish than would be an action which had only moderately adverse effects on someone else.

Brandt describes an optimific indirect theory as being concerned with acts which are *other*-involving. See "Fairness to Indirect Optimific Theories in Ethics," pp. 342 ff. Yet, it is not at all clear why the agent's happiness is not a part of the utility calculus and why actions which only involve the agent herself are somehow not appropriately evaluated within a normative theory. There may be reasons to establish why *external* sanctions are more appropriately imposed for other-harming actions than for self-harming actions, but that is a different matter.

7.   *Utilitarianism*, Ch. 2, Par. 18, p. 218.
8.   *A System of Logic*, Book 4, Ch. 4, Sec. 6, Par. 8, p. 684.
9.   *Ibid.*, Book 1, Ch. 5, Sec. 7, Par. 3 ff, pp. 106 ff.
10.   *Ibid.*, Book 5, Ch. 7, Sec. 1, see note on p. 812. For related comments, see Shelly Kagan, *The Limits of Morality* (Oxford: Oxford University Press, 1989), p. 266.
11.   *Principles of Political Economy*, Book 5, Chap. 11, Sec. 12, Par. 4, p. 960.
12.   "Bentham," p. 15.
13.   *Utilitarianism*, Ch. 2, Par. 18, p. 218.
14.   "Remarks on Bentham's Philosophy," p. 12.

Gauthier criticizes neo-Kantians for having "failed to relate our nature as moral beings to our everyday concern with the fulfillment of our individual preferences." Gauthier, *Morals By Agreement*, p. 184. Mill offers two suggestions to alleviate this lack of connectedness:

1.   We should try to change people's preferences, i.e., we should try to get them to prefer things which are in accord with the general good.
2.   We should arrange our laws, societal institutions, etc., to make sure that people will understand why their acting rightly will indeed fulfill their individual preferences, e.g., because they would presumably prefer not to be jailed.

15.   "Remarks on Bentham's Philosophy," p. 12.
16.   When we talk about something as prudent, we might mean what would be good for the individual, given her present desires, goals, etc., or we might mean what would be good for the individual, given the desires, goals, etc. which the person ought to have. When Mill talks about the prudent action and the utility-promoting action as being the same, he is assuming that the individual has the appropriate

attitudes, i.e., those which it would be utility-producing for her to have.

Of course, if the individual's attitudes and desires are inappropriate, then what is "prudent," i.e., what will lead to the fulfillment of those desires and goals, may not promote utility. By the same token, what is "prudent," i.e., what will lead to the fulfillment of *existing* desires and goals, may not be "prudent," i.e., may not lead to the fulfillment of those desires and goals which the person ought to have.

17. Presumably, Mill would judge the aesthetic aspect of an action differently than he would judge the aesthetic aspect of a work of art. The aesthetic aspect of an action would reflect the agent's character. The aesthetic aspect of a work, e.g., a painting, would also be judged by the principle of utility. However, the aspect would not involve a reflection of the agent's character. Rather, the aesthetic quality of a painting would be judged according to how much pleasure it produced in a cultured individual or, possibly, how constructive or uplifting it would be to a cultured individual. Mill doubts that "the word beautiful connotes the same property when we speak of a beautiful color, a beautiful face, a beautiful scene, a beautiful character, and a beautiful poem." *A System of Logic*, Book 4, Ch. 4, Sec. 5, Par. 7, p. 678. Of course, if the principle of utility is as fundamental as Mill believes it to be, he presumably believes that beauty is related to utility, although possibly in different ways for different kinds of beauty.

18. "Auguste Comte and Positivism," p. 339.

19. *Utilitarianism*, Ch. 2, Par. 23, p. 223.

20. Derek Parfit claims that imprudent actions may appropriately be called immoral, arguing that one's attitude towards one's future self might be likened to one's attitude towards others. See his *Reasons and Persons* (Oxford: Oxford University Press, 1984), pp. 318 ff. Thus, one's not getting a good education now would seriously affect the life of one's future self and hence would be immoral.

The claim offered here why imprudence may be immoral does not rely on Parfit's notions of personal identity. Further, this account does not entail that all imprudent actions are immoral, but that only those which result in over-all disutility are immoral. Of course, even if one does act immorally by acting imprudently, one may only deserve to have internal sanctions imposed, i.e., pangs of conscience. One does not necessarily deserve to have external sanctions imposed merely because one has acted imprudently.

21. "Auguste Comte and Positivism," p. 340.

22. Rees fails to appreciate this point, since he believes that Mill would argue that people must be allowed to smoke. See John Rees, *John Stuart Mill On Liberty* (Oxford: Oxford University Press, 1985), p. 153.

Mill might claim that although one's smoking is morally impermissible, one is not appropriately subjected to *external* sanctions for doing so. See *On Liberty*, Ch. 1, Par. 9, pp. 223-224. Or, Mill might claim that smokers are appropriately subject to certain external sanctions (e.g., public opinion), but not to others (e.g., fine or imprisonment). See *On Liberty*, Ch. 4, Par. 3, p. 276.

23. *On Liberty*, Ch. 4, Par. 6, p. 279.

24. *Ibid.*, Ch. 4, Par. 7, pp. 279-280.

25. See Berger, *Happiness, Justice and Freedom*, p. 278.

26. *On Liberty*, Ch. 4, Par. 4, p. 277.

27. "Auguste Comte and Positivism," p. 338.

28. "Thornton on Labour and Its Claims," *CW* Vol. 5, pp. 650-651. Edwards cites this passage, but does not seem to appreciate its import. Edwards, "J. S. Mill and Robert Veatch's Critique of Utilitarianism," p. 184.

29. "Thornton on Labor and Its Claims," p. 650.

30. *On Liberty*, Ch. 4, Par. 4, p. 277.

31. "Bentham," p. 98.

32. *On Liberty*, Ch. 3, Par. 1, p. 260 ff.

33. *Ibid.*, Ch. 3, Par. 3, p. 262.

34. *CW* Vol. 15, p. 649. Brown cites this letter, but does not seem to appreciate that it may militate against his own interpretation. Brown, "Mill on Liberty and Morality," p. 155.

35. See Lyons, "Benevolence and Justice in Mill," p. 57.

36. *Utilitarianism*, Ch. 2, Par. 2, p. 210. Both Gaus and Edwards attribute to Mill a minimizing utilitarian position. See Gaus's "Mill's Theory of Moral Rules" and Edwards's "The Principle of Utility and Mill's Minimizing Utilitarianism."

37. *On Liberty*, Ch. 1, Par. 11, p. 225.

38. It is in "Auguste Comte and Positivism" that Mill makes the non-maximizing nature of his system eminently clear. See pp. 338 ff.

39. "Auguste Comte and Positivism," p. 338.

40. *Utilitarianism*, Ch. 2, Par. 18, p. 218.

41. "Auguste Comte and Positivism," p. 338.

42. *Utilitarianism*, Ch. 2, Par. 24, p. 224. For related comments concerning how custom (and thus what people in fact think) affects

morality, see "Austin on Jurisprudence," *CW* Vol. 21, p. 183. For related and illuminating comments on how the customary morality develops and on the origin and function of the moral sentiments, see Alexander Bain's chapter, "The Ethical Emotions or the Moral Sense," in his *The Emotions and the Will* (London: Parker, 1859), pp. 286-323. Mill describes it as an "admirable chapter" which "enforce[s] and illustrate[s]" his point. *Utilitarianism*, Ch. 5, ftnt to Par. 14, p. 246.

43. *Utilitarianism*, Ch. 3, Par. 4, p. 229.

44. *Ibid.*, Ch. 3, Par. 8, p. 230.

45. *Ibid.*, Ch. 3, Par. 11, p. 233.

46. *Ibid.*, Ch. 3, Par. 10, p. 232. For related comments, see "De Toqueville" (2), *CW* Vol. 18, p. 181.

47. Clearly, Mill does not believe that all societies advance at the same rate. See, e.g., *On Liberty*, Ch. 1, Par. 1, p. 217 for suggestive comments.

Thomas Scanlon discusses how morality might be culturally dependent. See his "Contractualism and Utilitarianism" in *Utilitarianism and Beyond*, Amartya Sen and Bernard Williams eds., p. 112.

48. "Whewell on Moral Philosophy," p. 172.

49. *Ibid.*, p. 179.

50. *Utilitarianism*, Ch. 5, Par. 2, p. 240.

51. "Auguste Comte and Positivism," p. 337.

52. *Ibid.*, p. 338. Henry West realizes that Mill's view of what is morally required is closely connected to the commonly held moral views, although it is not clear whether he would subscribe to the position offered here. See his "Mill's Moral Conservatism," *Midwest Studies in Philosophy* 1 (1976), pp. 74 ff.

Wendy Donner realizes that, according to Mill, society plays an important role in shaping one's moral values and judgments, although the thesis for which she is arguing is very different from the one which is offered here. See her "Mill on Liberty of Self-Development," *Dialogue* 26 (1987), especially pp. 229 ff.

53. *On Liberty*, Ch. 3, Par. 3, p. 262 and Ch. 3, Par. 15, p. 271.

54. "Sedgwick's Discourse," p. 71.

55. *Ibid.*, p. 74.

56. "Whewell on Moral Philosophy," p. 169. Mill suggests in *On Liberty* that various moral systems capture aspects of the truth rather than the whole truth. Further, he suggests that, for example, the Gospels *improve* existing morality rather than simply supplant it.

See *On Liberty*, Ch. 2, Par. 37, p. 254 and Ch. 2, Par. 38 ff., pp. 256 ff.

57. "Whewell on Moral Philosophy," p. 169.

58. Thus, for Mill, the moral feelings will be concerned both with election and with justification. For a related discussion, see Chapter 5 of my *Francis Hutcheson's Moral Theory.*

59. "Bentham," p. 112.

60. "Blakey's History of Moral Science," pp. 26-27.

61. *The Subjection of Women*, Ch. 1, Par. 4, p. 263.

62. *Ibid.*, Ch. 1, Par. 3, p. 262. See also *Utilitarianism*, Ch. 5, Par. 36, pp. 258 ff.

63. "Whewell on Moral Philosophy," p. 196.

64. *Ibid.*, p. 197.

65. See "Chapters on Socialism," p. 740.

66. *Utilitarianism*, Ch. 3, Par. 5, p. 229.

67. *Ibid.*, Ch. 5, Par. 14, p. 246.

68. *Ibid.*, Ch. 5, Par. 21, p. 249.

69. *Ibid.*, Ch. 3, Par. 8, p. 230.

70. See Marcus Singer, "Consequences, Desirability and the Moral Fanaticism Argument," *Philosophical Studies* 46 (1984), p. 228.

71. However, it is not argued here that Mill "recommend[s] examples of non-conformity and eccentricity for their own sakes." Levi, "The Value of Freedom: Mill's Liberty (1859-1959)," p. 42. For example, Mill would certainly disapprove of non-conformity and eccentricity which were (foreseeably) disutility-producing both for the agent herself and for humankind in general.

72. See, e.g., Berger, *Happiness, Justice and Freedom*, p. 65.

CHAPTER SIX

Conscience

The importance of the role played by conscience in Mill's moral theory cannot be overemphasized. However, Mill's dependence on conscience may pose a problem. If all (foreseeably) disutility-producing actions are wrong and if all wrong actions should be punished by conscience, then it would seem that consciences should punish all (foreseeably) disutility-producing actions.

Clearly, actions which are malicious and destructive should be punished by conscience. However, reasonable, well-intended actions do not seem to be blameworthy — they are exactly the sorts of actions which we want agents to perform. Yet, if all disutility-producing actions are blameworthy by conscience, then some actions, which from a forward-looking perspective *we would want agents to perform*, are blameworthy by conscience nonetheless.

To some extent, the analysis of the roles of conscience will depend upon whether Mill is presenting a 'reasonably foreseeable consequence' utilitarian position, a 'foreseeable consequence' utilitarian position, or an 'actual consequence' utilitarian position. However, basically, the roles and functions of conscience will remain the same, regardless of which of these positions Mill actually espouses. Further, if we distinguish between two types of pangs of conscience — pangs of guilt and pangs of regret, we shall find that Mill's type of act-utilitarian conscience behaves exactly as we (both deontologists and utilitarians) would want consciences to behave.

The Utility and Disutility of Blaming

Mill sometimes writes as if he is presenting an 'actual consequence' utilitarian position, sometimes a 'foreseeable consequence' utilitarian position, and sometimes a 'reasonably foreseeable consequence' utilitarian position. When he writes that "the good of the human race is the ultimate standard of right and wrong"[1] or that the promotion of happiness is "the test by which to judge . . . all human conduct,"[2] he is offering an 'actual consequence' utilitarian position. The moral rightness or wrongness of the action will be determined by looking at the actual consequences of the action, regardless of whether those consequences could have been foreseen. When he writes that "actions are right as they *tend* to promote happiness, wrong as they *tend* to promote the reverse of happiness [my italics]"[3] or that "the morality of an action depends on its foreseeable consequences,"[4] he is proposing a 'foreseeable consequence' or a 'reasonably foreseeable consequence' utilitarian position. Insofar as the foreseeable consequences are determined by looking at those consequences which would have been foreseen by someone with a command of all of the known causal laws whether the agent herself knew of those causal laws, then Mill is offering a 'foreseeable consequence' position. Insofar as the foreseeable consequences are determined by looking at which consequences a reasonable person would have foreseen, Mill is offering a 'reasonably foreseeable consequence' utilitarian position.

No matter which of the above formulations is appropriately attributed to Mill, certain problems are raised. If actual consequence utilitarianism is the system Mill proposes, then an agent may be blameworthy for consequences which no one could have foreseen. If 'foreseeable consequence' or 'reasonably foreseeable consequence' utilitarianism is the system which Mill proposes, then an agent may be responsible for consequences which *she* could not have foreseen, as long as those consequences would have been foreseen by *someone else*. In all of these systems, the agent seems to be potentially blameworthy for something which she could not have anticipated.

Current theorists propose a solution to this problem, explaining that we should not always blame agents for their immoral actions. Our praising or blaming someone is itself an action. As an action, it, too, is to be judged by the principle of utility.[5]

For example, suppose that Jones is visiting Smith. Smith says, "You know, Agnes, I have this terrible heart condition. If I have an attack, I need to take one of my pills within five minutes or else I will suffer a great deal of pain. I just bought a gadget the other day which is supposed to send out a radio signal to a medic in case I'm going to have a heart attack. Of course, I don't know that it works and I doubt that the medic could get here quickly enough anyway. That's why I keep my tablets with me at all times." Smith takes a vial out of his left pocket, shows it to Jones, and puts it on a nearby table. As luck would have it, Smith has a heart attack. Jones grabs the vial, takes out a pill, and gives it to Smith. Smith grabs it, swallows it, and dies immediately, much to the consternation of Jones and the medic, who arrives three minutes later.

Unbeknownst to Smith and Jones, Anderson has tampered with the vial. He has substituted a fast-acting poison for the heart pills. Jones has unwittingly helped to cause Smith's death. Ironically, had Jones done nothing, Smith would have suffered no pain (since the medic arrived so quickly) and would not have died (since the medic arrived with his own bottle of pills which, of course, would have helped Smith.) The issue here is whether we should blame Jones. She helped to cause a death. Yet, she acted as any reasonable, well-intentioned agent would have acted.

Our saying that we should not blame Jones is quite appealing. Our calling an agent blameworthy implies that she, in this case Jones, has somehow been lax. If the agent has acted exactly as a good utilitarian would have acted, then it seems quite unfair to blame her. Were she in the future to be confronted by similar circumstances, we would want her to act in a similar manner. Calling her action 'blameworthy' would be counter-productive. Such blame would not change her future behavior. Or, if the behavior were changed, there would be yet another disutility produced by the blaming, since no one would want the agent's future behavior to be changed. *Prospectively*, the actual consequence utilitarian, the foreseeable consequence utilitarian, and the reasonably foreseeable consequence utilitarian all would have acted in the same way — each would have unintentionally poisoned Smith.

By pointing out that praisings and blamings are also actions, theorists are following Mill's lead in claiming that external sanctions against immoral actions are not always warranted. However, Mill realizes that this solution is only partially helpful. That *external* sanctions are not warranted does not imply that *internal* sanctions are also not warranted. In their discussions, theorists do not address whether an agent should blame herself for her own immoral (albeit reasonable and well-intended) action — they do not address whether internal sanctions are appropriately imposed in cases like the one described above. Had they addressed that issue, they would have seen that they must choose between offering:

    a.   a position like the one described here in which all disutility-producing actions should be punished by conscience (through the imposition of either pangs of guilt or pangs of regret), or

    b.   a position in which *not* all disutility-producing actions are immoral (a position which is not even a modified act-utilitarian position).

In their writings, these theorists assume that the punisher and the punishee will not be the same person. Yet, one of the most important areas of morality involves a time when the punisher and punishee are the same person — when the agent is punished by her own conscience. I can think that *someone else* has acted immorally without expressing my condemnation to the agent. However, I cannot think that *I* have acted immorally without expressing my moral condemnation to the agent, i.e., to myself. Using the word 'immoral' is a kind of blaming.

The rightness of an action is not equivalent to the wrongness of others' imposing sanctions to discourage that action. The two notions are quite distinct. On the actual consequence utilitarian account, an action which is disutility-producing is immoral. Imposing a sanction is immoral if so doing is disutility-producing. *An action can be immoral, even if others' imposing sanctions against that action would also be immoral.*

When theorists claim that blaming is also an action which must be utility-producing, they *are not* talking about whether an onlooker should have moral disapprobation for the agent's action. Even in those cases in which an observer should not express blame, she may correctly believe that the agent has acted immorally.

This may seem paradoxical.[6] Yet, there is nothing paradoxical in an observer's judging a utility-maximizing act to be right but refraining from expressing that judgment to the agent. The act is right and should be so judged. However, the act of *expressing* the praise is not warranted. An analogous point can be made with respect to judgments and expressions of blame.[7]

The issue here is not whether an observer should feel disapprobation when she sees someone perform a disutility-producing action, but merely whether that disapprobation should be expressed. Even if correct that the agent has acted immorally, the onlooker is morally prohibited from expressing or acting upon that belief unless so doing would itself be utility-promoting. The claim, then, is not that the well-intentioned, reasonable agent acts morally permissibly when she fails to promote utility. Nor is the claim that the reasonable, well-intentioned agent acts amorally when she fails to promote utility. *If the actual consequence, act-utilitarian agent performs a disutility-producing action, then she acts immorally.* The point in contention is whether the agent should be informed that she has acted immorally.

The foreseeable consequence utilitarian might evaluate Jones's action differently than would the actual consequence utilitarian. If Anderson's tampering could not have been foreseen or if the effects of giving these pills to Smith could not have been foreseen, then the foreseeable consequence theorist will say that Jones has acted morally permissibly and deserves no sanctions imposed against her, not even the guilt pangs of conscience. Thus, there may be some occasions on which an actual consequence utilitarian would call an agent's action immoral when the foreseeable consequence theorist would not call that action immoral.

Yet, the foreseeable consequence theorist cannot completely escape the charge that her moral evaluations of actions may somehow be unfair. Suppose that Anderson's psychiatrist did foresee that Anderson might tamper with Smith's medicine. (We shall not address the culpability of Anderson's psychiatrist here.) The poisoning was foreseeable, although not foreseeable by Jones. Or, suppose that any pharmacist would have realized that the pills in Smith's vial were not of the appropriate size, weight, or color and thus were not likely to be pills which would help him. Indeed, perhaps the pharmacist would realize that the pills were poisonous. The adverse result of giving Smith these pills was foreseeable, although not foreseeable by Jones. If the foreseeable consequence utilitarian merely requires that the effects be foreseeable and not that the effects be foreseeable *by the agent herself,* then the foreseeable consequence theorist might also have to call Jones's action immoral, even though Jones was acting as any reasonable agent would have acted.

The reasonably foreseeable consequence utilitarian might evaluate Jones's action differently than either the actual consequence utilitarian or the foreseeable consequence utilitarian would, since the reasonable person presumably would not have the psychiatrist's or the pharmacist's knowledge. Nonetheless, the reasonably foreseeable consequence utilitarian may still face a problem. Suppose that a reasonable person would at least have suspected that these pills were poisonous, perhaps because there was a skull and crossbones on the container. However, Jones did not know that a skull and crossbones indicated that the contents were poisonous, perhaps because she never paid attention in the past when people explained what the symbol meant.[8] At the moment she gave the pills to Smith, there was neither time to find out the relevant information nor even any reason to think that she would need to check the pills. Nonetheless, a reasonable person would have acted differently.

The claim here is *not* that there would be as many counter-intuitive blamings if one adopts reasonably foreseeable consequence utilitarianism as there would be were one to adopt foreseeable consequence utilitarianism. Nor is the claim here that there would be as many counter-intuitive blamings if one adopted a foreseeable consequence utilitarian system as there would be were one to adopt actual consequence utilitarianism. Rather, the claim here is that each of these systems would sometimes countenance these counter-intuitive blamings.

Regardless of whether one adopts actual consequence, foreseeable consequence, or reasonably foreseeable utilitarianism, one has adopted an achievement-oriented moral system. If one is an actual consequence utilitarian, then one should perform the action which *will* be productive of utility; if one is a foreseeable consequence utilitarian, then one should perform the action which, given the known causal laws, is "*objectively*" most likely to produce utility; if one is a reasonably foreseeable consequence utilitarian, then one should perform the action which *a reasonable agent would foresee to be* the most likely to produce utility. There are a variety of reasons why a sincere, well-intentioned agent might nonetheless not perform the action which the achievement-oriented system deems morally right. For example, the agent might miscalculate or might overlook some important information.

The problem for Mill or any achievement-oriented moral theorist *is not* how to justify society's refraining from punishing individuals' immoral acts in certain instances. Their problem *is* explaining either:

1.   how a consistent agent who subscribes to a particular achievement-oriented moral theory can see that he has failed to perform the correct action and nonetheless *not* blame himself for his failure, or

2.   how it can be appropriate for a conscience to impose sanctions in a situation in which the sincere agent did as well as she could have, given the obtaining conditions.

When Does a Properly Developed Conscience Punish?

We might say that a properly developed conscience will only punish an agent when the punishment itself would promote utility. Or, we might say that a properly developed conscience will punish all actions which are deemed immoral by the utilitarian system under discussion.

The former view has the drawbacks previously discussed, plus the additional drawback (from the actual consequence, act-utilitarian perspective) that we could no longer claim that actions are right if they promote the requisite amount of utility and wrong if they do not. We would have to admit that there might be disutility-producing actions which would not be wrong to perform.

The foreseeable consequence and the reasonably foreseeable consequence utilitarians will face analogous problems. If conscience should only punish when it would be productive of utility to do so, then the foreseeable consequence utilitarian must admit that there might be actions which were foreseeably disutility-producing and were nonetheless not wrong to perform, e.g., the action which the pharmacist would foresee would be disutility-producing even though Jones would not so foresee.

Such a result might seem desirable, since Jones's action might not seem blameworthy if a reasonable person would not have foreseen that it would be harmful. However, one's accepting the appropriateness of that evaluation implies that one does not accept the foreseeable consequence theorist's standard for the rightness and wrongness of actions. Certainly, the foreseeable consequence theorist could not so cavalierly accept that a foreseeably disutility-producing action was not morally objectionable.

Even the reasonably foreseeable consequence theorist must admit that there might be some actions which would not be productive of utility for conscience to punish, even though those actions would be foreseen by a reasonable person to be disutility-producing. Suppose that someone who is not particularly foresightful (and who cannot be made more foresightful) performs an action which a reasonable person would have known would be harmful, even though this person believes that the action will be utility-maximizing. Basically, if the reasonable person standard does not merely involve a claim about what would have been reasonable for *this* person to have performed but instead involves a claim about what a reasonable person would have performed, then the reasonably foreseeable consequence theorist may also be open to the charge that her theory sometimes blames unfairly.

The problem here is not merely that there are difficulties in determining which actions are wrong. The problem is that if we claim that:

1. consciences should only impose sanctions when that imposition would itself be utility-producing,
2. if actions are wrong then they are blameworthy by conscience, and

3. actions are wrong if they do not promote whatever the achievement-oriented system holds should be promoted,

then we countenance the possibility that there will be actions which are both morally wrong and not morally wrong. An action would be morally wrong according to (3) if it did not promote whatever the achievement-oriented system holds should have been promoted, and the action would not be wrong according to (1) and (2) if its punishment by conscience would be productive of disutility.

The imposition of external or internal sanctions against disutility-producing actions does not always promote utility. Let us designate set S as the set of disutility-producing actions against which the imposition of external or internal sanctions would be disutility-producing. Insofar as actions are morally wrong if they do not promote utility, all of the actions in S are morally wrong. Insofar as actions are morally wrong only if the imposition of either external or internal sanctions would be utility-producing, none of the actions in S would be morally wrong.

If a system holds that if an action is disutility-producing then it is morally wrong and also holds that an action is morally wrong only if its punishment would be utility-producing, then some actions (any members of S) would be both morally wrong and not morally wrong. An analogous argument can be made against both foreseeable and reasonably foreseeable consequence utilitarianism. For the former, we simply must let S be the set of foreseeably disutility-producing actions which would be disutility-producing to punish. For the latter, we simply must let S be the set of actions which a reasonable person would foresee would be disutility-producing, which would nonetheless be disutility-producing to punish.[9]

Mill's View

Mill argues, "Utilitarians are ... aware that a right action does not necessarily indicate a virtuous character, and that *actions which are blamable often proceed from qualities entitled to praise* [my italics]. When this is apparent in any particular case, it modifies their estimation, not certainly of the act, but of the agent."[10]   This distinction helps the actual consequence utilitarian, the foreseeable consequence utilitarian, and the reasonably foreseeable consequence utilitarian.

Insofar as Mill is offering an actual consequence utilitarian account, the distinction between assessing actions and assessing characters will be used in the following way. Jones's *action* was wrong and deserved censure from conscience. However, Jones *herself* deserves praise, because her action manifests admirable character traits.

Mill would say that we, as people *external* to the agent, should not express our blame of the agent for her reasonable, well-intended, disutility-producing actions. However, he would then be talking about expressing blame rather than about blaming, *per se*.

Mill clearly believes in the importance of distinguishing between blaming an agent for her character and blaming an agent for her action. We can believe that an agent's character is blameworthy without believing that her action is blameworthy, and vice versa. However, blaming an agent for her action is still a blaming, just as blaming an agent for her character is still a blaming.[11] If either the agent's action or her character deserves blame, then we cannot say that the agent is blameless. Even if *we* should not express our blame to the agent, she is still blameworthy *by her own conscience* as long as either her action or her character deserves blame.

When explaining that there are situations in which one should not express one's blame, Sidgwick makes very clear that he is talking about the expression of blame and not about blaming, *per se*. "In such cases [i.e., when we refrain from blaming others] the line seems drawn by a more or less conscious consideration of what men ordinarily do, and by a social instinct as to the practical effects of *expressed* [my italics] moral approbation and disapprobation: we think that moral progress will on the whole be best promoted by our ... confining censure ... to acts that fall clearly below [the level of ordinary practice]."[12] Sidgwick is referring to what we should *express*, not to what we should *think*. It is acceptable to think that our neighbors have acted immorally, even when it is unacceptable for us to express that thought.

When Bernard sees that Howard has acted immorally, Bernard can withhold that judgment from Howard. However, Howard cannot see that he himself has acted immorally and withhold that judgment from himself. That judgment, i.e., that Howard has acted immorally, is itself a kind of blaming.

In order for Bernard to express his moral disapproval of Howard's action, he need not do anything *in addition* to uttering, "Howard, you've acted immorally." That alone will suffice. If Howard thinks to himself, "I have acted immorally," he thereby morally condemns his own action. He does not need to do something *in addition* to realizing that he himself has acted immorally in order to express his moral condemnation of his own action. He might do something in addition, e.g., act in some way to make amends for his action, but he need not do so in order to have 'successfully' morally condemned (and thus punished) himself.

The question is not whether Howard *intends* to blame himself. Indeed, a salient difference between self-blaming and other-blaming involves intention. When Bernard realizes that Howard acts immorally, Bernard must *in addition* form an intention to express that blame in order for the agent to hear the blaming. When Howard realizes that he himself has acted immorally, he need *not* in addition form an intention to express that blame in order for the agent to 'hear' the blaming. An individual cannot *realize* that she has acted immorally without also blaming herself.[13]

A critic of the position outlined here might agree that an expresson of moral disapprobation, e.g., "I acted immorally" or "You acted immorally," is a form of blaming. However, she might point out that just as one does not always feel the pangs of conscience when someone else expresses moral condemnation of one's action, one may not always feel the pangs of conscience when one expresses moral condemnation of one's own action, since the realization that one has acted immorally and the imposition of pangs of conscience are two distinct events.

Certainly, that is true. The realization that one has acted immorally might *result* in one's feeling pangs of conscience but is not *identical to* one's feeling pangs of conscience. However, too much should not be made of that point.

Although the realization that one has acted immorally and the feeling of the pangs of conscience are two distinct events, once one realizes that one has acted immorally one does not need in addition to *intend* to feel badly in order for conscience to do its work. One will feel the pangs of conscience 'automatically'. Thus, although the events are not identical, that point is not as helpful as might first appear.

Before we actually express our blame of others, we should consider whether the blaming would itself promote utility. If it would not, then we should not express that blame. However, a self-blaming (i.e., an imposition of the pangs of conscience) is not the same *kind* of act as is an other-blaming. A self-blaming is not something which we *choose* to do and hence its appropriateness should not be evaluated in the same way as an other-blaming should be.

Our not being able at a moment's notice to control whether our consciences will impose sanctions might simply seem to be a failing in our natures. Even if we cannot prevent these disutility-producing punishments by conscience, that does not undermine the claim that we *should not* punish ourselves when the imposition of those punishments would be disutility-producing.

Certainly, the important issue here does not involve when consciences *do* punish but when they *should* punish, since our conciences are not infallible and may punish or fail to punish at inappropriate times. Further, they may impose very weak pangs when much stronger ones would be appropriate. Mill realizes this, pointing out that consciences may have no "binding efficacy" for those people whose consciences are not properly developed.[14]

Mill argues that an action is wrong only if it is blameworthy by conscience. If I realize that I have acted immorally, then I *should* feel pangs of conscience. If a properly developed conscience does not impose a sanction after the performance of a particular action, then the action is not immoral. If all disutility-producing actions are immoral, then the properly developed conscience must and should impose sanctions against all disutility-producing actions.

The proposal offered by current theorists involves the claim that a disutility-producing action can be *immoral*, and yet *not* something for which we should feel pangs of conscience, i.e., not something which is blameworthy by conscience. According to Mill, the notion of 'immoral' implies that the agent should feel pangs if she so acts; it implies that her conscience should punish her. Mill, *qua* actual consequence utilitarian, would claim that one is confused if one says that a disutility-producing action is immoral but not blameworthy — one would have misused the term 'immoral'.

This confusion might be traced to an ambiguity in our language. If we say, "Smith should not blame Jones," we might mean:

a. Smith should not think that Jones is culpable, since Jones is innocent, or

b. Smith may think, but should not *express* the thought, that Jones is culpable.

(a) implies that Jones has not acted immorally. (b) implies that Jones should not be told that he has acted immorally, even though he has indeed acted immorally.

Only (b) would allow one to say that the action is immoral, although the agent should not be punished for it. As long as the punisher and the punishee are different people, (b) allows one to say that all disutility-producing actions are immoral and yet not necessarily blameworthy. However, as soon as an agent must judge his own action, we cannot sensibly say that the punisher knows that the punishee has acted immorally, and yet the punisher refuses to express his knowledge to the punishee. The punishee must know. If the punisher and the punishee are the same person and the punishee is not blamed for his *immoral* action (i.e., his conscience should not and does not punish him), then the word 'immoral' has been used improperly. To say that an action is immoral is to condemn the action. Condemnation is a form of blaming. Thus, if indeed an action is immoral, then it is also blameworthy.

An analogous argument can be used for the foreseeable consequence utilitarian. If Jones could not foresee the effects of her action but someone else (the pharmacist) could, her action would still be wrong, since it would not have been the action which, even foreseeably, had good consequences. If her action was wrong, then it was blameworthy by conscience, even if she was trying to perform the best action, given what she could foresee.

An analogous argument can also be made with respect to reasonably foreseeable consequence utilitarianism. Even if the agent does what she believes will be best, her action is immoral if the action which she chooses would be foreseen by a reasonable person to be harmful. If her action is immoral, then it is blameworthy by conscience.

The Impartiality of Conscience

Mill, like many utilitarians, claims that moral agents should be disinterested and benevolent. "As between his own happiness and that of others, utilitarianism requires [the agent] to be as strictly impartial as a disinterested and benevolent spectator."[15] This impartiality requirement is included to assure that the agent's own interests will not cloud her judgment about which action should be performed. By the same token, the requirement is included to assure that an agent will blame herself only when the agent, *qua* impartial observer, would say that the action was blameworthy.

When we talk about when an agent should blame herself, we are discussing when the agent's conscience should impose pangs of guilt or regret. When we say that an agent's conscience should blame her only when an impartial spectator would blame her, we might have one of two meanings in mind:

Possible Meaning 1. The agent's conscience should blame her whenever an impartial being would *express* blame to the agent. If this is the utilitarian's meaning, then our consciences occupy a special moral position only insofar as they have a better vantage point than most observers have. It is easier for our consciences to "see" all of our actions than it is for others. Thus, our consciences should act exactly as impartial, *omniscient* spectators would act. When such a spectator would express blame, our consciences should blame us. When such a spectator would not express blame, our consciences should not blame us.

Sometimes, other agents should not blame us, because they do not know all of the facts. In such cases, our consciences may occupy a privileged position. They, like omniscient spectators, would "know" all or most of the relevant information and thus might be in a position to make a moral judgment while others might not be in such a position. However, there are other times when other people should not blame us for our immoral action, even though they know all of the relevant information, i.e., even though they are in the position of an omniscient spectator.

When Sidgwick refers to those cases in which we should not blame agents for their immoral actions, he is referring to both types of cases.[16] It is the second type of case (in which we should not be blamed even though all of the relevant facts are known) which is more interesting, since it is hardly surprising that those who do not have all of the relevant information should not express their blame to the agent. In those cases in which we should not blame the agent even though we know all of the relevant information, the agent's conscience is in no better position than we are. If we (as omniscient observers) should not expressly blame the agent and conscience should not blame in those cases in which an omniscient observer would not express blame, then in these cases no one should blame the agent, neither other people nor the agent's conscience. However, if others should not blame the agent and the agent's conscience should not blame him, then the claim that the agent has acted immorally loses its meaning. He would have committed an immoral, blameless action.

An immoral, blameless action involves:

a. a contradiction in terms. Mill says that if one has acted immorally, then one is blameworthy, if only by conscience. One cannot be both blameworthy and blameless. There cannot be blameless, immoral actions.

OR

b. a new use of the term 'immoral'. 'Immoral' would no longer mean 'blameworthy'. It would have no pejorative content. It would merely mean what 'non-utility-maximizing' means to (some) deontologists. However, to separate 'immoral' from its pejorative connotation would in effect simply negate the function of the word. It would no longer be particularly surprising that one could act immorally and yet blamelessly. By the same token, it would no longer be morally significant to claim that all disutility-producing actions are immoral. Such a claim would *not* imply that disutility-producing actions were wrong. Nor, alternatively, would it be significant to claim that all foreseeably disutility-producing actions are wrong or, alternatively, that all actions reasonably foreseen to be disutilty-producing are wrong. *If 'immoral' lost its pejorative content, then it would no longer be clear why we as moral agents should not act immorally.*

When actual consequence act-utilitarians liken the way one's conscience should behave to the way an impartial omniscient spectator would behave, they cannot mean that one's conscience should express blame only when an impartial, omniscient spectator would express blame. Such a claim would imply:

a. that not all disutility-producing actions are immoral,

OR

b. that utilitarians rely on a contradiction in terms when explaining the praising and blaming of actions,

OR

c. that it is not clear why one should not perform immoral actions. One's calling an action 'immoral' would not imply that the action was wrong or blameworthy.

The actual consequence utilitarian cannot accept any of these possibilities. Nor could the foreseeable or reasonably foreseeable consequence utilitarians accept any of the analogous possibilities.

They must have a different interpretation in mind when they say that one's conscience should blame whenever an impartial observer would blame.

Possible Meaning 2. The utilitarian might mean that the agent's conscience should blame the agent whenever an impartial, omniscient spectator would blame the agent — not just those times when the spectator would express the blame, but also those times when the spectator would blame the agent but would refrain from expressing the blame.

There might be cases in which an impartial, omniscient spectator would say, "I blame Black for his action. He acted immorally. However, because I am an outsider, it would be disutility-producing for me to express the blame. Fortunately, it would be productive of utility for Black's conscience to blame Black."

Suppose that I, an impartial, omniscient spectator, know that Black will repeat his immoral action if I upbraid him for it. I also know that Black will not repeat his immoral action if he is upbraided by his own conscience for performing it. I, as an impartial, omniscient spectator, should not upbraid Black, although his conscience should upbraid him.

There might be cases in which it would be improper for a spectator, *qua* outsider, to express blame, even though it would be quite proper for the agent's conscience to express blame. Unfortunately, there are some cases in which the agent acts immorally and yet it seems that neither an impartial spectator's expressing blame nor the agent's conscience's expressing blame would promote utility.

We could say that neither the benevolent spectator nor the agent's conscience should blame the agent in these cases. However, if no one (*including the agent's conscience*) should blame him, then the agent has not performed a wrong action. If we claim that the agent should neither be punished by others nor by his own conscience, then we would be denying the basic tenet of our moral theory — we would be denying that the non-achievement of the appropriate end was wrong.

If we say that the agent's conscience should punish him because the conscience should blame whenever a disinterested, benevolent spectator would blame, then we have achieved a rather ironic result. Every time that a disinterested, benevolent, omniscient spectator would blame but would refrain from expressing the blame (because expressing the blame would be disutility-producing), the conscience would both blame and express the blame. By blaming whenever an

impartial, benevolent spectator would blame but not refraining from
expressing the blame whenever an impartial, benevolent spectator
would refrain, the properly developed conscience would not seem to be
behaving properly.

We *seem* to have a contradiction in terms. If the properly developed conscience should punish all disutility-producing actions and if
indeed we determine which actions are immoral by looking at which
actions a properly developed conscience would punish, then we are in
the uncomfortable position of both affirming that the action should be
punished (because conscience should punish all harmful actions) and of
denying that the action should be punished (because the punishment
itself would be counter-productive). In reality, this position is not
only *not* self-contradictory, but actually represents many people's
intuitions regarding when agents would appropriately feel pangs of
conscience. (Of course, this position's being in accord with people's
intuitions does not thereby *validate* it, but does refute one of the
charges frequently made against act-utilitarianism, *viz.*, that it is so
counter-intuitive.)

Which Actions Are Immoral?

Act-utilitarian theorists might define the rightness and wrongness
of actions in a variety of ways, e.g., in terms of actual consequences,
foreseeable consequences, or reasonably foreseeable consequences.
However, one should not infer that the choice is either arbitrary or
unimportant.

All of the examples offered above are achievement-oriented. If
one, despite the best of intentions and motivations, fails to perform
the correct action, then one has acted immorally. Theorists might
instead adopt a system in which the agent's intention and motivation
determine the moral worth of the action.[17] However, there would be
certain costs to doing so, e.g., one would seem to lose a sort of
objectivity.[18]

Suppose that one claims that the imposition of great suffering on
innocent individuals is "objectively" morally wrong. There is no
exception appended to that claim, e.g., that causing such suffering is
morally permissible as long as one does not intend to do so or as long
as one is motivated by benevolence. The subjective considerations
(those considerations involving the subject, i.e., agent) of intention
and motivation are not included in the prohibition against causing
needless, undeserved suffering.

Just as one might perform a morally wrong action even though one might have had the best of intentions or motivations, Mill argues that one can perform a morally right action, even if it is performed for the wrong reason. "[U]tilitarian moralists have gone beyond almost all others in affirming that the motive has nothing to do with the morality of the action, though much to do with the worth of the agent."[19] Mill, for one, would not want to define as wrong only those harmful actions which involved evil intentions and were badly motivated.

Mill argues that the promotion of humankind's utility is the principle by which actions should be judged. We consider a situation in which the action which will *foreseeably* promote utility is not the action which will *actually* promote utility. Were Mill to adopt either foreseeable or reasonably foreseeable consequence utilitarianism, he would have to call the action which in fact did not promote utility morally *right*, and the action which in fact would have promoted utility morally *wrong*. Certainly, the foreseeable consequence utilitarian would do this. Further, there seems to be support for such a claim in Mill's writings. He argues that "whatever incidental and unexpected benefits may result from crimes, they are crimes nonetheless."[20] However, if the principle of utility really is the ultimate principle, then Mill will have some difficulty in consistently supporting the claim that a utility-maximizing action can nonetheless be immoral.

Perhaps Mill is simply inconsistent with respect to reasonably foreseeable, foreseeable, and actual consequence utilitarianism. However, a line is suggested which would make Mill's view consistent.

Insofar as we talk about the imposition of external sanctions, we might restrict their imposition (*ceteris paribus*) to those actions which would be reasonably foreseen to be harmful. Thus, the crimes alluded to by Mill would still deserve external sanctions because their fortuitous effects could not have been predicted. However, if Mill really believes that the principle of utility is the Supreme Principle and that a properly developed conscience will punish all immoral actions, then he must believe that conscience will punish all harmful actions. He must believe that the "ultimate sanction . . . of all morality,"[21] "in properly cultivated moral natures," will punish or prevent any violation of duty[22] (any insuffficiently utility-producing action).

On the Disutility of Conscience' Punishing Certain Immoral Actions

According to the view ascribed to Mill here, conscience will punish even at disutility-producing times. Suppose that there is a situation in which the imposition of neither external nor internal sanctions would promote utility — no beneficial changes in the agent's behavior would be produced thereby and no one other than the agent would be beneficially affected by the agent's undergoing some sort of punishment. The agent performs an action which she sincerely believes will maximize utility, even though a reasonable person would have known that it would be disastrous. Whether one subscribes to a reasonably foreseeable consequence, a foreseeable consequence, or an actual consequence utilitarian position, one must say that the agent should have an internal sanction imposed against her at the very least.

The fortuitously utility-maximizing crime mentioned above suggests another problem. Should the person who committed it be punished by his conscience? Neither the foreseeable consequence nor the reasonably foreseeable consequence theorist would have any difficulty in saying 'Yes' and remaining consistent. However, the actual consequence act-utilitarian would seem to have difficulty insofar as he wanted to claim that conscience *should* punish a utility-maximizing action.[23]

Mill has no problem in explaining why the criminal alluded to above should feel guilty, i.e., should have internal sanctions imposed against him. The criminal who performed the utility-maximizing action should feel guilty, not for his *action* but for his *character* (for being the sort of person who would willingly perform actions which he believed would be harmful). The only difficulty for Mill's position as outlined here is in explaining why the benevolent, well-intended individual who performs a harmful action which he, *qua* reasonable agent, believed would be utility-maximizing, nonetheless *should* feel the pangs of conscience.[24]

Assessments of Actions and Characters

Before we continue, one point must be made clear. When Mill distinguishes between assessing actions and assessing characters, he is *not* claiming that an agent with a good character who performs a blameworthy action should have *no* sanctions imposed against her, not even by conscience. Indeed, it is not clear what it would mean to say that the action, but *not* the agent, is blameworthy. We cannot punish actions, *per se*. We cannot even condemn actions without also condemning the agent. To say that an action is immoral but that no agent deserves punishment denies the essentially condemnatory nature of 'immoral'. There would be no point in talking about immoral actions if there was no one who was responsible for those actions. Certainly, Mill would deny that an action could be wrong if the agent should not suffer the pangs of conscience for its performance.[25]

Yet, one might argue, if conscience is really to have the role ascribed to it here, it would have to punish agents at inappropriate times — at times at which it would be *counter-intuitive* to claim that the agent deserves to undergo pangs of conscience. That alone should establish the falsity of the view presented here.

Yet, Mill denies that "we ought to take the feelings as we find them, as accident or design has made them."[26] He discusses the power of "the customary morality, [i.e.] that which education and opinion have consecrated," arguing that "when a person is asked to believe that this morality *derives* its obligation from some general principle round which custom has not thrown the same halo, the assertion is to him a paradox; the supposed corollaries seem to have a more binding force than the original theorem; the superstructure seems to stand better without, than with, what is represented as its foundation."[27] Thus, Mill recognizes that some dictates of the principle of utility, e.g., about which actions deserve punishment and which do not, will not be in accord with our intuitions.

Indeed, the difficulty that we do not and believe we should not feel pangs of conscience for some of the actions for which the principle of utility dictates we should feel pangs of conscience "will always present itself . . . until, by the improvement of education, the feeling of unity with our fellow creatures shall be . . . as deeply rooted in our character, and to our own consciousness as completely a part of our nature, as the horror of crime is in an ordinarily well-brought up young person."[28] Thus, Mill believes that once the principle of utility and its implications have been adequately instilled within people, these conflicting intuitions will cease to exist. He believes that "the object of education should be to form the strongest possible associations of the salutary class; associations of pleasure with all things beneficial to the great whole, and of pain with all things hurtful to it."[29] Presumably, anyone with this very strong painful association with everything hurtful to humankind would feel quite badly were she to cause harm.

Merely because one would feel badly does not imply that one would feel *guilty*. For example, if one could not have foreseen one's producing disutility, it seems rather difficult to justify one's deserving to feel guilty, nonetheless. Indeed, Mill argues that "the *tendency* [my italics] of actions to promote happiness affords a test to which the feelings of morality should conform."[30] Yet, this apparent contradiction can be explained away if we distinguish between different types of "feelings of morality." On the account offered here, one should not feel *guilt*, but *regret*, for producing disutility which could not have been foreseen.

The Dual Role of Conscience

Conscience has two distinct roles. (1) It preserves and reinforces, and (2) it punishes. Conscience imposes different kinds of pangs in performing these functions — pangs of regret and pangs of guilt, respectively. These two roles are described below:

1. Conscience preserves and reinforces. This sort of punishment does not imply that the agent was at fault. The agent would feel regret or sorrow, not because she felt guilty (not because she felt that she had been negligent), but simply because her action was harmful. She would not feel that anyone (including herself) was accusing her of having been lax. She, as a benevolent agent, would simply feel sorry that she had produced harm. By imposing pangs of regret, the conscience would be helping to preserve and reinforce attitudes of benevolence and consideration for others. If I feel as good for performing a reasonable, well-intended action which has bad results as I would feel for performing a reasonable, well-intended action with good results, then I have become hardened to the plights of others. By feeling regret, I am forced to remember that my intention is not the only important element of my actions — the effects on other people are important as well.[31]

2. Conscience corrects. It helps to build character. This sort of punishment does imply that the agent was at fault. The agent would feel guilty because he had been lax. Indeed, he should feel somewhat guilty even if his action was utility-maximizing, not because his action was utility-maximizing, but because he was lucky to have maximized utility. The most likely result of his action would have been harmful.

Mill suggests that "ninety-nine hundredths of all our actions are done from other motives [i.e., motives other than a feeling of duty], and rightly so done if the rule of duty does not condemn them."[32] Of course, even if the act is right, the agent may deserve blame. Certainly, an omniscient spectator would admonish a person who accidentally maximized utility out of malice and miscalculation,[33] if only because the person's character was defective. An agent with a bad character would be more likely to produce disutility the next time, *ceteris paribus*, than would be an agent with a good character. If an omniscient spectator would rebuke an agent for his utility-maximizing action, i.e., not for the action but for his motives, then the agent's conscience also should rebuke the agent.

Thus, the utilitarian conscience has a dual role.[34] It imposes sanctions against all harmful actions. It also imposes sanctions against all actions performed from improper motives (motives that would tend to produce harmful results). Had Mill explained the dual role of the utilitarian conscience, he could have avoided many of the criticisms which were and are aimed at utilitarians.

This dual role of conscience is not surprising. As far as the preserving role of conscience is concerned, we would want an agent who produced harm to feel at least somewhat regretful. It would hardly be appropriate for him to feel completely cheerful and proud of himself if he caused general disutility, even if he did act reasonably and with the right intention. As far as the correcting role of conscience is concerned, we would want an agent who was merely lucky to have maximized utility to feel somewhat guilty. If he continues to act in this manner, he will probably produce much disutility.

If an agent acts contrary to the standard maxims of morality because he has good reason to believe that his so doing would be utility-maximizing, then we would not characterize his maximizing utility as merely lucky. If an agent tries to produce disutility but ends up maximizing utility nonetheless, then we would characterize his utility-maximization as 'merely lucky'.

Thus, we might talk about two different "feelings of morality." If an agent performs an action which will not foreseeably produce utility, then he should feel guilty. Indeed, if the action which the agent performs happens to correspond to the action which is most likely to maximize utility but the agent does not know this, then he too should feel guilty. The "test to which the feelings of morality [i.e., in this case, the feelings of guilt] should conform" is "the *tendency* of actions to promote happiness." However, the test to which the feelings of

regret should conform is the production of that which is "beneficial to
the great whole."

The foreseeable consequence utilitarian and the reasonably foreseeable consequence utilitarian might also adopt this account. They
would not believe that the agent deserved to feel guilty for
unforeseeable negative consequences. However, presumably, they too
would want agents who produced disutility to feel some regret.[35]

Why Conscience Must Punish All Disutility-Producing Actions

If 'immoral' has the pejorative connotation which both utilitarians
and deontologists currently ascribe to it, then utilitarians cannot talk
about immoral, blameless actions. Nor can they sensibly talk about
immoral actions performed by blameless agents. To say that an action
is immoral is to say that someone is blameworthy, however slightly,
for its performance.[36]

If the expression 'disutility-producing actions are immoral' is going to have any pejorative content, then immoral actions cannot be
blameless actions. Or, if the expression 'foreseeably disutility-
producing actions are immoral' is going to have any pejorative
content, then foreseeably disutility-producing actions cannot be
blameless actions. Both of these achievement-oriented systems must
hold that an agent who fails to perform the correct action, despite his
having had the best of motivations and intentions, acts immorally
nonetheless. While a particular immoral action may not deserve
blame from others, it must deserve blame from the agent himself. As
soon as an agent realizes that he has committed an immoral action, he
will necessarily blame himself — he will necessarily feel somewhat
badly for his action. Unless we radically change the meaning of
'immoral', using the word 'immoral' is a blaming.

Mill convincingly argues that there are many times when immoral
actions do not deserve blame from others. However, merely because
others should not blame an agent does not mean that the agent has not
acted in a blameworthy fashion. It is perfectly consistent and coherent
to claim that an action is immoral and yet should not be blamed by
others. However, 'should not be blamed by others' is not equivalent to
'blameless'. 'Blameless' means 'not blameworthy by anyone, including
the agent herself'.

To call an action 'immoral but blameless' is to deny the condemnatory nature of an essentially pejorative term (viz., 'immoral').
Philosophers cannot talk about immoral actions which do not merit

censure from conscience. Nor can they talk about immoral actions for which the agent should not blame herself. If an action is harmful, then (on the actual consequence act-utilitarian account) the action is immoral. To call an action immoral is to express blame. An actual consequence act-utilitarian agent cannot see that she has acted in a harmful manner without blaming herself.

By the same token, if an action would be reasonably foreseen to be harmful, then the reasonably foreseeable consequence theorist and the foreseeable consequence theorist must call that action immoral, even if the agent had the best of intentions and motivations. A reasonably foreseeable consequence utilitarian agent or a foreseeable consequence utilitarian agent could not see that he had performed an action which a reasonable person would have known would be harmful without blaming himself.

Utilitarians, including Mill, must talk about the dual role of conscience. Consciences should impose sanctions against actions which are harmful and against actions which are reasonably foreseen to be harmful. Agents should feel some sorrow or regret for performing an action of the first sort and they should feel some guilt for their performing an action of the second sort. If utilitarians talk about the dual role of conscience, they will neither be forced to resort to incomprehensible defenses (and talk about blamable actions performed by blameless agents) nor to deny the essentially condemnatory nature of the term 'immoral'.[37]

NOTES

1. "Auguste Comte and Positivism," p. 335.
2. *Utilitarianism*, Ch. 4, Par. 9, p. 237.
3. *Ibid.*, Ch. 2, Par. 2, P. 210.
4. "Bentham," p. 112.
5. See, e.g., Sartorius, *Individual Conduct and Social Norms*, p. 19, and Smart, "Extreme and restricted utilitarianism," p. 198. These theorists are *not* offering the kind of act-utilitarian position suggested by Mill. Nonetheless, their comments are applicable when suitably modified. For ease of explication, when I talk about Mill's requiring that actions be utility-producing, one should understand the implicit 'to the required extent'.
6. See Marcus Singer, "The Paradox of Extreme Utilitarianism," *Pacific Philosophical Quarterly* 64 (1983), p. 244.

7. A different point is suggested by M. Singer's remarks, *viz.*, whether the 'act' of judging is itself appropriate only if it would be utility-producing to do. I suspect that Mill would deny that most acts of judgment are voluntary and hence would not be willing to subject them to this kind of evaluation.

8. Jones's character might be blameworthy if, on a series of occasions in the past, she neglected to do something which a reasonable agent would have done. However, the blameworthiness of her character might *not* affect the moral quality of her *action*.

9. For a related discussion, see my "Conscience and the Right to Do Wrong," *Philosophia* 17 (1988), pp. 411-420.

10. *Utilitarianism*, Ch. 2, Par. 20, p. 221.

11. Singer makes an analogous point. See Marcus Singer, "Incoherence, Inconsistency, and Moral Theory: More on Actual Consequence Utilitarianism," *Southern Journal of Philosophy* 20 (1982), p. 390.

12. Henry Sidgwick, *The Methods of Ethics* (7th ed., 1907) (Indianapolis: Hackett Publishing Co., 1981), p. 221.

13. Insofar as we are considering the agent herself, Singer's point about the difficulties of separating the judgment of the moral worth of an act from the expression of that judgment to the agent is well-taken. See M. Singer, "The Paradox of Extreme Utilitarianism," p. 244.

14. *Utilitarianism*, Ch. 3, Par. 5, p. 229.

15. *Ibid.*, Ch. 2, Par. 18, p. 218. See also Smart in Smart and Williams, *Utilitarianism For and Against*, p. 32; and R. M. Hare, "Ethical theory and utilitarianism," *Utilitarianism and Beyond*, Amartya Sen and Bernard Williams eds. (Cambridge: Cambridge University Press, 1982), p. 26.

16. Sidgwick, *The Methods of Ethics*, p. 221.

17. For a modified utilitarian view in which the intentions and motivations are included within the assessment of the action, see my *Francis Hutcheson's Moral Theory.*

For Mill, the importance of the intention lies in its determining *what* the action is. See *Utilitarianism*, Ch. 2, footnote to Par. 19, pp. 219-220. See also *A System of Logic*, Bk. 1, Ch. 3, Par. 5, p. 55.

18. See Gruzalski, "Foreseeable Consequence Utilitarianism," p. 167.

19. *Utilitarianism*, Ch. 2, Par. 19, p. 219. However, Mill believes that the motivation affects the *aesthetic* worth of the action.

20. *Three Essays on Religion, CW* Vol. 10, p. 387.

21. *Utilitarianism*, Ch. 3, Par. 5, p. 229.

22. *Ibid.*, Ch. 3, Par. 4, p. 228.

23. Smart presumably would argue that, even on an actual consequence account, the criminal's action would be blameworthy. Smart argues, "In considering questions of praise and blame it is not the expediency of the praised or blamed action that is at issue, but the expediency of the praise. It can be expedient to praise an inexpedient action and inexpedient to praise an expedient one." Smart, "Extreme and restricted utilitarianism," p. 198.

See also Narveson on the efficacy of blaming in his *Morality and Utility*, p. 167.

24. The 'should' here does not imply that conscience' punishing the agent would be productive of utility in this case. Rather, the should is a 'functional' one, i.e., if it is the 'function' of conscience to punish all harmful actions and the action in question is harmful, then conscience 'should' punish the action, i.e., it is conscience' function to punish the action.

25. Parfit talks about "blameless wrongdoing," where "it is the act and not the agent that is immoral." See his *Reasons and Persons*, p. 32.

Certainly, Parfit and Mill are both correct insofar as they are implying that an action can be blameworthy even if the agent's character (i.e., standard disposition to act or refrain from acting in certain ways) is not at all blameworthy. However, insofar as actions are essentially related to agents, it is rather odd to talk about blameworthy actions performed by agents who are completely blameless in all respects.

26. "Whewell on Moral Philosophy," p. 172.

27. *Utilitarianism*, Ch. 3, Par. 1, p. 227.

28. *Ibid.*, Par. 2, p. 227.

29. *Autobiography*, p. 141.

30. "Whewell on Moral Philosophy," p. 172.

31. It might be true that feelings of regret would not always be productive of utility. Sometimes, a person who is suitably benevolent might feel regret for his disutility-producing action, even though the regret would not serve an important enough function to warrant its existence. For example, conscience' reminding the person this additional time of the need to consider others may not be necessary if he is already suitably benevolent.

Deontologists must resist the temptation to claim (triumphantly) that consciences sometimes act in harmful ways and thus act immorally. At most, consciences *behave* 'immorally'. Behaviors seem to be out of the realm of moral praise and blame, especially if performed by beings without consciences.

In any case, consciences do not 'deserve blame from others' for punishing at disutility-producting times, since their function is to punish harmful actions even at disutility-producting times, and they cannot blame themselves, because they do not themselves have consciences. Thus, consciences do not act (or behave) wrongly insofar as wrong actions/behaviors should be punished by others or themselves.

On the account offered here, we might talk about two kinds of regret which the agent might feel after having faultlessly brought about bad consequences. She might feel regret (1) that there were bad consequences (e.g., that someone else had suffered), and (2) that *she* had been the agent who had brought about those bad consequences. For related comments, see, e.g., Loren Lomasky, *Persons, Rights and Moral Community* (New York: Oxford University Press, 1987), p. 166.

32. *Utilitarianism*, Ch. 2, Par. 19, p. 219.

33. Parfit argues that consequentialism may be indirectly self-defeating in that the motivations which consequentialism dictates that agents have may cause consequentialists to perform fewer good actions than they would have, had these people had different motivations. See *Reasons and Persons*, pp. 27 ff.

There are two objections to Parfit's claim. First, even maximizing act-utilitarians do not demand that people try to cause themselves to become "do-gooders," especially if some other attitude would produce a greater number of utility-maximizing actions. Mill would accuse Parfit of having made a mistake made by Comte. "He committed the error which is often, but falsely, charged against the whole class of utilitarian moralists; he required that the test of conduct should also be the exclusive motive to it. Because the good of the human race is the ultimate standard of right and wrong, and because moral discipline consists in cultivating the utmost possible repugnance to all conduct injurious to the general good, M. Comte infers that the good of others is the only inducement on which we should allow ourselves to act." "Auguste Comte and Positivism," p. 335. Thus, insofar as Parfit believes that utilitarianism demands that actions be performed out of benevolence, he is mistaken.

Second, Mill denies that there is any *single* motivation which is morally required. He believes that one's acting out of any of several motivations, e.g., out of benevolence *or* out of a sense of virtue, is morally acceptable, as long as one performs a morally permissible action.

Parfit may be correct insofar as he is implying that humans may be so constituted that they cannot have the motivational structure which would produce utility-producing actions in all situations — such motivations may not be compossible within human characters. Of course, all moral theories may have to face the same problem, viz., that humans may not be able to have the motivational structure recommended by that theory. Kant, for example, is skeptical that humans can have the proper motivational structure for virtuous action.

34. One might claim that conscience imposes pangs of guilt, but some other faculty imposes pangs of regret. By the same token, one could claim that pangs of guilt are sometimes imposed by conscience and sometimes by a different faculty. My point here is that we might want an agent to feel somewhat badly for her reasonable, well-intended, harmful actions. I am not trying to argue about which faculties perform which functions. I do not even know how one would go about establishing which faculties performed which functions, short of offering definitions.

Slote understands the importance of making a distinction between guilt and regret, although he thinks that regret "acknowledges no wrongdoing," whereas guilt is appropriate for one's "doing wrong things." See Michael Slote, "Utilitarianism, Moral Dilemmas and Moral Cost," *American Philosophical Quarterly* 22, (1985), p. 165.

In an actual consequence system, if the agent acted in a harmful way then he would have acted wrongly. Hence, regret would be appropriate for wrong, i.e., harmful, actions. Of course, on either the foreseeable consequence or the reasonably foreseeable consequence views, regret would sometimes 'acknowledge no wrongdoing'.

35. For further discussion of this and related topics, see my "Guilt, Regret and Prima Facie Duties," *Southern Journal of Philosophy* 25 (1987), pp. 133-146.

36. On this account, utilitarians would not necessarily have tremendous loads of guilt or regret on their shoulders, since they only have the duty to promote a certain degree of utility — they need not maximize utility. Further, one can feel slightly guilty or slightly regretful for a long or short period of time. Hence, on this account, utilitarians would not necessarily be guilt- or regret-ridden individuals.

37. Admittedly, there is something dissatisfying here. The problem could be, as some of Mill's comments would suggest, that

we do not have 'properly developed' act-utilitarian consciences. I do not know whether the account here solves the achievement system dilemma. However, I believe that the act-utilitarian is committed to something like the account offered here whether she is an actual consequence, a foreseeable consequence, or a reasonably foreseeable consequence utilitarian. If act-utilitarians are willing to adopt a "strict liability" type of ethics, the ramifications of all harmful actions' being immoral will not seem to be particularly problematic.

A different way to attack at least one of the problems posed here is to deny that actions appropriately include unforeseeable consequences. However, the analysis required for such a position is too extensive to be appropriately included within this book.

One of the problems here is related to the problem raised by moral dilemmas. Many claim that an agent (when faced with conflicting duties) should feel compunction for failing to fulfill her lesser duty, even though she has done nothing to deserve that feeling. These theorists claim that she should feel compunction, even if she has acted as any reasonable, well-intentioned agent would have acted.

There is an extensive literature about moral dilemmas. See, for example, John Rawls, *A Theory of Justice* (Cambridge: Harvard University Press, 1971), p. 341; W. D. Ross, *The Right and the Good* (Oxford: Oxford University Press, 1930), p. 28; Bernard Williams, "Ethical Consistency" in his *Problems of the Self* (Cambridge: Cambridge University Press, 1973); Ruth Barcan Marcus, "Moral Dilemmas and Consistency," *Journal of Philosophy* 77 (1980), pp. 121-136; and my "Guilt, Regret and Prima Facie Duties."

CHAPTER SEVEN

Imperfect Duties and Supererogatory Actions

Critics of utilitarianism sometimes argue that since moral systems must account for perfect duties, imperfect duties, and supererogatory actions and since act-utilitarians cannot do so, act-utilitarianism cannot be a valid moral system. This argument is much less powerful than might originally be supposed, since standard act-utilitarians can offer a system which has perfect duties, imperfect duties, and a *modified* version of supererogatory actions. Further, and more importantly for the purposes of this book, because Mill is not a maximizing act-utilitarian, he *can* account for these different categories.

Mill distinguishes between justice and the rest of morality by distinguishing between perfect and imperfect duties, "the latter being those in which, though the act is obligatory, the particular occasions of performing it are left to our choice, as in the case of charity or beneficence, which we are indeed bound to practice but not toward any definite person, or at any prescribed time."[1] Many utilitarians follow Mill's lead in maintaining such a distinction.

Critics maintain that act-utilitarians thereby ignore the basic tenet of act-utilitarianism — that one should promote the greatest good for the greatest number. If more utility is produced by requiring donations at particular times to particular people, then it would seem that act-utilitarians must admit that donations must be given at those times to those people. Act-utilitarians can easily refute this charge as well as the charge that they are unable to account for imperfect duties. Indeed, were they to adopt Mill's form of act-utilitarianism in which it is morally best to maximize utility but morally acceptable merely to promote a certain degree of utility, they would have no difficulty in accounting for supererogatory actions as well.

Does Utilitarianism Require Excessive Contributions?

Whether one is a (standard) actual consequence act-utilitarian, foreseeable consequence act-utilitarian, or reasonably foreseeable consequence act-utilitarian, one believes that one has a duty to maximize some kind of utility — actual, foreseeable, or reasonably foreseeable utility, respectively. Often, one correctly foresees that one would produce more good by donating to charity than one would have produced had one used the money for a different purpose. Each of these forms of utilitarianism would mandate that one give the money to charity in such cases.

These utilitarian positions would presumably promote more charity-giving than would many deontological systems. A deontologist might feel that she had satisfied her duty to be charitable after making her initial donation. Thereafter, she might buy many luxuries with a clear conscience. However, were she an act-utilitarian, her initial donation might not satisfy her duty to give charity. If she would produce more good by donating to charity than she would by using the money as she normally would have, then she would be morally required to make additional donations.

Offering some variation of the above analysis, some philosophers contend that act-utilitarianism requires that one make excessive contributions to charity.[2] However, that charge often misses its mark. For example, it is inappropriate insofar as it implies that act-utilitarianism requires that individuals be subjected to *external* sanctions for failing to donate the requisite amount of charity. It is also inappropriate insofar as it implies that act-utilitarianism would require an individual to donate an amount which exceeded the amount which would be utility-maximizing for her to donate.

It seems likely that some critics of utilitarianism would make the excessiveness charge, even were utility maximized by these stringent demands.[3] Suppose, for example, that the recipients would be benefited much more than the donors would be harmed. Some donors might feel that the charity requirements would still be excessive, even if such requirements would maximize the general good.

The use of 'excessive' in these latter cases would be somewhat misleading. I would not be forced to donate excessively in at least one objective sense of the word, i.e., donate so much that more utility would have been produced had I donated less. Rather, I would be forced to donate excessively in the sense that *I* thought the amount excessive. My being forced to donate 'excessively' would maximize general utility, although it might not maximize my own utility. Often, the accusation that utilitarianism would force one to donate excessively really means that utilitarianism would force one to donate more than one would have wanted to — utilitarianism assigns moral duties which are sometimes difficult to perform.

The claim here is *not* that all critics who make the excessiveness charge are simply attempting to defend selfishness. Sometimes, the critics are pointing out that the demands are excessive in that they are greater than what some other system (which the critics accept) demands. However, such a criticism faces certain difficulties. For example, unless there is independent justification for accepting the nonutilitarian system's dictates, this criticism seems reducible to the claim that not all systems yield the same dictates. Presumably, the standard act-utilitarian would claim that the nonutilitarian system requires too little charity-giving.[4]

Usually, when critics charge utilitarianism with demanding too much charity or with disallowing certain practices which should be allowed, the critics have maximizing act-utilitarianism in mind. Those charges which do not miss their mark are usually inappropriately made against a nonstandard utilitarian system like Mill's. Indeed, it is precisely because commentators on Mill have misunderstood his standard for obligatoriness that they have been misled into believing that Mill is a maximizing utilitarian and have made these charges against him.[5] Mill writes, "There is a standard of altruism to which all should be required to come up, and a degree beyond it which is not obligatory, but meritorious. ... What those limits are, it is the province of ethical science to determine; and to keep all individuals and aggregations of individuals within them, is the proper office of punishment and of moral blame."[6] Thus, Mill denies that agents are appropriately subjected even to *internal* sanctions for failing to live up to the utilitarian ideal, although they are appropriately punished for failing to meet the standard "to which all should be required to come up."

Some theorists argue that the nonutilitarian standard of charity is preferable because it is the one which we all intuitively accept. Mill denies the unanimity of our 'intuitions', arguing that theorists who claim such general agreement "assume the utmost latitude of arbitrarily determining whose votes deserve to be counted. They either ignore the existence of dissentients or leave them out of the account, on the pretext that they have the feeling which they deny having, or if not, that they ought to have it."[7]

In discussing the utilitarian position on charity, two issues should be distinguished:

1. Is the utilitarian ideal of disinterested benevolence a goal towards which we should aspire?

2. Should the State or society impose the utilitarian ideal of disinterested benevolence on people and force them to donate the utility-maximizing amount of charity?

Some critics of utilitarianism argue that the answer to (1) is 'No', because the pursuit of that goal precludes the pursuit of other worthy goals.[8] Mill disagrees, arguing that the utilitarian ideal is something towards which all of us should strive. Of course, it merits repeating that Mill's understanding of what promotes the utilitarian ideal is very inclusive. For example, he would deny that individuals cannot appropriately pursue philosophy or the arts.

The more often-discussed issue is (2). Many agree with the act-utilitarian view that the goal of disinterested benevolence is an attitude towards which we should aspire, but disagree with the (alleged) act-utilitarian view that it is an attitude which the State should enforce.

While standard act-utilitarian might believe that the State should enforce an attitude of disinterested benevolence, Mill does not. He criticizes Comte for not having followed the example provided by the Catholic Church, writing that "the distinction which we have drawn was fully recognized by the sagacious and far-sighted men who constructed the Catholic ethics. . . . It has one standard which, faithfully acted up to, suffices for salvation, another and a higher which when realized constitutes a saint." Mill criticizes Comte because "like the Calvinists, he [Comte] requires that all believers shall be saints, and damns them (after his own fashion) if they are not."[9] It is precisely because maximizing act-utilitarians require agents to be moral saints that Mill would never subscribe to that system.

Mill might object to the State's punishing agents for not acting like saints because:

a. individuals have no such duty and thus their being punished for failing to be saints would be wholly undeserved and inappropriate, or

b. although individuals have the duty to act like saints, they are not appropriately subjected to *external* sanctions for failing to fulfill that duty.[10]

Since Mill believes that one merely has a duty to *promote* (rather than maximize) utility, he does not believe that individuals are morally blameworthy for failing to act like saints. Blamings for such failures are inappropriate, since they involve a confusion between what is morally best and what is morally obligatory. They would be extremely inappropriate were they other-blamings — they would be both undeserved and counterproductive. Certainly, they would be quite unfair and would cause justified resentment, an obvious disutility.[11]

Thus, Mill chooses (a) above — people do not deserve any punishment whatsoever for merely failing to be saints. However, even had he been a mazimizing act-utilitarian, he still might have chosen (b) and claimed that individuals do not deserve to have *external* sanctions imposed against them for merely failing to maximize utility. (Thus, even standard act-utilitarians are not committed to the claim that the State should *enforce* attitudes of disinterested benevolence.)

The Creation of Charity Boards

Mill explicitly states that individuals have a duty to give *some* charity. The question then becomes who should receive those donations. According to Mill and most contemporary utilitarians, that decision is left up to the individual donor. However, it is difficult to see why I am not morally obligated to donate only to particular persons. If my duty to give charity is based upon my duty to promote the good of humankind, then it would appear that I should not donate my charity to individuals or groups who would not promote utility.

The utilitarian might object that part of the notion of charity involves my choosing when and to whom to donate. Such a response begs the question. Charity as 'voluntary donation to the donor's chosen recipient' is a concept within deontological ethics. The issue at hand is whether such a concept can also be maintained within utilitarian ethics.

Deontologists can consistently maintain that donors should be allowed the freedom to choose when and to whom to give their charity. Within deontological ethics, there is no recognized obligation to promote the good of humankind (almost) every time we act. One does not perform a morally better act by donating to an extremely needy person who can greatly benefit society than by donating to an extremely needy person who is unlikely to promote any net utility at all. One can help a particular needy individual without fearing that one has acted immorally.

Within the various forms of act-utilitarianism considered here, actions are right if they produce (or can be expected to produce) utility for humankind. A donation is an action. Thus, one would expect that a morally acceptable donation is one which would promote (foreseeable) utility. Donors cannot fulfill their obligation to give charity by simply giving to whomever they like without considering whether the recipient would promote humankind's utility.

One might pity the potential donor. She will not know who deserves her donation unless she is willing to do (possibly a lot of) research. As a further responsibility, the donor would have to keep track of how much each potential recipient had already received. (The utilities might change depending upon how much each donee had already been given.) The donor is, needless to say, in a difficult position.

One solution would involve setting up a centralized charity board. Each donor would regularly send money to the board, which would be as waste-free as possible. The board would know which individuals had already received charity and how much each had already received.[12]

Do Donees Have Rights to Donations?

The charity board would determine the worthy charity recipients, i.e., the people whose receiving the money would promote the good of humankind. Those people might seem to have rights to the money.[13] If, for example, I have been determined by the board to be deserving, then it would be in society's interest that I receive the money. (If there were not enough money to go around, then it might not be in society's interest that I get the money. However, that would not be a problem here, since the determination of who was deserving would be made in light of how much money there was — the board would not only be determining who should get the money but also how much each recipient should get.)

According to Mill, a right is something which "society ought to defend me in the possession of." Society should defend me "for no other reason than general utility."[14] To grant someone a right is to promise him protection insofar as he wishes to exercise that right. Such protections have costs.[15] In the case of charity, there are a variety of disutilities produced by granting a particular donee the right to a donation, especially if that donation must come from a particular individual. Smith might be upset because she is morally required to donate to Jones, even though she wants to donate to Robinson. Even if it turns out that Robinson has the right to the donation and thus Smith can donate to him, Smith might be upset that she has no say in who receives her money. Her desire to donate to Robinson has been gratified only as a result of a fortunate coincidence. Suppose, she might ask herself, she had wanted to donate to Anderson. What then?

There are still further costs if donors must give their charity to particular recipients. If Jones has a right to charity from Smith, then Jones might ask Smith for the money too often or too soon, thus producing disutility for Smith. Or, Smith might be 'late' in her payment, forcing Jones to go through the embarrassment of asking for it or the embarrassment of getting a court order to obtain the money. The embarrassment caused by personal contact might be avoided if the government were to set up a centralized charity board.

One might imagine a process which would minimize disutility as much as possible. The criteria for determining worthiness might be developed by a committee. The candidates would be evaluated according to the criteria. The results would be fed into a computer. The names, addresses, checks, etc., would be printed up and mailed out automatically. To alleviate problems of collection, the computer might send out reminders each month. Or, a small amount might automatically be deducted from paychecks.

One might further imagine that each month every donor would have the opportunity to send in a list of potential donees ranked in order of preference. A complicated algorithm would be used to *include* the donor's preferences within the calculation of the particular recipient's utility quotient (the utility likely to be produced by the donee's receiving the money).[16]

A good utilitarian might not send in a list. Her only preference would be that the recipient would be someone who would promote utility. The donor might fear that, not having done all of the research that the board had done, she would suggest a recipient who would not produce utility. Those who did send in preferences would include:

1. good utilitarians who thought that their own analysis of who would promote utility was (likely to be) better than the board's analysis, and
2. people who were not good utilitarians.

According to deontologists, one can fulfill one's moral duty to be charitable by giving to one's favorite charity, even if that charity does not promote general utility. The morally relevant consideration is that one donates, not to whom one donates. However, within utilitarianism, to whom one donates is also morally important, since some charities are more deserving than others.[17] Indeed, some are not deserving at all. Mill suggests in a letter that "the charities which are not useful, *as the majority are not* [my italics], should be reformed altogether instead of being taxed."[18]

Mill on Distribution

One way to assure that the more deserving individuals/charities received donations would be to set up the type of charity board described earlier. As long as the charity board would distribute monies in the way which would promote (foreseeable) utility, this would seem to be a fine solution. However, such a board might abuse its position and give money to totally undeserving individuals.

Mill was rather distrustful of boards. In a different context, he writes, "What 'the Board' does is the act of nobody; and nobody can be made to answer for it. The Board suffers, even in reputation, only in its collective character, and no individual member feels this further than his disposition leads him to identify his own estimation with that of the body." Mill somewhat pessimistically concludes that boards "are not a fit instrument for executive business; and are only admissible in it when, for other reasons, to give full discretionary power to a single minister would be worse."[19]

Mill understood that the deserving might not receive as much as they should if charity were only distributed by private individuals or groups. However, he feared that were decisions about who were the most deserving solely left up to a public board or to a single minister, even less utility would thereby be produced.

Mill is not claiming that a private board would be any better than a public board, since either might make irresponsible decisions. He presumably believes that even if the private charities would be as irresponsible as the public board, their 'mistakes' would help to cancel each other out. Were there a *single* private board, this canceling out process would not occur.

Nonetheless, Mill does not trust private charity enough to let them completely control the distribution of charity. "[C]harity almost always does too much or too little: it lavishes its bounty in one place, and leaves people to starve in another." He suggests a compromise in which both public and private concerns distribute charity. The government should provide a certain base amount of charity. "[T]he administrators of a public fund ought not to be required to do more for anybody, than that minimum which is due even to the worst." The government should not "undertake to discriminate between the deserving and the undeserving indigent. It owes no more than subsistence to the first, and can give no less to the last."[20]

Mill does not impose the same conditions on private charity, which "can give more to the more deserving." A private charity is entitled to make its distributions "according to its own judgment." The charity "is commendable or the contrary, as it [distributes] with more or less discernment."[21] Basically, the question of who should distribute charity is based on empirical considerations. Mill believes that government would be more likely to overdistribute to the undeserving than would private charity. However, to assure that everyone gets something, government should provide the basic necessities for those who cannot provide for themselves.

Mill is quite wary of promoting a lack of self-reliance. "[I]f assistance is given in such a manner that the condition of the person helped is as desirable as that of the person who succeeds in doing the same thing without help, the assistance . . . is mischievous." However, as long as charity does not promote this lack of self-reliance, it is good. "[I]f, while available to everybody, it leaves to everyone to do without it if he can, it is then for the most part beneficial."[22]

Imperfect Duties

Mill clearly believes that charity-giving is important, since he argues that there should be both public and private charity. He also obviously believes that charity is an imperfect duty. Nonetheless, some critics charge that utilitarians cannot account for the notion of an imperfect duty.

Imperfect duties seem to be problematic. If giving charity is an imperfect duty, then merely because a person has failed to donate charity on a particular occasion does not imply that the person has acted immorally. If there is no particular time at which an imperfect duty must be performed, then it would seem that we cannot say that at any particular time a person has acted immorally in breaching his duty to give charity.[23]

Mill says that an action is not wrong unless we think it blameworthy.[24] If we cannot ever infer that an agent has failed to fulfill her moral obligation to be charitable and thus acted wrongly,[25] then it would seem that we cannot ever say that an agent is blameworthy for having failed to give charity.[26] However, if we cannot say that an agent is ever wrong for having failed to give charity, then imperfect duties seem rather peculiar. They seem to be the sort of duties which one need not ever fulfill, even if one wishes never to act wrongly. Yet, this plainly cannot be, at least for Mill, who says, "It is a part of the notion of duty in every one of its forms [i.e., both perfect and imperfect duties] that a person may rightfully be compelled to fulfill it."[27]

Various critics talk about Mill's tri-partite system.[28] However, Mill's writings imply that he has a quadra-partite system.

He distinguishes between perfect and imperfect duties,[29] the non-performance of either being blameworthy. He talks about meritorious actions which are praiseworthy if performed but not blameworthy if not performed. He talks about expedient actions (which might fall into any of the other three categories). Thus, we have:

1. expedient actions
2. meritorious actions
3. imperfect duties
4. perfect duties

Meritorious actions are utility-producing actions the non-performance of which is not blameworthy. (Although Mill can talk about the non-performance of meritorious actions as blameless, maximizing act-utilitarians cannot call them *completely* blameless. However, they can still benefit from Mill's system by claiming that meritorious actions are not blameworthy by *others*.)

Sidgwick echoes Mill's distinction by pointing out that "there seem to be acts and abstinences which we praise as virtuous or meritorious, without imposing them as duties upon all who are able to do them; as for a rich man to live very plainly and devote his income to works of public beneficence."[30] Were the rich man (in Sidgwick's example) to exist, Mill would say of him that he acts virtuously and rightly. His action is aesthetically pleasing, since it indicates fine qualities of character: generosity, selflessness, etc.

Suppose that the rich man above had already donated the requisite amount of charity for the year. On a particular occasion he decided to spend his money on himself or on his family rather than donate this amount to charity as well. Mill would say that the man could have acted in a better way (in that he could have produced more utility had he been more public-spirited). Yet, Mill would deny that the man had acted wrongly (in the sense of having failed to perform a duty). As long as the man had donated an acceptable amount of money (given his level of income), any donations beyond that would be "not obligatory, but meritorious."[31] Meritorious actions correspond to supererogatory actions (within deontological ethics).

Duties may be characterized as those actions which promote utility, the non-performance of which we do think blamable. If someone else can claim *as her right* that the duty be performed, then the duty involved is a perfect one. If no one can claim that she has a right to the performance of that duty, then it is an imperfect one.

When we distinguish between perfect and imperfect duties by looking at whether someone has a right to the performance of the action, we are not tempted to make a mistake made by some contemporary theorists who believe that one cannot be morally culpable for failing to fulfill an imperfect duty. Mill makes clear that "in the case of charity or beneficence, . . . we are indeed bound to practice [it] but not toward any definite person or at any prescribed time."[32] Mill does not thereby preclude saying that the acts of charity must be performed *by* a prescribed time. For example, he might say that unless a person of sufficient means donates every year, the person has acted immorally by not donating. Such a statement does not force Mill to pinpoint the time at which the person has acted immorally, since he would merely be saying that because of a series of neglected opportunities to donate, the agent has breached his duty to give charity.

Indeed, perfect duties are sometimes defined in terms of a particular time *by* which the action must be performed. For example, I owe Brown $50. I have promised to pay him *by* next Tuesday. I can pay him any time until Tuesday. That I must pay him *by* next Tuesday (rather than *on* Tuesday) does not negate that my repaying the debt is a perfect duty.

Thus, the difference between a perfect and an imperfect duty even in deontological ethics is that no one has a right to the performance of the imperfect duty. It is a mistake to believe that a perfect duty must be performed *at* a particular time, while an imperfect duty need not be performed at any particular time. Both perfect and imperfect duties must be performed *by* a particular time. In the limiting case, the duty must be performed *by* a minute from now or *by* three seconds from now.

It is quite clear that Mill feels that one has a duty to donate at least some charity, since he claims that there "is a standard of altruism to which all should be required to come up." However, because he is not a maximizing utilitarian, he does not have to say that one has a duty to donate amounts of charity vastly exceeding societal standards.

Nor does he have to claim that one has a duty to donate charity to the most deserving candidate.

Imperfect Duties Versus Supererogatory Actions

Supererogatory actions are neither equivalent to nor a subset of imperfect duties.[33] An imperfect duty is still a duty. It involves an action which one is required to perform. If one fails to perform an imperfect duty, then one is blameworthy. True. There may be some difficulty in establishing the point by which the imperfect duty to give charity must be performed, but that is a different matter.

A supererogatory action need not ever be performed. One is not blameworthy, even if one never performs a supererogatory action during one's entire lifetime.

It is important to distinguish between imperfect duties and supererogatory actions because the failure to perform imperfect duties is blameworthy, whereas the failure to perform supererogatory actions is never blameworthy. On one's deathbed, one is blameworthy for having failed to perform imperfect duties; one is not blameworthy for having failed to perform supererogatory actions.

We remember Mill's claiming, "We do not call anything wrong, unless we mean to imply that a person ought to be punished in some way or other for doing it. ... This seems the real turning point of the distinction between morality and simply expediency. It is a part of the notion of Duty in every one of its forms that a person may rightfully be compelled to fulfill it."[34]

Some theorists interpret the above quotation as providing Mill's distinction between the spheres of morality and expediency. Morality involves those actions the commission or omission of which would deserve punishment. Expediency involves those actions the commission or omission of which would not deserve punishment.

These theorists are correct *insofar as we are talking about the part of Morality which involves Duty.* If I have a duty to X, then my failure to X deserves punishment, if only by conscience. If I have a duty to refrain from X-ing, then my X-ing deserves punishment, if only by conscience. If my X-ing (or refraining from X-ing) would be expedient but is nonetheless not required by duty, then its non-performance would *not* be blameworthy.

Yet, *Morality is not exhausted by Duty.* Some acts, i.e., meritorious acts, are within the moral realm in that their performance is morally praiseworthy. However, since their non-performance *does not deserve punishment even from conscience*, they are not within the moral realm in that they are not required by Duty.

Morality is concerned with those acts which are morally best, morally worst, and all acts in between. Since Duty is concerned with those actions which we are obligated to perform, it is a part of morality, although not exhaustive of it.

Mill might more felicitously have said that the turning point of the distinction between *Duty* and simple expediency is that the failure to do the former (but *not* the failure to do the latter) is blameworthy. (If one closely examines the relevant passage, one sees that Mill is using 'morality' as a synonym for 'duty'.)   Something is *simply* expedient in that it is not, *in addition*, a duty.

It is worth emphasizing that acts required by Duty are also expedient. Mill is not setting up two non-overlapping spheres of action. He is merely pointing out that since not all expedient acts are required by duty, the non-performance of an expedient act may not be blameworthy.

The above analysis bears repeating, since it provides the key to understanding the crucial distinction which has caused so much confusion among Mill commentators. An action is *simply* expedient if it is not required by Duty. When Mill distinguishes between "Morality" (i.e., "Duty") and expediency, he is distinguishing between those acts which one is blameworthy for not performing and those acts which one is *not* blameworthy for not performing. Simply expedient acts are *meritorious*, i.e., their performance is morally praiseworthy although their non performance is not morally blameworthy.

Mill writes, "The object should be to stimulate services to humanity by their natural rewards; not to render the pursuit of our own good in any other manner impossible, by visiting it with the reproaches of others *and of our own conscience* [my italics]."[35] Thus, Mill clearly believes that some acts are supererogatory,[36] since in some instances our not rendering certain services to humanity (e.g., charity-giving) and our instead pursuing our own good by doing something else *would not even deserve the sanctions of conscience.*

Mill is *not* implying that conscience should only punish when others can rightfully punish. He is merely claiming that certain meritorious actions are beyond the call of duty and hence one is not appropriately subjected to moral punishment for refraining from performing those acts.

People should not be held (even by conscience) to a standard which is greatly above general societal standards. Mill realizes that he is committed to a position in which an action might not be appropriately punished today, but might be appropriately punished in several years. "What once was uncommon virtue becomes common virtue, it comes to be numbered among obligations, while a degree exceeding what has grown common, remains simply meritorious."[37]

Someday, there *may* not be a category of meritorious actions — it may be that society will so much "improve" that all of the acts which we now would call "meritorious" will become "common virtue." However, that would require a continually "improving society" for a long time to come.

Mill and present-day utilitarians can easily explain charity as a perfect duty, an imperfect duty, or as both. Those critics who wrongly accuse utilitarians of being unable to account for imperfect duties do not understand that utilitarians can easily explain how it is possible for a donor to be morally culpable for failing to fulfill his imperfect duty to donate *by* the end of a specified time period, despite no one's having a right to the donation. The standard act-utilitarian's difficulty lies solely in explaining charity as a meritorious action (i.e., in explaining how an action, which should be performed because it is utility-maximizing, is not wrong not to perform, despite the failure's being (foreseeably) non-utility-maximizing and the theory's tenet that (foreseeably) non-utility-maximizing actions are morally wrong).

Mill chides Comte for not perceiving "that between the region of duty and that of sin there is an intermediate space, the region of positive worthiness." Mill claims that "it is not good that persons should be bound, *by other people's opinion* [my italics], to do everything that they would deserve praise for doing." Mill wants to be sure that donors "will not be compelled to this conduct [i.e., charity-giving] by any *external pressure* [my italics]."[38]

Quite clearly, Mill is not a maximizing utilitarian. He criticizes Comte for being a "morality-intoxicated man"[39] and obviously does not want to hold that position himself. Mill especially wants to deny that individuals should be forced by law to do everything which they morally should do. He talks about the principle that "it is the absolute social right of every individual that every other individual shall act in every respect exactly as he ought; that whosoever fails thereof in the smallest particular violates my social right and entitles me to demand from the legislature the removal of the grievance." He argues, "So monstrous a principle is far more dangerous than any single interference with liberty; there is no violation of liberty which it would not justify; it acknowledges no right to any freedom whatever, except perhaps to that of holding opinions in secret, without ever disclosing them."[40] Thus, even if, for example, individuals should donate large amounts of charity, this does not imply that a law requiring large donations would be justified.

Mill's comments above underscore his commitment to the importance of the difference between the appropriateness of the imposition of internal sanctions and the appropriateness of the imposition of external sanctions. Even if the failure to donate a certain amount of charity does not deserve the imposition of external sanctions, one's doing so may nonetheless be one's imperfect duty. Mill's wanting to make sure that people who give charity "are in no way compelled to this conduct by any external pressure" in no way implies that one's not performing one's imperfect duty to give charity (by the end of the relevant time period) is morally permissible. Such a refraining deserves to be punished, although (possibly) only by the agent's conscience.[41]

Standard maximizing act-utilitarians can coherently maintain that some failures to give charity are punishable *only* by conscience. Thus, they can offer a *modified* version of supererogatory acts in which supererogatory acts are those non-utility-maximizing acts which do *not* deserve punishment from others. On such an account, imperfect duties would involve those acts which:

1. one has a duty to perform,
2. need not be performed for a particular person, and
3. are punishable by *others* if not performed.

However, unlike Mill, standard act-utilitarians cannot maintain that one's not giving charity (where doing so would maximize utility) is not appropriately punished even by conscience.

One might wonder how Mill can justify his being a non-maximizing utilitarian. He cannot simply appeal to common intuitions and argue that it is counterintuitive to claim that we have a duty to maximize utility. Were he to do that, he would be open to the criticism which he himself levels against others, *viz.*, that our intuitions are sometimes in need of correction.

Certainly, some current theorists argue that our intuitions may be in error with respect to supererogation.[42] Yet, Mill offers reasons to believe that our maintaining a supererogatory realm is in accord with the principle of utility. He believes that one's not making extreme moral demands of individuals will actually promote the interests of humankind. By not demanding too much, "society, in any tolerable circumstances, obtains much more; for the natural activity of human nature, shut out from all noxious directions, will expand itself in useful ones."[43] Mill worries that enforced sacrifice (assuming that unusual circumstances do not obtain) may be counter-productive, believing that "the notion of a happiness for all procured by the self-sacrifice of each, if the abnegation is really felt to be a sacrifice, is a contradiction."[44] As society improves, the level of sacrifice which individuals once thought burdensome might no longer be thought burdensome. Thus, as society progresses one will have to give greater and greater amounts of charity in order to fulfill that imperfect obligation.

According both to Mill and to various deontologists, imperfect duties and supererogatory actions can be differentiated by looking at whether the failure to perform the action is blameworthy. The non-performance of a supererogatory action is not blameworthy (does not merit the imposition of sanctions), whereas the failure to perform one's imperfect duty is blameworthy. Deontologists (and utilitarians) have some difficulty in determining at what point the failure to perform one's imperfect duty is blameworthy, but that is a different matter.

The claim here is *not* that deontologists and utilitarians use the same criterion by which to decide when an act is blameworthy. Rather, the claim here is that just as the deontologist may distinguish between a supererogatory act and an imperfect duty by talking about whether the failure to perform the act is blameworthy, the non-maximizing utilitarian can distinguish between the supererogatory act and the imperfect duty by talking about whether the failure to perform the act is blameworthy.

On this account, Mill can talk about a "region of positive worthiness." One has an imperfect duty to donate a certain amount of charity — any donations beyond that would be expedient (utility-producing) and worthy (indicative of good character traits), but not morally right (in the sense in which morally right actions are morally required).

Certainly, deontologists might disagree with Mill about whether one's donating to a worthless charity would indeed satisfy one's imperfect duty. However, there, Mill seems to have the more commendable position.

The claim here is *not* that maximizing systems are invalid, since they can only offer a modified account of supererogation. The claim here is merely that Mill can account for that area. Yet, Mill should not be thought to be merely recommending a minimizing utilitarian system. Society should always be inculcating and reinforcing utility-promoting attitudes. By doing that, it will cause the domain of obligatory actions to be ever-widening. At the same time, since this process will occur relatively slowly, one need not worry about the system's imposing 'unfair' burdens. Further, Mill's point about the importance of the difference between internal and external sanctions still remains. Agents who fail to perform certain actions which are within the realm of duty may nonethless not be appropriately subjected to the imposition of external sanctions. Just as one might justly be criticized for being morally intoxicated, one might also be justly criticized for trying to impose external sanctions against all violations of duty. As we shall see in the final section of this book, Mill believes that a variety of actions, *even if morally impermissible*, must not be subjected to external sanctions. In the next three chapters, we shall examine Mill's protection of individual liberties and rights from the interference of the State and society.

NOTES

1. *Utilitarianism*, Ch. 5, Par. 15, p. 247.
2. See Richard Brandt, *A Theory of the Good and the Right* (Oxford: Oxford University Press, 1979), p. 276; R. I. Sikora, "Utilitarianism, Supererogation and Future Generations," *Canadian Journal of Philosophy* 11 (1979), pp. 461-466; and Terrance McConnell, "Utilitarianism and Supererogatory Acts," *Ratio* 22 (1980), pp. 36-38.
3. When figuring out the various utilities and disutilities produced by a particular charity requirement, one would have to include any tendencies of a worker to work less hard because of that requirement. She might feel that the lower return per work hour (since some of the return would go to charity rather than to her) would not merit her working as hard as she would have, had there been no such charity requirement. Brandt suggests that the demands of charity might affect the incentive to work. See Brandt, *A Theory of the Good and the Right*, p. 276.
4. Singer argues that our reluctance to be as charitable as utilitarianism demands should not be taken to be a criticism of utilitarian standards, but rather "a criticism of our ordinary standards of behavior." Peter Singer, "Famine, Affluence and Morality,"

Philosophy and Public Affairs 1 (1972), reprinted in Vincent Barry ed., *Applying Ethics* (Belmont: Wadsworth, 1985), p. 347.

5. But see Gaus's "Mill's Theory of Moral Rules," *Australasian Journal of Philosophy* 58 (1980), pp. 265-279.

6. "Auguste Comte and Positivism," p. 337. Joel Feinberg's position on the duty to help seems similar to Mill's in a variety of important respects. See Feinberg's "Failure to Prevent Harm" (Chapter 4) in his *Harm To Others* (New York: Oxford University Press, 1984), especially pp. 137 ff.

7. "Whewell on Moral Philosophy," p. 179.

8. See, e.g., Susan Wolf, "Moral Saints," *Journal of Philosophy* 79 (1982), p. 426.

9. "Auguste Comte and Positivism," p. 338.

10. For related comments, see Sidgwick, *Methods of Ethics*, p. 221; J. O. Urmson, "Saints and Heroes," reprinted in *Moral Concepts*, Joel Feinberg ed. (Oxford: Oxford University Press, 1969), p. 64.

11. Singer discusses another argument designed to show that punishing people for failing to give charity may be counterproductive. If "we tell people that they ought to refrain from murder and give everything they do not really need to famine relief, they will do neither, whereas if we tell them that they ought to refrain from murder and that it is good to give famine relief but not wrong not to do, they will at least refrain from murder." P. Singer, "Famine, Affluence and Morality," p. 347. But see Kagan, *The Limits of Morality*, p. 35.

12. There is support for such a board in the literature today. Brock suggests that there are "utilitarian grounds for setting up a system of aid provision to which everyone would be required to contribute." See Dan Brock, "Utilitarianism and Aiding Others," *The Limits of Utilitarianism*, eds. Harlan Miller and William Williams, (Minneapolis: University of Minnesota Press, 1982), p. 230.

13. Lyons remarks that "it is not implausible to suggest that the individuals we are *morally bound to help* may be said to *have a right* to our assistance . . . in the . . . sense that they would individually be wronged if denied it." David Lyons, "Benevolence and Justice in Mill," *The Limits of Utilitarianism*, p. 63. See also Lomasky, *Persons, Rights and the Moral Community*, p. 126.

14. *Utilitarianism*, Ch. 5, Par. 25, p. 250.

15. See Jan Narveson, "Rights and Utilitarianism," *New Essays on John Stuart Mill and Utilitarianism*, p. 145.

16. Donors (like Ms. Smith above) do not merely derive pleasure from the act of giving. They also derive pleasure from knowing that

their money has been contributed to what they believe to be a worthy cause. Thus, the donors' preferences must also be given some weight.

17. Smart talks about having made a promise to a dying man that the man's money would be donated to the South Australian Jockey Club. After the man dies, the money is given to the Royal Adelaide Hospital for a badly needed X-ray machine. Smart maintains that no one, without being open to the charge of heartlessness, could accuse him of having acted wrongly. Smart and Williams, *Utilitarianism For and Against*, p. 62.

18. *CW* Vol 15, p. 892.

19. *Considerations on Representative Government*, Ch. 14, Par. 33, p. 521.

20. *Principles of Political Economy*, Book 5, Ch. 11, Sec. 13, Par. 7, p. 962.

21. *Ibid.*

22. *Ibid.*, Par. 6, p. 961.

23. Lyons, "Benevolence and Justice in Mill," p. 47.

24. *Utilitarianism*, Ch. 5, Par. 14, p. 246.

25. Lyons, "Benevolence and Justice in Mill," p. 47.

26. Lyons suggests that one can breach a moral obligation without acting wrongly, but he does not explain how this is possible.

27. *Utilitarianism*, Ch. 5, Par. 14, p. 246.

28. David Lyons, "Mill's Theory of Justice," *Values and Morals*, eds. A. I. Goldman and J. Kim (Dordrecht: D. Reidel Publishing Co., 1978); and Jonathan Harrison, "The Expedient, the Right and the Just in Mill's Utilitarianism," in *Canadian Journal of Philosophy* Supplementary Volume #1, Part 1.

29. *Utilitarianism*, Ch. 5, Par. 15, p. 247.

30. Sidgwick, *The Methods of Ethics*, p. 221.

31. "Auguste Comte and Positivism," p. 337.

32. *Utilitarianism*, Ch. 5, Par. 15, p. 247.

33. Peter Jones makes this point in his "Toleration, Harm and Moral Effect" in *Aspects of Toleration*, John Horton, Susan Mendus eds. (London: Methuen, 1985), p. 150.

34. *Utilitarianism*, Ch. 5, Par. 14, p. 246.

35. "Auguste Comte and Positivism," p. 338.

36. Berger, *Happiness, Justice and Freedom*, p. 111. See also P. Singer, "Famine, Affluence and Morality," p. 346.

37. "Auguste Comte and Positivism," p. 338. Copp's interpretation of Mill's writings also involves the claim that an action may be a duty one day and not a duty on a different day. However,

Copp's theory is based upon the differing qualities of discernment of conscience. Mill's theory is based upon the claim that conscience should not demand much more than society demands.

38. *Ibid.*, pp. 337 ff.
39. *Ibid.*, p. 336. Mill might more felicitously have called him a 'Duty-intoxicated' man.
40. *On Liberty*, Ch. 4, Par. 19, p. 288.
41. For related comments, see Kagan, *The Limits of Morality*, p. 397.
42. Kagan suggests that "if the intuition that consequentialism demands too much remains impossible to defend, we may have to face the sobering possibility that it is not consequentialism, but our intuition, that is in error." See Shelly Kagan, "Does Consequentialism Demand Too Much? Recent Work on the Limits of Obligation," *Philosophy and Public Affairs* 13 (1984), p. 254.
43. "Auguste Comte and Positivism," p. 339.
44. *Ibid.*, p. 338.

CHAPTER EIGHT

Some Initial Considerations Concerning Rights

Even if Mill can account for imperfect duties and supererogatory actions, he may be unable to refute what is often thought to be the most serious charge against him, *viz.*, that he cannot account for the protection of individual rights. In this chapter, some important aspects of theories of rights in general and Mill's theory of rights in particular will be examined.

Mill distinguishes between the two areas of Duty by pointing out that one area (matters of justice) involves perfect obligations, whereas the other area involves imperfect obligations. "Duties of perfect obligation are those in virtue of which a correlative *right* resides in some person or persons; duties of imperfect obligation are those moral obligations which do not give birth to any right."[1]

Rights protect our interest in security, "the most vital of all interests." Security is the "most indispensible of all necessaries, after physical nutriment."[2] It is precisely because justice and rights are concerned with such an essential area that people react so differently to questions of justice than to questions which involve utility-promotion but which do not involve rights. "Our notion . . . of the claim we have on our fellow creatures to join us in making safe for us the very groundwork of our existence gathers feelings around it so much more intense than those concerned in any of the more common cases of utility that the difference in degree (as is often the case in psychology) becomes a real difference in kind."[3] (Mill claims that this psychological difference is what accounts for our viewing matters of Justice as so much more important than matters involving Expediency.)

If the feelings which gather around rights are as strong and universal as Mill believes them to be, then much disutility would be produced by the trampling of rights. In order for one to abridge someone else's rights justifiably, one must produce a great deal of utility by doing so. Ordinarily, a right-abridgement would not produce enough utility to offset the insecurity produced by the right-abridgement.

In order to discuss whether Mill adequately protects rights, we must first establish:

1. what a right is.
2. that Mill presents an internally consistent position.
3. what an adequate defense might entail.
4. whether Mill gives such a defense.

What Is A Right?

Mill defines a right by saying, "To have a right ... is ... to have something which society ought to defend me in the possession of."[4] If to have a right is to have something society ought to defend me in the possession of, and society should protect that right because it would promote utility to do so, then it would seem that there could be no conflicting rights[5] (since it would not promote utility to defend each of two competing rights).

The above quite reasonably assumes that society cannot defend *both* of two opposing parties. Otherwise, a utilitarian might claim that society could weakly defend A in his possession of object X, e.g., by instilling within the general populace the idea that his keeping X would be a good thing, while strongly defending A_1 in her possession of object X, e.g., by imprisoning (or beheading) anyone who prevents her from keeping X. In some sense, both A and A_1 would be defended, although the defense of A would be quite weak.

Suppose that A is a pauper and A_1 is a rich, miserly man. A steals a lot of money from A_1, although not so much that A_1's lifestyle would be markedly changed. Society might believe that A_1 deserves to be condemned for his miserliness and that, in some sense, it would be a better world were A to have the money than were A_1 to have it. However, society might also believe that the institution of property is important to maintain. Thus, society might claim that A should be punished severely (imprisoned) for stealing, whereas A_1 should be punished mildly (be subjected to public expressions of disapproval) for not donating some of his wealth to A.[6]

If we talk about the possession of a right as implying that society will defend the right-holder in her possession of the object and will not also defend someone else who also wants the object, then the above claim is correct. There can be no conflicting rights, at least not in the sense that the society would defend two people in their pursuit of the same object, unless the object could be shared in some way. Society would only defend one of them.

If my right to X is outweighed by Smith's stronger right to Y, then I do not have the right to X in that particular case. The right to X is qualified — it is *not* a right when it is in conflict with the 'stronger' right Y. On this interpretation of a right, one cannot speak of a stronger or a weaker right. A right exists (it corresponds to what would otherwise be called a "stronger" right) or it does not exist (either it corresponds to what would otherwise be called a "weaker" right or it does not correspond to any right at all).

For example, physicians usually have a right to be free from coercion. However, "to save a life, it may not only be allowable, but a duty, . . . to kidnap and compel to officiate the only qualified medical practitioner."[7] The right to X (the physician's right to freedom from coercion) did not suddenly disappear. She did not cease to have the right to X because of the stronger conflicting right Y (someone else's right to life). The physician simply never had the right to X when such an action would conflict with the stronger right (to) Y.

Deontologists might complain that such an explanation is merely making use of a semantic distinction to allow utilitarians to wriggle out of a difficulty. Yet, deontologists have the same problem. When there is a conflict between a stronger and a weaker right, a deontologist can describe the result in two ways:

1. She can say that the weaker right has ceased to exist. Such an explanation would be open to the criticisms aimed at utilitarianism. Rights which cease to exist do not seem to be rights. If a right only guarantees that one will sometimes be able to perform the action in question, then the right to X does not really seem to be a right.

2. She can say that the weaker right still exists; however, it exists in an ineffective state. Such a claim is also open to the criticism that it involves either a basic misunderstanding or a basic reformulation of the notion of a right. We would be claiming that there exists a right to X which does not entail that, should one desire, one should be allowed to X.

Prima Facie Rights

Some theorists try to avoid the above-mentioned difficulties by talking about *prima facie* rights. A prima facie right is an apparent right which will be respected as long as other conditions, e.g., the presence of a competing and stronger prima facie right, do not obtain. If those other conditions do not obtain, then the prima facie right will be an actual right. If those other conditions do obtain, then the prima facie right will not be a right at all.[8] Thus, in a situation in which a relatively weak prima facie right and a relatively strong prima facie right conflict, the latter is the (actual) right which must be respected.

Yet, the difficulty with a theory of weaker and stronger rights also obtains when one speaks of weaker and stronger prima facie rights. If the stronger prima facie right is respected, then one might ask what role the weaker prima facie right plays. If the right is simply to be ignored, then the weaker prima facie right would seem to have no function — the outcome would have been no different had the weaker prima facie right never existed.[9] Of course, what was the weaker prima facie right in this case might be a stronger prima facie right in a different case. In that *different* case, the prima facie right would affect the outcome. However, in *this* case, it is not at all clear what role the prima facie right plays in determining the outcome.[10]

If one refuses to adopt a prima facie rights account and none-theless wants to talk about conflicts of rights, one will have to offer a different kind of account in which some right-abridgements are justifiable. For example, one might adopt a system in which rights can be overridden, although with a spirit of reluctance and apology.[11]

Some theorists distinguish between two kinds of overridings of rights. An *infringement* of a right is a justifiable overriding of a right, whereas a *violation* of a right is an unjustifiable overriding of a right.[12] The question then becomes whether infringements of rights are blameworthy, since an infringement of a right is still a right-abridgement, even if in the final analysis it was justified.

Certainly, a theorist might claim that a right-infringer is properly punished for the infringement.[13] By the same token, a 'prima facie rights' theorist might claim that one is blameworthy for overriding a weaker prima facie right in favor of a stronger one. Thus, the fear that the prima facie account would simply negate the existence of the weaker prima facie right may be unwarranted. However, insofar as that fear is unwarranted, another problem presents itself.

If a theorist maintains that an individual is blameworthy for over-riding a prima facie right or for infringing an actual right, then she seems to be simultaneously affirming and denying that the overrider has acted rightly. The overrider should have so acted and nonetheless should feel guilty for having so acted.

The underlying intuition that an agent should feel some compunction for overriding a right (whether actual or prima facie) seems correct. Yet, we do not want the right-overrider to feel that he has acted wrongly. This case is exactly the sort in which the distinction between guilt and regret is useful. (Further, 'compunction' can mean either 'feelings of guilt' or 'feelings of regret'.) We want the agent to feel regret because a benevolent person would feel it — she would feel sorry that the conditions of the world necessitated her having disappointed someone else's expectations.

Our invoking 'weaker rights' (whether prima facie or actual) clouds the issues. The agent should feel regret, not because she acted wrongly by abridging someone's right, but because her acting rightly caused someone else to have pain. If we talk about weaker rights, we are tempted to think that the person who abridged the weaker right did not act as she should have — which is exactly what we *do not* want to say.

We do not want to present the agent with a double-bind by saying that the agent has acted both rightly and wrongly. We must say that the agent has acted rightly and should not feel guilty for her action. If we are going to talk about right-*infringements*, as opposed to right-*violations*, we should say that since right-infringements are justified, right-infringers do not deserve to feel guilty. At most, they should feel regret for their right-infringements. We must not simultaneously affirm and deny that the right-infringer acted rightly by upholding the 'stronger' prima facie or actual right.

Mill would not have accepted either an account in which there were prima facie rights or an account which distinguished between right-infringements and right-violations. The former would have been unacceptable because a prima facie right would not necessarily be "something which society ought to protect me in the possession of." The latter account would be unacceptable, precisely because it countenances justified injustice. Mill would argue that a case of justified injustice would simply be a case in which "what is just in ordinary cases is . . . not just in this particular case." He especially wants to avoid "the necessity of maintaining that there can be laudable injustice."[14]

Irresolvable Conflicts of Rights

The above discussion is concerned with situations in which there is a resolvable conflict of rights — situations in which there are stronger and weaker prima facie or actual rights or situations in which the alleged right does not apply to the case at hand. A utilitarian rights theorist can explain such conflicts of rights by offering:

    a. an analysis in which there are prima facie rights,
    b. an analysis in which there is a distinction between an infringement and a violation of a right, or
    c. an analysis in which the scope of the right is carefully delimited so that apparent conficts turn out not to be actual conflicts.

When theorists argue that there cannot be conflict of rights within utilitarianism, they do not mean that utilitarianism cannot countenance a conflict between a stronger and a weaker prima facie or actual right in which the stronger right is respected because its being protected would promote more utility than would the protection of the other right. Were that their meaning, they would be wrong. The utilitarian has no difficulty in describing conflicts in which that is the outcome.

Such theorists might have a different kind of conflict in mind. Suppose that two rights of equal strength were to conflict. This kind of conflict would seem to be irresolvable, since the protection of one would produce no more utility than would the protection of the other. This would seem to involve a situation in which the right-abridger could not help but act in a way for which she should feel guilt. No matter what she did, she would be violating one of the rights.

Suppose that Jones has promised Brown to answer his questions truthfully. Suppose further that Jones has promised Black that certain information would never be revealed to anyone. Jones is asked a question which, if answered truthfully, would reveal the information.

She might explain her predicament to Brown — that if she truthfully answered the question a confidence would thereby be broken. Perhaps Brown will be considerate enough to refrain from repeating the question. However, if Brown insists that an answer be given, then Jones has a problem.

To avoid the question is no solution, since she has promised to answer the question truthfully. She must decide whether to betray a confidence (break a promise that the information in question will remain a secret) or to refrain from speaking the truth (break her promise to answer Brown's question truthfully). If the two duties are of equal strength, then she seems to be in the unenviable position of necessarily neglecting to fulfill her duty without the excuse that a stronger duty prevailed and thus that the neglect of the weaker duty was 'permissible'.

Within utilitarianism, there can be situations in which there are two actions, the amount of utility produced by the performance of one equalling the amount of utility produced by the performance of the other. Suppose that Action E produces exactly as much utility as Action F. Either action would be morally correct, since either action (we will assume) would produce the required amount of utility. One might have a right to perform or have performed either E or F rather than certain other possible actions. However, one would not have the right to E rather than F.

Within Mill's utilitarianism, there cannot be irresolvable conflicts *between* rights. Yet, there can be conflicts *about* rights. It cannot be that two (or more) opposing parties have moral rights to the same object, where no right outweighs the other(s), since according to Mill one's possessing a right implies that society should protect one in the possession of it. If each of two people has a right to an object which cannot be shared, then society cannot protect *each* rightholder in the possession of her right.

It is preferable to have conflicts about rights (where one is trying to figure out what one's right is or, possibly, who has a right to a particular object) rather than irresolvable conflicts between rights. An irresolvable conflict between rights seems to invalidate the notion of rights and, possibly, the moral system which allows the conflict.

Mill does not adopt a stronger/weaker actual or prima facie rights account, because he believes that there cannot be laudable injustice and because he believes that society must protect all rights. If it is not the case that society should defend me in the possession of all objects to which I have a right or justified claim, then one must question the force of saying that I have a justified claim.[15] A justified claim which does not deserve to be protected does not seem to be much of a claim or, perhaps, does not seem to be particularly justified. For present purposes, a right is a justified claim which should be protected.

Mill's Position as Internally Consistent

Before we can discuss the relative merits of Mill's system, we must establish that it is consistent. Unsurprisingly, many critics maintain that it is self-contradictory.[16] In *Utilitarianism*, Mill says that "actions are right in proportion as they tend to promote happiness, wrong as they tend to produce the reverse of happiness."[17] In *On Liberty*, he says that a man "cannot rightfully be compelled to do or forbear because it will be better for him to do so, because it will make him happier, because, in the opinion of others, to do so would be wise or even right. These are good reasons for remonstrating with him, or persuading him, or entreating him, but not for compelling him, or visiting him with any evil in case he do otherwise."[18]

Yet, one might wonder why these "are good reasons for remonstrating with him . . . but not for compelling him." If forcing him to act or forbear would indeed make him happier, and actions are right if they promote happiness, then why is it not right to compel him to do something which will make him happier?

Mill could say that if I, with the intention of making her happier, force someone to perform an action against her will, then I am doomed to failure from the start. The disutility of forcing someone against her will to perform an action would be more than enough to counteract any benefits gained thereby.

Such a claim could only be supported or refuted by empirical evidence. Certainly, there are cases which would support that contention. Often, my being forced to attend certain social functions causes sufficient amounts of resentment to insure that I will not enjoy myself. However, Mill seems to be making a much stronger claim, *viz.*, that forcing people against their wills to perform actions *necessarily* produces more disutility than utility.

Such a claim is not very credible. Often, parents force their children to perform actions which the children do not want to perform, e.g., tasting a new food, going to some new activity which they are reluctant to attend, etc. However, after performing the action, the children would have to admit, were they to be honest, that they were happier as a result of having performed the action than they otherwise would have been. Mill would not be concerned by such a counterexample. "It is, perhaps, hardly necessary to say that this doctrine is meant to apply only to human beings in the maturity of their

faculties. We are not speaking of children, or of young persons below
the age which the law may fix as that of manhood or womanhood."[19]

A problem not quite so easy to solve is suggested. Children are
not old enough to make decisions, because they are not sufficiently
mature or experienced or rational. Knowing that children are often
incapable of making certain judgments, the State sets minimum age
levels, the attainment of which allows one to enjoy certain privileges.
However, many adults (out of prejudice, ignorance, stubbornness, or
whatever) make incorrect choices. If it is right to force children
against their wills to perform actions (because children are not capable
of making correct decisions), then why would it not be right to force
fools (who are also incapable of making correct decisions) to perform
certain actions?

Mill can make a variety of responses as to why it is improper to
regulate the lives of fools. (However, these objections do not indicate
why age is an appropriate criterion by which to judge whose lives
should be regulated — why it is permissible to regulate the lives of
younger fools but not of older fools.) Mill can say that, even if I am
a fool, others cannot know my interests as well as I do. For example,
others may say that I should go to business school so that I can make
a lot of money. However, I might not be interested in making a lot of
money. They would be incorrect in thinking that forcing me to
acquire this training would make me happier.

The fact that others' opinions are fallible supports Mill's claim
that a man "cannot rightfully be compelled to do or forbear . . . ,
because, in the opinion of others, to do so would be wise or even
right."[20] Others should not force me to make my actions comply with
what they think is wise or right, because they might be wrong. (Here,
Mill is denying that even *competent judges* should make decisions for
fools.) Merely because most of the people in a society think that a
particular course of action is the right one does not make it so.
Sometimes, public opinion is merely a means of enforcing an
unhealthy and stagnating conformity to certain 'acceptable' modes of
behavior. Mill argues that "there needs protection also against the
tyranny of the prevailing opinion and feeling; against the tendency of
society to impose . . . its own ideas and practices as rules of conduct
on those who dissent from them; to fetter the development and, if
possible, prevent the formation, of any individuality not in harmony
with its ways, and compel all characters to fashion themselves upon
the model of its own."[21]

Society tends to resist change — it sometimes insists on conformity where innovation might produce more benefit. Unfortunately, one does not know when the dictates of society are in error. To be on the safe side, society should not force anyone to act or forbear as long as the person's actions would not be harmful to others.

Suppose, however, that one knew that preventing Jones from hurting himself would yield much more utility than would allowing Jones to hurt himself. Mill argues that a person should not be forced to perform actions, even though it *will* make him happier.[22] Mill is not solely relying on the assertion that society sometimes makes mistakes and thus, for fear of being in error, society should not prevent self-harms. Even if society is correct that prohibiting the performance of certain actions would increase utility, the actions still should not be prohibited.

Mill might *seem* to be ignoring the principle of utility by refusing to allow someone to be forced to be happier. Mill argues that forcing someone to act or forbear might produce disutility because:

1. One might have incorrectly assessed the person's tastes. Forcing her to X would yield much disutility because the person hates X-ing.

2. Even if X-ing would normally be pleasurable, the fact that the person would be forced to X would make X-ing very unpleasurable.

3. Even if forced X-ing would be pleasurable, a precedent has been set. Forcing people against their wills to perform actions will now become more prevalent. Much disutility will thus be produced because people at improper times will be forced against their wills to act or to refrain from acting in a manner contrary to their choosing. Thus, even though the "consequences, in the particular case, might be beneficial,"[23] one still should not force the person to X.

4. People will become very insecure about the possibility that they will be forced to perform actions against their will. The insecurity will yield much displeasure. Even if the belief is unfounded, the insecurity and unhappiness thereby produced will be quite real.

Thus, there are many reasons why, even if I know that Jones would be happier were he X-ing, I should not force him. (Some of the reasons include 2 - 4 mentioned above.) However, if one takes all of these reasons into consideration and one's forcing Jones to act or forbear would still promote utility, and one's doing nothing would promote disutility, then one presumably should force Jones to so act, since Mill claims that by "a wise practitioner, . . . rules of conduct [e.g., not forcing people to perform or refrain from performing certain actions] will only be considered as provisional."[24]

Mill's statement that "the only purpose for which power can be rightfully exercised over any member of a civilized community, against his will, is to prevent harm to others"[25] sounds as if it is a hard and fast rule. He sounds as if he is condemning all acts of force which are perpetrated for reasons other than the prevention of harm to others. However, upon reexamining the statement, one discovers an ambiguity. Mill's notion of harm is rather unclear and must be better understood before one can determine how much Mill is actually protecting individual liberties.

Mill's Notion of Harm

'Harm' is a somewhat difficult word to define. One might say that harmful actions are those that "tend to produce . . . pain and the privation of pleasure."[26] However, the term is still somewhat ambiguous. Harmful actions might be limited to those actions which produce pain. Or, they might include all actions which lead to the privation of pleasure.

'Pain' and 'the privation of pleasure' are not synonymous. For example, suppose that Jones is very pleased. A doctor comes along and injects Jones with a powerful drug. Jones goes into a coma and is in neither a pleasurable nor a painful state. She has been deprived of pleasure, but is not in pain.

There may be even more important differences between 'pain' and 'the privation of pleasure', depending upon how one construes the latter term. On the one hand, one is deprived of pleasure only when one is pleased and then subsequently becomes displeased as a result of someone's actions. On the other hand, one might construe the 'privation of pleasure' as occurring every time that one does not have as much happiness as one might have had.

Suppose that another individual and I are going to spend an evening together. I am to choose the restaurant. He is to choose the evening's entertainment. I choose the best restaurant, where 'best' involves the most delicious food, appealing ambience, convenient location, etc., for the money that we want to spend. Unfortunately, he chooses the inferior of the two musical comedies which had been under consideration. If harm = privation of pleasure, and privation of pleasure = the enjoyment of fewer utiles than one might have enjoyed, then he has harmed me. Although I enjoyed the comedy which we did see, I would have enjoyed the other one even more. I have not been harmed in the sense that he has caused me pain. Nor have I been harmed in the sense that as a result of his action I am enjoying less pleasure than I had been enjoying before he acted. I have been harmed in the sense that I did not enjoy as many utiles of pleasure as I might have enjoyed.

If I am harmed every time that I do not enjoy as many utiles as I could have, then Mill does very little to restrict the use of power. Anytime that anyone else acts in a way which results in my enjoying fewer utiles than I might have enjoyed, he is harming me. For example, if my neighbor takes his car to town thereby preventing me from getting to town, then he has harmed me. The fact that he has worked hard in order to purchase his car is irrelevant. If my being harmed is a sufficient reason to compel someone else to refrain from acting in a certain way, then my neighbor can be compelled to refrain from using his own car. To make matters more complicated, compelling my neighbor to refrain from using his car, because his using it would harm me, would cause my neighbor to have fewer utiles of enjoyment than he might have had. Thus, by being compelled to refrain from harming me, my neighbor is being harmed.

The problem might seem to lie in the definition of 'harm'. However, if one defines 'harm' as 'causes one to have fewer utiles of enjoyment than one had been enjoying' or as 'causes pain', then one may accomplish nothing. For example, if I am caused pain by the thought that I have not enjoyed as many utiles of pleasure as I might have enjoyed or even if I lose pleasure at such a thought, then the same problems which were encountered with the former definition will be encountered with the latter definitions.

Suppose that a friend of mine is drinking too heavily. I might be very unhappy that he is harming himself that way. My unhappiness might prevent my working effectively. To define harm in terms of one's enjoying fewer pleasure utiles than one might otherwise have enjoyed or in terms of displeasure produced as a result of another's action or in terms of an induced inability to operate as well as one, otherwise, would have been able to, would mean that almost any action is potentially harmful to others — I might be displeased by anyone's doing practically anything. That displeasure might translate itself into reduced work efficiency.

Thus, unless our notion of harm allows us to avoid some of the problems mentioned above, Mill's prohibition of compulsion may not be very helpful. In saying that harm to others justifies force, Mill may not be limiting the use of force very much at all.[27]

Mill admits that many self-harming actions affect others in some way. "I fully admit that the mischief which a person does to himself, may seriously affect, both through their sympathies and their interests, those nearly connected with him, and in a minor degree, society at large." Mill even admits that the rationale used to support the right to regulate children's lives (that it is for their own good) might also be used as a rationale to support the right to regulate the lives of older people. "If protection against themselves is confessedly due to children and persons under age, is not society equally bound to afford it to persons of mature years who are equally incapable of self-government?"[28]

Nonetheless, Mill thinks that a person should be allowed to perform these self-harming actions, even if such actions seriously affect those nearly associated with him. "[W]ith regard to the merely contingent, or as it may be called, constructive injury which a person causes to society, by conduct which neither violates any specific duty to the public, nor occasions perceptible hurt to any assignable individual except himself; the inconvenience is one which society can afford to bear for the sake of the greater good of human freedom."[29] Thus, that others may be harmed does not suffice to give the State the right to compel people to refrain from performing an action. In order to qualify as the sort of action which one can be compelled to refrain from performing, the action must:

    a. violate a specific duty to the public, e.g., one's duty to join in the common defense, or

    b. occasion perceptible hurt to an assignable individual other than himself.

(b) must be explained more fully. 'Perceptible hurt to any assignable individual' sounds like it means 'a non-trivial hurt to any particular individual'. Yet, such an interpretation would be a misreading of Mill.

For example, emotional distress can be extremely harmful. Inability to concentrate, poor health, etc., might all be manifestations. Yet, Mill would not include emotional distress, *per se*, as a perceptible hurt to an assignable individual, since "the mischief which a person does to

himself may seriously affect . . . those nearly connected with him."
For example, my friend may hurt me every time that he drinks too
much, but my very real pain does not negate his right to drink
excessively. A man may act as he wishes, even if by so acting, he
causes his family or friends to suffer greatly. It is only if he is
violating a "distinct and assignable obligation . . . that the case is
taken out of the self-regarding class, and becomes amenable to moral
disapprobation in the proper sense of the term."[30]

Suppose that someone "through intemperance or extravagance, becomes unable to pay his debts, or having undertaken the moral
responsibility of a family, becomes from the same cause incapable of
supporting or educating them." This person "is deservedly reprobated,
and might be justly punished, but it is for the breach of duty to his
family or creditors, not for the extravagance."[31] Had this man been
able to pay his debts and sup-port and educate his family, he would
have been allowed to act in ways which cause pain or unhappiness.
He could not rightfully have been compelled to forebear from so
acting.

Mill explicitly considers the example of religious bigotry sometimes offered as a counter-example to his theory.[32] "[M]any . . .
consider as an injury to themselves any conduct which they have a
distaste for, and resent it as an outrage to their feelings; as a religious
bigot, when charged with disregarding the religious feelings of others,
has been known to retort that they disregard his feelings, by persisting
in their abominable worship or creed." However, the bigot's response
is without merit, since "there is no parity between the feeling of a
person for his own opinion, and the feeling of another who is offended
at his holding it; no more than between the desire of a thief to take a
purse, and the desire of the right owner to keep it."[33]

Mill does not adequately explain *why* there is no parity between
the feelings of a person for his own opinion and the feelings of a
bigot. Certainly, the discomfort of the bigot is as real as is the
discomfort of the person who is prevented from holding or acting upon
an opinion. From Mill's writings, we infer that when he says that
there is no parity between the two, he means that society's protecting
freedom of religion would produce much more utility for humankind
than would society's enforcing the bigot's desires.

Yet, Mill seems to be creating a problem for himself. Suppose
that we modify the example and say that the bigot is the person who
has a feeling for his own opinion and that there is a do-gooder who,
when charged with disregarding the bigot's feelings, retorts that the

bigot disregards her feelings. If indeed it is utility-producing to promote religious tolerance, then one might think that the bigot could justifiably be punished for his beliefs.

According to Mill, we might try to educate the bigot. We might point out that the people with the 'abominable' creed are just as good or law-abiding or whatever as the people with more acceptable creeds. We might avoid the bigot's company for as long as he continues to hold his objectionable position. However, we cannot jail or fine him for his views.

Mill's comment about parity is a bit difficult to understand because we are not sure of the identity of the objects or states between which there is no parity:

1. He might be saying that there is no parity between someone's opinion and someone else's opinion about that opinion.

2. He might be saying that there is no parity between a tolerant attitude and a bigoted one.

3. He might be saying that there is no parity between the long-term utilities which would result from the enforcement of the different desires.

If we are correct that Mill would claim that the bigot should not be punished by society for having bigoted opinions, then option #2 cannot be right. Option #1 may be correct, but it does not go far enough. Differentiating between an agent's feelings for his own opinions and others' feelings and opinions about his opinions is not helpful unless we can show why that is the proper distinction to make.

We might claim that Jones feels more strongly about his own opinions than Smith feels about Jones's holding those opinions. However, Jones might only be mildly attached to his religious views, whereas Smith might be fanatically attached to his hatred of that religion.[34]

We could say that Jones *needs* to have his own opinions. However, Smith might have an even greater need to have his own opinion or even to have that opinion confirmed. Smith's whole understanding of the world might be predicated upon his hatred.

Perhaps Mill's comment will be easier to understand if we look at his analogy. He compares the parity between the believer and the bigot to the parity between a thief and a rightful owner of a purse. When we take into account the thief/purse analogy, we realize that

Mill cannot merely be talking about a parity between individual desires or needs. Mill denies the thief's right to the purse, despite the possibility that the thief needs and desires the purse and its contents a great deal more than the rightful owner does.[35]

A deontologist would have no difficulty in explaining the thief example or the bigot example. He would simply point out that there is no parity between the believer and the bigot or between the thief and the owner, because the believer has a right to practice his religion while the bigot does not have a right to suppress its practice and the owner has a right to keep his purse while the thief does not have a right to steal the purse.

Mill would agree. However, he would point out that these rights are based on utility. Mill "regard[s] utility as the ultimate appeal on all ethical questions."[36] He very much wants to protect the freedoms of worship, thought, and expression, precisely because doing so promotes the utility of humankind.

My having a freedom to perform or have performed a particular action is not necessarily a right. However, if I have a freedom which society should protect, then that freedom is a right.

There is no parity between the thief and the purse-owner and between the bigot and the believer because the purse-owner and the believer have rights. Mill believes that it would promote humankind's utility for society to protect property at this time and and to protect one's ability to practice the religion of one's own choosing.

The bigot should be allowed to express his own opinions, too, as long as they are not being expressed to an angry crowd. That, too, is included within the freedom of expression, a freedom which is utility-promoting for society to protect.

When Mill talks about harm here, he is talking about disutility (pain, indignation, etc.) which *should be prevented by the State or society*, i.e., disutility which would not promote the long-term interests of humankind. If we talk about harm in the sense in which it is more commonly used (where harm = disutility-producing), then we would say that the bigot is harmed, but it is an acceptable harm which should not cause the harmer to change her actions, since the bigot's attitudes should not be promoted. Humankind will be much better off if attitudes of tolerance, rather than bigotry, are promoted.

Mill does not make his notion of harm sufficiently clear. Yet, it is important to emphasize that if an action *only* causes disutility for the agent, then there obtains a sufficient but not necessary condition for the action's being free from outside interference. There are a variety of non-trivial, other-injuring actions which are not appropriately regulated by the State. Merely because a bigot objects to one's religion and suffers pain at the thought of one's practicing that religion does not warrant the prohibition of one's practicing that religion. The notion of harm, as a determinant of whether societal interference is justified and thus whether rights are involved, is based upon the long-term interests of humankind. A harm does not merely involve the production of pain. Those critics who argue that Mill in *On Liberty* only protects trivial activities do not understand his position.[37]

Indeed, there is a more important misunderstanding of Mill that seems to run through the literature. The misunderstanding is briefly discussed in Chapter 4, but bears repetition. *Utilitarianism* is a moral tract. *On Liberty* is a political tract. Mill explicitly states his purpose in *On Liberty*. "The subject of this essay is . . . civil or social liberty, the nature and limits of the power which can be legitimately exercised by society over the individual."[38]

In each of the chapters in this book starting with Chapter 4, a great deal of emphasis is given to Mill's definition of wrong — an act is wrong if it is blameworthy by *law, public opinion, or conscience.* When Mill writes about the sanctions which the State or society can impose, he is talking about the sanctions of law and public opinion. *He is not talking about the sanction of conscience.* Merely because an action should not be punished by society or the State does not imply that the action is morally permissible.[39]

The Protection of Liberty

While Mill is not extremely clear in explaining his notion of harm, he argues articulately and convincingly that people should be allowed to have certain liberties.[40] He must further explain why such liberties should be *protected* by the State. If he can establish that the State should protect these liberties, then he will have established that individuals have *rights* to the objects rather than are merely *permitted* to pursue the objects.

Utilitarianism states that actions are right if they (foreseeably) promote happiness and wrong if they (foreseeably) promote unhappiness. Mill must explain why the protection of individual liberties would tend to promote happiness. He explains that "individuality is one of the leading essentials of well-being." Were it properly appreciated, "the adjustment of the boundaries between it and social control would present no extraordinary difficulty."[41] Unfortunately, liberty is not valued sufficiently and Mill feels compelled to praise it.

Mill discusses a "morality grounded on large and wise views of the good of the whole, neither sacrificing the individual to the aggregate nor the aggregate to the individual, but giving to duty on the one hand and to freedom and spontaneity on the other their proper province."[42] He believes that "different persons . . . require different conditions for their spiritual development; and can no more exist in the same moral, than can all the variety of plants in the same physical, atmosphere and climate. The same things which are helps to one person towards the cultivation of his higher nature, are hindrances to another."[43] Thus, by preserving liberty, we assure that the greatest number of people will be able to 'cultivate their higher natures'. The cultivation of one's higher nature will lead to more happiness for the individual, for society, and for humankind.[44]

Mill offers other reasons to show why the protection of certain liberties leads to happiness. For example, freedom of speech is important because it is through the exchange of ideas that one can arrive at truth.[45] Further, because man is not infallible, man has no way to be absolutely sure that the opinions which he wants to censor are *not* the truth.[46] Finally, if the to-be-censored opinions are false, then they still should be aired to provide support through contrast for the true opinions. Even if the false opinions are dangerously specious, airing them will force the listener to rigorously examine the arguments. Only then can he really understand why the true opinion is indeed the truth.[47]

Mill sometimes seems too confident that people will be able to discern the truth. Individuals (in many current societies) are constantly subjected to false or misleading information from a variety of media — there is no guarantee that individuals will be able to separate the wheat from the chaff.

Mill realizes that individuals are inundated with information and that it grows exceedingly difficult to know what is true. However, rather than argue that we should therefore censor materials, he argues that we should double our efforts to assure that we have an educated populace.[48] Such a populace would more easily detect specious argumentation and, further, might acquire the ability to distinguish among kinds of information and sources so that it would be unnecessary to read or listen to everything before making reasonable, informed decisions.

Of course, one takes a risk when refusing to look at all relevant material. However, the alternatives are plainly less preferable. We imagine the individual who refuses to form an opinion and continues to look for additional information for fear that she might miss something relevant to the topic. She presumably would never reach any conclusions.

Or, we imagine a different situation in which the *government* decides which information is relevant. Mill rightly worries about the dangers posed by the possible abuse of the 'privilege' of censorship and believes that such potential dangers far outweigh the potential benefits.[49]

Perhaps Mill assigns too much utility to knowing the truth — the ignorant fool's euphoria, were there a guarantee that it would continue, might be very desirable. A false sense of security does help produce bliss and thus has utility. It is only if and when the security is put to the test that the unwarranted feelings have disutility.

Even if Mill has assigned too much utility to knowing the truth, he may be able to justify the protection of free speech in other ways. People might feel more secure in having the freedom to speak. They might feel afraid that, were their freedom to speak abridged, they would be living in a world of false security, a world which could be destroyed at any moment by an unfortunate turn of events. Were they certain that no harm would befall them, they might prefer the bliss of the fool.

It may only be because these people lack a credible guarantee of future security that they would not prefer the fool's bliss. Although the truth does not *necessarily* promote utility, perhaps it happens to promote utility, nonetheless.

Indeed, despite Mill's eloquent insistence upon the necessity of protecting individual liberties, he says, "It is proper to state that I forego any advantage which could be derived to my argument from the idea of abstract right, as a thing independent of utility. I regard utility as the ultimate appeal on all ethical questions."[50] Thus, Mill can argue eloquently in favor of protecting individual liberties. Yet, at the same time, he can base his argument on utility, claiming that the protection of liberties insures that the society will enjoy more happiness.

Mill claims that society's protecting rights will promote utility. One of the ways in which we define an agent's having a right to an object is in terms of the agent's being free from outside interference. If Jones has a right to X, then Jones should be allowed to X (or to receive *X*) — Jones should be free from outside interference when he *X*-es (or receives *X*). When Mill is talking about *society's protecting an agent's ability to act without external interference*, he seems to be talking about *an agent's having a right to act in a certain way.*

In both *Utilitarianism* and in *On Liberty*, Mill claims that rights should be protected because they promote utility.[51] If Mill is committing a written legerdemain by basing rights on utility, then he is committing it in both works. For Mill, the utility of humankind is the basis for every right, whether these rights are discussed in *Utilitarianism, On Liberty, Principles of Political Economy*, or wherever. Underlying Mill's entire system is the claim that utility is "the ultimate appeal on all ethical questions." Mill's position is internally consistent. The principle of utility is the ultimate moral criterion.

What Would Be an Adequate Defense of Rights?

If the principle of utility is the ultimate moral standard for *actions* (rather than, e.g., for rules), then any individual right can be overridden if sufficient utility is produced by doing so. Since it might seem that utilitarian rights would be overridden whenever "incremental" net utility would thereby be produced, one might claim that utilitarianism cannot adequately protect rights.[52]

Yet, it is a mistake to believe that mere incremental benefit will justify a right-abridgement. Abridging rights promotes disutility because:

1.   Rights are only granted when they would promote utility.[53] Thus, whatever large amount of utility which is produced by granting this right will be lost when the right is abridged.

2.   When another's right is abridged, one might become afraid that one's own right will also be abridged.

3.   When a particular right is abridged, all rights seem easier to abridge. Thus, insecurity about rights in general would be produced by abridging a right. For example, if I see someone else's right to free speech abridged, I will not only become concerned that my own right to free speech will be abridged, I will also become concerned that other rights of mine, e.g., my right to worship as I please, will also be (more likely to be) abridged — my seeing one right abridged will make me less confident that my other rights will not also be abridged.

4.   Whether the right-abridger is a person or government, the abridger's character might be affected, making other possibly improper right-abridgements more likely.

5.   People might grow to fear the right-abridger more, knowing that their rights might well be abridged again.

Thus, whenever any right is abridged, a great deal of disutility is produced.

Basically, there are hidden costs whenever one abridges rights. These costs must be considered before a right can justifiably be abridged. Incremental net utility *is not sufficient* to justify a right-abridgement if the calculation of the relative utilities *does not include* these hidden costs. Incremental net utility *is sufficient* to justify a right-abridgement if the calculation of the relative utilities *does include* all of the hidden costs.[54]

Utilitarians might seem to be required to constantly monitor costs in order for them to know whether a right-abridgement would be in order. Although such monitoring would sometimes be required, utilitarians would not need to monitor the costs most of the time. It is a good rule of thumb that rights should not be abridged. One would monitor costs only when there was a compelling reason to do so, i.e., when it appeared that the rights should be abridged.

A deontologist would claim that in order for Mill to protect rights adequately, he must protect them as much as most deontologists do. Or, at the very least, Mill must give plausible reasons which show why anyone's protecting rights more than Mill does would be a defect within that person's system.

Who Gets Rights to What?

Before we can address whether Mill protects rights as much as most deontologists do, we must establish who gets rights to what. To determine who has rights to what, we must establish whether protecting particular rights of particular (types of) people would indeed promote the general welfare. Rights promote utility because people feel more secure when they have rights. Rights promote disutility because there are costs in assuring that rights will be respected. (This is by no means an exhaustive list of the utilities and disutilities promoted by rights.)

Mill evaluates both attitudes and actions according to whether they promote the utility of humankind. I may have rights now which I would not have 2000 years from now. Just as training wheels may be necessary in order for one to learn how to ride a bicycle and yet are unnecessary as soon as one has mastered bicycling, certain rights may be necessary in the early stages of our development which will not be necessary later. Perhaps, 2000 years from now, we will neither have a need nor a right to own private property. "When private property in land is not expedient, it is unjust."[55] However, now, our having a right to own private property might promote utility. Indeed, our having that right now might help to develop other attitudes within us which eventually will eradicate the need to own private property.

Of course, I may not have rights now which I would have were I to live 2000 years in the future. For example, it might be too expensive for a society to guarantee all people the right to adequate medical care. It would neither be in the particular poor society's interests nor in the interests of humankind to grant rights to medical care if the rights could not be enforced. (The respect for rights would be severely diminished if one had unenforceable rights.)

Particular rights, then, need not exist through time. Individuals may have particular rights today which individuals living 2000 years in the future will not have. By the same token, individuals living 2000 years in the future may have rights which individuals today do not have.

Although rights need not exist eternally in order to be genuine rights, they cannot be so transitory that they exist today and yet will not exist tomorrow.[56] Mill points out that the possession of rights produces feelings of security. If rights could exist one day and yet not exist the next, then possessing them would not produce much security. My being able to pursue a particular object today would not imply that I could pursue it tomorrow.

As basic changes in attitudes and technology occur, we will have to re-evaluate which rights humans actually possess. However, only *basic* changes will warrant re-evaluations. To re-evaluate every day would seriously weaken the notion of a right and the security which the possession of rights produces. We could not grant rights today which would disappear tomorrow. If we did, then all rights would seem to be in jeopardy.

Mill says that rights promote "security, to everyone's feelings the most vital of all interests." Security is something that "no human being can possibly do without." Without security, we would lose "all immunity from evil and . . . the whole value of all and every good, beyond the passing moment, since nothing but the gratification of the

instant could be of any worth to us if we could be deprived of
everything the next instant by whoever was momentarily stronger than
ourselves." Security is the "most indispensible of all necessaries, after
physical nutriment." Thus, utilitarianism must respect rights, since
they are concerned with "the very groundwork of our existence."[57]

Mill is making a few arguments for the existence and protection
of security. He claims that humans have a need for security which is
almost as basic as the need for food. He also claims that security is a
necessary condition for long-term goods. Without security, we would
only seek immediate gratification.

Mill is describing security as an important goal because it fills a
basic need and because it is a necessary means to the attainment of an
important goal — the making and fulfilling of long-range plans.
However, "security cannot be had, unless the machinery for providing
it is kept unintermittedly in active play."[58]   Thus, justice and
individual rights must be protected, since they are the means by which
we acquire and maintain our security.

Does Utilitarianism Guarantee Equal Rights for All?

A different criticism of utilitarianism is that it does not grant
equal rights to all. Certainly, utilitarians have a response to that
criticism — when some people are granted rights and other people are
denied those rights, resentment often occurs. Yet, such a response
does not settle the matter — that resentment occurs is not itself
significant, since we "resent indiscriminately whatever anyone does
that is disagreeable to us."[59] The important question is concerned with
what we *should* resent, insofar as our resentments can be modified, not
with what we *do* resent. For example, six-year-olds should not resent
their not being allowed to drive. They are too young. Even though
some people have the right to drive while others do not, the
discrimination in this case is in society's best interests. It would
promote disutility to allow everyone to drive regardless of their age or
ability.

It is not true that everyone within utilitarianism has equal rights.
One can discriminate according to age, intelligence, or whatever if
such discrimination would promote the utility of humankind. "The
equal claim of everyone to happiness . . . involves an equal claim to
all the means of happiness *except in so far as the inevitable conditions
of life and the general interest in which that of every individual is*

included sets limit to the maxim [my italics]."⁶⁰ Thus, everyone may
not have an equal 'claim' to happiness. Mill offers two exceptions:

1. The inevitable conditions of life presumably refer to those
less than optimal conditions which usually prevail. For example, one
means to happiness involves access to certain types of medical care.
However, because of financial and geographical considerations, society
cannot guarantee that everyone will be able to benefit from life-saving
technology.
2. If it turns out that the happiness of the individual is in
conflict with the happiness of society broadly construed, then the
individual does not have a right to his happiness. The happiness of
the individual *should be* in conformity with the happiness of society.

Mill differs from other utilitarians in that he believes that we
must *also* talk about what *should* make an individual happy, given
certain natural constraints, rather than *solely* about what *does* make an
individual happy. An individual's happiness will coincide with the
general interests as long as the individual has the proper attitudes and
desires, where the criterion for the 'proper' attitudes will involve what
would promote humankind's utility and not merely what would
promote the currently existing society's utility.

Mill believes that utility is promoted when people live with each
other as equals, with the exceptions as noted above. Sometime in the
distant future, "[i]t will be impossible to live permanently on other
terms [i.e., any terms but equality] with anybody." Nonetheless, he
admits that the right to equal treatment is based on the principle of
utility and that exceptions can be made when the principle of utility so
dictates. "All persons are deemed to have a *right* to equality of
treatment, except when some recognized social expediency requires the
reverse."⁶¹

Sometimes, the social expediency which justified the inequality at
an earlier time no longer obtains. When that happens, not treating
people equally would not only be inexpedient, it would also be unjust.
"All persons are deemed to have a *right* to equality of treatment, except
when some recognised social expediency requires the reverse. And
hence all social inequalities which have ceased to be considered
expedient, assume the character not of simple inexpediency, but of
injustice."⁶²

Mill cannot guarantee that there will be an equal distribution of
goods. Nor can he guarantee that rights which exist now will exist

2000 years from now, nor even that rights which will exist 2000 years from now exist today. Both the distribution of goods and the duration of rights are dependent upon what would promote the interests of humankind. In the next chapter, the charges that Mill does not sufficiently respect considerations of justice and does not adequately protect individual rights will be discussed and evaluated.

NOTES

1. *Utilitarianism*, Ch. 5, Par. 15, p. 247.
2. *Ibid.*, Ch. 5, Par. 25, p. 251.
3. *Ibid.*
4. *Utilitarianism*, Ch. 5, Par. 25, p. 250.
5. See Harrison, "The Expedient, the Right and the Just in Mill's Utilitarianism," p. 105.
6. For a related argument, see my "Hutcheson on External Rights," *Philosophical Studies* 49 (1986), pp. 263-269.
7. *Utilitarianism*, Ch. 5, Par. 37, p. 259.
8. Martin and Nickel explain that the distinction is drawn from Ross's distinction between prima facie duties and duties *sans phrase*. "When this distinction is applied to rights, a right *sans phrase* is one which has always dictated the result that ought to be followed in cases to which it applies whereas a prima facie right is merely one that should so dictate unless stronger considerations intervene." Rex Martin and James Nickel, "Recent Work on the Concept of Rights," *American Philosophical Quarterly* 17 (1980), p. 173.
9. In my "Guilt, Regret and Prima Facie Duties," I argue that even if in conflicts of prima facie duties the *outcome* would have been no different had the weaker prima facie duty never existed, the *process* by which one decides what to do differs when a weaker prima facie duty is involved. Hence, it would be wrong to conclude that in cases of conflicts it is as if the weaker prima facie duty had never existed. An analogous argument can be made with respect to prima facie rights.
10. Morris worries that the prima facie account is dangerous and misleading, precisely because it might lead one to discount the weaker prima facie right completely. "It may be justifiable not to accord a man his rights. But it is no less a wrong to him, no less an infringement. It is seriously misleading to turn all justifiable infringements into noninfringements by saying that the right is only prima facie, as if we have, in concluding that we should not accord a

man his rights, made out a case that he had none." Herbert Morris, "Persons and Punishment," *The Monist* (1968), p. 499.

11. See Joel Feinberg, *Social Philosophy* (Englewood Cliffs: Prentice Hall, 1973), p. 75.

12. For this distinction, see Judith Thomson, "Self Defense and Rights" in her *Rights, Restitution and Risk* (Cambridge: Harvard University Press, 1986), p. 40.

13. See Richard Brandt, "Concept of a Moral Right," *The Journal of Philosophy* 80 (1983), p. 36.

14. *Utilitarianism*, Ch. 5, Par. 37, p. 259. It is because of Mill's desire to avoid maintaining that there can be "laudable injustice" that John Gray is likely in error when attributing to Mill the view that "none of the fundamental rights is indefeasible." See Gray's "Indirect Utility and Fundamental Rights," p. 86. I suspect that Mill would instead talk about appropriate delimitations of rights.

15. If one is willing to distinguish among justified claims and say that only some rights should be enforced by society, then one might be able to talk about rights which should not be enforced. See my "Hutcheson on External Rights."

16. See, e.g., Singer, "On Rawls, On Mill, On Liberty, and So On," p. 144; D. A. Lloyd Thomas, "Liberalism and Utilitarianism," *Ethics* 90 (1980), pp. 319-334; Himmelfarb, *On Liberty and Liberalism*, pp. 106 ff; James Stegenga, "J. S. Mill's Concept of Liberty and the Principle of Utility," *Journal of Value Inquiry* 7 (1973), pp. 281-89.

17. *Utilitarianism*, Ch. 2, Par. 2, p. 210.

18. *On Liberty*, Ch. 1, Par. 9, pp. 223-224.

19. *Ibid.*, Ch. 1, Par. 10, p. 224.

20. *Ibid.*, Ch. 1, Par. 9, pp. 223-224.

21. *Ibid.*, Ch. 1, Par. 5, p. 220.

22. *Ibid.*, Ch. 1, Par. 9, pp. 223-224.

23. *Utilitarianism*, Ch. 2, Par. 19, p. 220.

24. *A System of Logic*, Bk. 6, Ch. 12, Sec. 3, p. 946.

25. *On Liberty*, Ch. 1, Par. 9, p. 223.

26. *Utilitarianism*, Ch. 2, Par. 2, p. 210.

27. For related comments, see C. L. Ten, *Mill on Liberty* (Oxford: Clarendon Press, 1980), p. 10.

28. *On Liberty*, Ch. 4, Par. 9, p. 280.

29. *Ibid.*, Ch. 4, Par. 11, p. 282.

30. *Ibid.*, Ch. 4, Par. 10, p. 281.

For a discussion of Bentham's position on assignable individuals, see H. L. A. Hart's "Legal Rights" in his *Essays On Bentham* (Oxford: Clarendon Press, 1982), especially pp. 175 ff.

31. *On Liberty*, Ch. 4, Par. 10, p. 281.

32. See, e.g., Robert Paul Wolff, *The Poverty of Liberalism* (Boston: Beacon Press, 1968), p. 24.

33. *On Liberty*, Ch. 4, Par. 12, p. 283.

34. For related comments, see Albert Weale, "Tolerations, Individual Differences and Respect for Persons" in *Aspects of Toleration*, p. 25.

35. Rees suggests that Mill is interested in protecting the *interests* of others. However, interests "depend for their existence on social recognition and are closely connected with prevailing standards about the sort of behaviors a man can legitimately expect from others." J. C. Rees, "A Rereading of Mill on Liberty" in *Limits of Liberty*, Peter Radcliff ed. (Belmont: Wadsworth Publishing Co., Inc., 1966), pp. 87-107. Wollheim points out that Rees's interpretation makes Mill rather conservative, given that prevailing standards change rather slowly. J. Wollheim, "J. S. Mill and the Limits of State Action," *Social Research* 40 (1973), pp. 1-30. Since Mill is trying to prevent individuals from falling prey to the "tyranny of public opinion," Rees's interpretation is unlikely.

Rees himself points out that 'interests' is a vague term at best (p. 103). We are no closer to figuring out Mill's meaning, even if we adopt Rees's suggestion. Indeed, Rees's suggestion may cause us to misunderstand Mill's position. A case in point involves Rees's talking about a businessman's interests which "would be affected by a tax on business property no matter what his tastes." (p. 94) Yet, surely one of Mill's major contributions involves his protection of free speech, even if such speech were to cause the imposition of a large tax which might severely affect the interests of many people.

Or, we consider a very able, very well-known president of a publicly owned company whose resignation would severely affect the interests of many stockholders. (The value of their stocks would plummet were he to resign.) Yet, surely Mill would argue that even if their interests would be severely affected, the stockholders would have no right to the president's continuing in his position.

Gray seems closer to the mark when he suggests that "harm to others is best construed as 'injury to the vital interests of others'." John Gray, *Mill and Liberty: a defence* (London: Routledge and Kegan Paul, 1983), p. 95. Certainly, Mill is not interested in limiting someone's rights because doing so would slightly promote someone else's interests. Yet, we still have a problem.

The thief's possessing someone's purse and its contents might be vital to the interests of the thief. Yet, Mill still would not allow the thief to steal the purse, much less force the purse-owner to hand it over to the thief.

Mill presumably would want Jones to be forced to pay back the $70 which he owes Smith, even though Smith's 'vital interests' would not be affected by not receiving this money. We must find an informative way to talk about interests, a way which would help us to understand which liberties would be protected and which would not. However, if we change Rees's claim and link those of the "prevailing standards" which do promote utility to the amount of utility which one has a duty to promote, then his comments are quite compatible with the position offered here.

Riley argues that the "utilitarian standard for the *department of morality* holds that actions are right to the extent that they promote social harmony or unity, wrong to the extent that they promote instability." *Liberal Utilitarianism*, p. 198. Wollheim's comments seem quite correctly aimed at Riley's interpretation as well, given Mill's strong desire to assure that moral standards continue to *improve*.

Feinberg tries to define harms in terms of setbacks to interests, although it is not clear that he can escape the kinds of difficulties suggested here. See his *Harm To Others*.

36. *On Liberty*, Ch. 1, Par. 11, p. 224.

37. Mill's claim that one's maintaining one's own health can be an other-regarding duty implies that he believes that, sometimes, the enforcement of such a duty (through *external* sanctions) best serves the long-term interests of humankind. His claiming that parents have a duty to make sure that their children receive an education may be justified in the same way. (Semmel points out this education requirement of Mill's. See Semmel, *John Stuart Mill and the Pursuit of Virtue*, p. 171.) Mill may have some difficulty in establishing the point at which one need no longer be educated, e.g., through high school, junior high school, etc., and how unhealthily one may live, e.g., allowing one to eat red meat but not smoke tobacco, allowing one to consume one alcoholic drink per day but not two, etc., but that is a different matter.

Horton points out some of the difficulties which Mill faces if he tries to deny that the bigot's pain due to others' practicing their religion involves a harm. See Horton's "Toleration, Morality and Harm" in *Aspects of Toleration*, p. 115. Yet, Mill does not deny that the bigot's pain is a harm. Rather, he says that it is an acceptable harm, i.e., one the allowance of which would promote the general good.

38. *On Liberty*, Ch. 1, Par. 1, p. 217.

39. Not seeming to appreciate the importance of conscience for Mill, Riley writes, "According to Mill, then, if we say that a person has a moral obligation or duty to perform a particular action, then we imply that the person would be *right* to do the action and *wrong* not to do the action, *and that it would be right for society to punish him for inaction* [my italics]." *Liberal Utilitarianism*, p. 176.

40. See *On Liberty*, Ch. 1, Par. 9, 10, and 13, pp. 223-226..

41. *Ibid.*, Ch. 3, Par. 2, p. 261.

42. *Three Essays on Religion*, p. 421.

43. *On Liberty*, Ch. 3, Par. 14, p. 270.

44. *Utilitarianism*, Ch. 2, Par. 8-9, pp. 213-214.

45. *On Liberty*, Ch. 2, Par. 7, p. 231.

46. *Ibid.*, Ch. 2, Par. 8, p. 232.

47. *Ibid.*, Ch. 2, Par. 23, p. 245.

48. See "Civilization," pp. 135-136.

49. See, e.g., "Law of Libel and Liberty of the Press," *CW* 21, pp. 5-6.

50. *On Liberty*, Ch. 1, Par. 11, p. 224.

51. See *Utilitarianism*, Ch. 5, Par. 25, p. 250; and *On Liberty*, Ch. 1, Par. 11, p. 224.

52. Dworkin, "Taking Rights Seriously," p. 106.

53. Jan Narveson, "Rights and Utilitarianism," *New Essays on John Stuart Mill and Utilitarianism*, p. 145.

54. For related comments, see Richard Brandt, "Utilitarianism and Moral Rights," *Canadian Journal of Philosophy* 14 (1984), p. 2.

55. *Principles of Political Economy*, Book 2, Ch. 2, Sec. 6, Par. 4, p. 230. See also Levi's discussion of Mill's view of the state appropriation of land in *A Study in the Social Philosophy of John Stuart Mill*, pp. 72 ff.

56. Gauthier criticizes utilitarian rights theory because he claims that rights would be subject to continual readjustment. However, that criticism is based on an (at best) unusual reading of Mill. Further, the only 'support' which Gauthier offers for his interpretation is Mill's claim that rights are based on utility. That claim of Mill's can be used to support a variety of conflicting interpretations and thus can hardly

be thought to establish that Gauthier's interpretation is correct or even plausible. See David Gauthier, *Morals by Agreement* (Oxford: Oxford University Press, 1986), pp. 106 ff. The important question here would not be whether they were continually adjusted, but how often, e.g., every day or every decade.

57. *Utilitarianism*, Ch. 5, Par. 25, p. 251.
58. *Ibid.*
59. *Utilitarianism*, Ch. 5, Par. 21, p. 249.
60. *Ibid.*, Ch. 5, Par. 36, pp. 257-258.
61. *Ibid.*, p. 258.
62. *Ibid.*, Ch. 5, Par. 36, p. 258.

CHAPTER NINE

On Justice and Individual Rights

When theorists criticize utilitarianism, they often claim that it cannot adequately account for considerations of justice and cannot adequately protect individual rights. In order for utilitarians to argue that their system is not open to these charges, they must respond to several major criticisms:

1. They do not take the distinction between persons seriously. This criticism might involve the claim that utilitarians arrive at (possibly) correct conclusions for the wrong reasons. (See #3 below.) It might also mean that utilitarianism does not weigh individual wants and needs heavily enough, that individual rights will sometimes be violated so that aggregate utility can be promoted.

2. Within utilitarianism, the notion of a right is superfluous. The assumption underlying this criticism is that there are no times when the protection of rights is not utility-maximizing. Since maximizing utilitarianism dictates that (foreseeable) utility must always be maximized, the possession of a right would never change anything. One only has rights to that which is (foreseeably) utility-maximizing, and the (foreseeably) utility-maximizing action should be performed whether or not one has a right to it.

3. The justificatory basis of utilitarianism is invalid. Even if utilitarians come up with the 'right' answers, their system has an improper basis. Or, their system makes use of an improper method by which to arrive at answers — they look at aggregate utilities rather than at individual rights or needs.

On the Distribution of Goods

One of the most commonly made charges against utilitarianism is that it does not take the distinction between persons seriously.[1] This criticism might have a variety of meanings.

For example, it might mean that utilitarianism does not guarantee an equal distribution of goods. Suppose that there are 100 utiles of happiness to be distributed among four people. Utilitarianism would allow:

a.   the happiness to be distributed equally — each person would receive twenty five utiles, or

b.   the happiness to be distributed unequally — one person would receive ninety-four utiles while each of the other people would receive two utiles.[2]

Utilitarians respond by pointing out that there are diminishing marginal returns in the acquisition of wealth. All else equal, an extra $1000 would produce a lot more happiness for someone earning $10,000 per year than for someone earning $100,000 per year. Further, unequal distributions of wealth will cause anger, resentment, envy, etc. These disutilities must be included in any attempt to determine what the best distribution would be like.[3]

Critics might counterclaim that the resentment would presumably be outweighed by the greater utility produced by an unequal distribution. Further, the diminishing marginal returns might be outweighed by the benefits produced by an accumulation of wealth (which might be used to create jobs, good working conditions, etc.).

Were theorists honest, they would admit that utilitarianism simply does not say how the money should be distributed. We cannot demonstrate conclusively that an unequal distribution of wealth would best promote happiness. Nor can we say that an equal distribution of wealth would best promote happiness. We simply do not know and thus cannot say which is the more morally desirable distribution.[4]

Even were utilitarianism to dictate that all income be distributed equally, the debate between deontologists and utilitarians would not be resolved. Basically, the debate is centered around the utilitarian's notion of desert. The utilitarian claims that the only applicable criterion of desert is whether a particular distribution would best promote utility. (This is at least one way to view the dispute. Another way would be to claim that utilitarians deny that desert is an appropriate criterion to determine how goods should be distributed.)

Suppose that more utility would be promoted were Anita to receive Julia's salary, even though Julia works hard for her money and Anita does nothing to earn it. A utilitarian would claim that Anita's receiving the money would involve a morally better state of affairs than would Julia's receiving it. The deontologist would not criticize the utilitarian's giving the money to Anita on the ground that such a distribution would be unequal. (Anita might be getting the money, precisely because her getting the money would assure an equal distribution of income). Rather, the deontologist who wanted to criticize the distribution would claim that Anita did not deserve the money, even if her getting it would be a more equitable distribution of wealth.

Not all deontologists would claim that Anita does not deserve the money. Mill points out, "Some Communists consider it unjust that the produce of the labour of the community should be shared on any other principle than that of exact equality, others think it just that those should receive most whose needs are greatest; while others hold that those who work harder, or who produce more, or whose services are more valuable to the community may justly claim a larger quota in the division of the produce." Mill believes that "the sense of natural justice may be plausibly appealed to in behalf of every one of these opinions."[5] (He suggests settling the dispute by seeing which distribution would indeed promote humankind's utility, but that is a different matter.) Insofar as this is a matter of *justice*, these theorists would be disagreeing about a question of *desert*.

Even if Anita's having received the money would be a better state of affairs than would Julia's having received it, this would not imply that were Julia to receive the money, she would have an enforceable obligation to give it to Anita. Indeed, if we view the discussion above in light of the *imperfect* duty to give charity, we can see how both deontologists and utilitarians *might* talk about the state of affairs in which Anita ends up with the money as being morally preferable to the state of affairs in which Julia ends up with the money, *without imposing on Julia or on her employer the duty to give the money to Anita.*

In the example above, it would presumably be disutility-producing for Anita to get Julia's money, since Julia would then lose her incentive to work. Others' happiness would not be the same whether Julia or Anita received the money, because Julia would produce less in the future if Anita were awarded the money and thus others would be less happy if Julia's wages were awarded to Anita.[6] However, if Julia would work no less hard even were Anita to receive the money, if all other other-affecting considerations would not affect the relevant utilities, and if Anita's happiness would be increased more than Julia's would be decreased, then utilitarians should agree that Anita should receive the money.

It is somewhat surprising that so much time is spent trying to show that utilitarianism would yield an egalitarian distribution of goods, precisely because of the difficulty in showing that each individual's receiving exactly the same amount of goods would promote more utility than would individuals' receiving differing amounts. Further, it would not be particularly telling if utilitarianism did not require equal distributions of wealth, since *most deontological systems also do not require that each person receive exactly as much as her neighbor does.*

Some argue that utilitarianism does not adequately respect the separateness and autonomy of persons because it uses some individuals for the benefit of others.[7] Yet, the question at hand is *why* such persons are not being *sufficiently* respected. A moral system mandating that one follow the dictates of reason might require that one individual make great sacrifices for someone else. So, presumably, might most moral systems. The "separateness of persons" argument (in many of its variations) does not refute utilitarianism *while not at the same time refuting most moral systems.*

Needs Versus Desires

If deontological and utilitarian systems can only be distinguished in terms of *why* each person receives what she receives rather than in terms of *how much* each person receives, then the difference between the two types of systems may not be particularly important. However, deontologists claim that utilitarian and deontological notions of desert yield different dictates, e.g., certain individuals' needs may be sacrificed so that other individuals might enjoy frivolous desires.[8]

Utilitarians can distinguish between needs and desires.[9] Further, they can use different scales by which to come up with some objective composite scores to assist one in the evaluation of different desires. However, we must be careful not to make a distinction in kind with respect to which needs or desires must *always* be respected. Were we to do that, we would have incommensurability difficulties.

When Mill talks about security, he says that "the very groundwork of our existence gathers feelings around it so much more intense than those concerned in any of the more common cases of utility that the difference in degree (as is often the case in *psychology* [my italics]) becomes a real difference in kind."[10] Insofar as this is a question of degree, we can make measurements along *one* scale. However, if security is different in kind than other goods, then we run into the same problem which we encounter with the higher pleasures (if one believes that the higher pleasures must always be pursued over the lower pleasures), viz., that security must always be promoted over any other good. We must have some scale by which we can compare the promotion of security (or the promotion of the higher pleasures) with the promotion of other goods, if we are going to choose the promotion of security sometimes and the promotion of other goods at other times.

Theorists fear that if utilitarianism does not distinguish between needs and desires (and treats security, for example, as being comparable to other goods), then individual rights will be sacrificed to promote the general good. An incremental increase in utility for a very large number of people would more than offset a very significant amount of disutility for one person. For example, it is often argued that the principle of utility would justify the punishment of innocent persons if societal security could thereby be enhanced.[11]

Mill disagrees with those who contend that "punishment must have some other and higher justification than the prevention of crime [and] . . . that if punishment were only for the sake of example, it would be indifferent whether we punished the innocent or the guilty, since the punishment, considered as an example, is equally efficacious in either case." Such theorists seem to forget that "if the person punished is supposed to be innocent, or even if there be any doubt of his guilt, the spectator will reflect that his own danger, whatever it may be, is not contingent on his guiltiness, but threatens him equally if he remains innocent, and how therefore is he deterred from guilt by the apprehension of such punishment?"[12] Thus, were utilitarianism known to allow the punishment of the innocent, punishment itself would become less effective if not totally ineffective as a deterrent.

Mill does not thus preclude utilitarianism's ever countenancing the punishment of the innocent. Were one able to avoid a nuclear holocaust by punishing an innocent person, Mill would presumably countenance doing so. Other steps would also be taken, e.g., finding ways to assure that such a conflict would never arise again, but that is a different matter.

Utilitarians are morally required to protect individual rights if the non-protection of these rights would be harmful. People who fear that individual rights will not be respected are more insecure and unhappy than they would have been, had they felt that individual rights would be respected. Utilitarians are not permitted to act in ways which do not sufficiently respect individual rights, if not sufficiently respecting rights would promote insecurity and unhappiness.

The abridgement of an individual's rights does not only harm that individual. Society, in general, is harmed. Many people in Socrates' society were pleased that Socrates was forced to take hemlock. They were thus able to rid themselves of a painful gadfly. Yet, Socrates' death produced much disutility. Critical thought and expression were discouraged, since vocal critics might have ended up as Socrates did. Progress was thereby slowed and some future happiness lost. Although a superficial calculation of utilities might show that there was utility in executing Socrates, a careful and deliberate calculation of the utilities involved (including the effects of others' hearing of his execution) would show that Socrates' execution was disutility-producing.[13]

Nonetheless, one might be able to imagine circumstances in which the fulfillment of frivolous wants might produce more pleasure than would the fulfillment of basic needs. However, before one can dismiss utilitarianism for such a fatal flaw, one must first realize that deontologists might also be subjected to the same criticism. Very few deontologists would claim that Brown has a moral duty not to spend his honestly earned money on an additional car rather than use it to help feed starving people in Ethiopia. However, by buying an additional, unneeded car, Brown is fulfilling one of his own frivolous wants rather than a basic need of someone else.

Even were deontologists correct that their systems protect individual needs while utilitarian systems do not, we would still have to ascertain whether this 'fact' was telling. To do so, we would have to distinguish between two different questions:

1.   Are there any cases in which the dictates of deontological distributive justice would not produce the most aggregate happiness? To be more specific, are there any cases in which net utility would be produced by abridging someone's rights or by not giving someone her due?

2.   If there are conflicts between aggregative happiness and distributive justice, what does their existence imply about the validity of utilitarianism?

Let us assume that Question 1 should be answered in the affirm-ative.[14] We must also answer the second question — what are the implications if conflicts between aggregative happiness and distributive justice exist?

For utilitarians, the conflict between aggregative happiness and distributive justice is not problematic in the sense that they would have difficulty in knowing which of the two principles to choose. Their choice is simple. For them, the conflict is between a primary principle (aggregative happiness) and a secondary principle (distributive justice). Rather, the utilitarians' problem is that their resolution of the conflict is not in accord with everyone's intuitions.[15]

Yet, utilitarians do not claim to reflect all ethicists' intuitions. Mill, who thinks that utility does account for many of our intuitions, still insists that we must have utility-promoting attitudes. Even Mill is unwilling to admit that *all* of our attitudes are based on the principle of utility. If a moral system must yield dictates which are in accord with everyone's moral intuitions in order to be valid, then utilitarianism is not a valid moral system. By the same token, no other moral system is valid either.[16]

Merely because we do not have unanimity does not imply that we cannot say anything about the validity of moral systems. Perhaps unanimity is too severe a criterion for validity. "The universal voice of mankind, so often appealed to, is universal only in its discordance. What passes for it is merely the voice of the majority, or failing that, of any large number having a strong feeling on the subject."[17]

If indeed there is a conflict between aggregative happiness and distributive justice, then there is a serious problem. However, the problem is everyone's. Deontologists will accuse utilitarians of being too nonchalant about the preservation of justice and utilitarians will accuse deontologists of being too nonchalant about the promotion of humankind's happiness. Thus, those deontologists who claim that utilitarianism is invalid because it yields dictates which are not in accord with their own intuitions have a problem — utilitarians claim that deontological systems are invalid because such systems yield dictates which are not in accord with the utilitarians' intuitions.[18] There simply is no satisfying way to resolve this kind of debate.[19]

On the Pursuit of Personal Projects

Some critics charge that utilitarianism is flawed because it does not allow individuals to pursue their own projects but instead requires them to pursue those projects required by the principle of utility.[20] Yet, this criticism is weak for two very different reasons:

a. It is not at all clear that *my* having chosen a particular project rather than having had *someone else* choose that project for me makes the project *intrinsically* more valuable. Suppose that I chose a project which was not in accord with the dictates of reason and which would be harmful both to myself and to others. Most if not all deontologists and consequentialists would call my pursuit of that project morally impermissible. Further, that project would not have been any less worthy merely because someone else had chosen it for me.

   b.   The extent to which utilitarianism limits the pursuit of projects is exaggerated. Mill writes, "It is incumbent on everyone to restrain the pursuit of his personal objects within the limits consistent with the essential interests of others."[21] Thus, while the pursuit of certain projects is prohibited by utilitarianism, one's projects need not be in strict accord with what would maximize utility.

Mill devotes *On Liberty* to establishing that society must protect the right of individuals to make a variety of choices. People should be allowed to choose their own projects, because allowing them to do so will promote utility in the long run. Were the government to assign projects to different individuals, it would be too likely to make those assignments to the wrong people and at the wrong times.

Mill would offer three responses to those who would criticize utilitarianism for not allowing individuals to pursue their personal projects:

1.   He would say that he disagrees with their assessment of the psychological nature of human beings, since the "wonderful pliability of the human mind"[22] would allow humans to value their own projects as the principle of utility dictates that they should.

2.   He would point out that if what people naturally want to do does not coincide with the dictates of the principle of utility, this hardly establishes that the *principle* needs modification. Were humans naturally selfish, this would hardly establish that they should be selfish. "That a feeling is bestowed on us by nature does not necessarily legitimate all its promptings."[23]

3.   He would claim that the relevant utilities have been incorrectly calculated. If we consider the long-term utilities, we shall see that *the long-term interests of humankind are best served by allowing individuals to make their own plans and to pursue their own goals. On Liberty* is devoted to establishing that the State's allowing individuals to make their own choices is the best way to promote humankind's utilities. In criticizing Comte, Mill asks rhetorically, "Why is it necessary that all human life should point to one object, and be cultivated into a system of means to a single end? May it not be the fact that mankind, who after all are made up of single human beings, obtain a greater sum of happiness when each pursues his own,

under the rules and conditions required by the good of the rest, than when each makes the good of the rest his only object, and allows himself no personal pleasures not indispensible to the preservation of his faculties?"[24]

Thus, Mill would respond to such theorists that they:

1. do not understand the psychological nature of humankind,
2. do not understand that what people naturally do is not necessarily what they should do, and
3. do not understand that the long-term happiness of humankind is best served by allowing individuals to choose their own projects.

The Problem of Secrecy

Right-abridgements will cause people to feel more insecure only if they hear about the right-abridgements. Sidgwick remarks that "it may conceivably be right to do, if it can be done with comparative secrecy, what would be wrong to do in the face of the world."[25] Sidgwick's point negates one of the major safeguards protecting individual rights. If no one knows about a particular right-abridgement, then no one will feel more insecure as a result of it.

This is not the same issue as was discussed earlier in this chapter with respect to publicity. There, the issue was publicity concerning *rules* or *secondary principles*. Here, the issue is publicity concerning *actual practices* — whether in practice those rules are actually being followed.

The distinction can be explained in the following way. If the utilities would so dictate, utilitarianism would countenance the punishment of innocent persons. *That* utilitarianism countenances the punishment of innocents is known and, if Mill is correct, somewhat diminishes the efficacy of punishment. Diminishes it by how much? That would depend on how often such a practice would take place. If it is known that utilitarianism would countenance the punishment of the innocent in only a few possible scenarios and if it is also known that those scenarios hardly ever occur, then the knowledge that utilitarianism would countenance such punishments were the appropriate conditions to obtain might not cause too much insecurity. However, there is a greater likelihood that enough utility would be produced to warrant the punishment or murder of an innocent *were society allowed to act in secret.* The costs would then not be as great, since general insecurity would not thereby be produced.

Mill argues that the costs of society's acting secretly are too high. Society makes mistakes. Secrecy would result in many unjustified abridgements. Requiring public disclosure provides a check on the abuse of power. Without this check, much unhappiness will result from many unwarranted exercises of power.[26]

The more often that secret right-abridgements are performed, the more likely it is (*ceteris paribus*) that these secret right-abridgements will be discovered. Such a discovery would promote insecurity and lead to unhappiness. If a secret right-abridgement is to be permissible, then it will have to produce enough utility to counteract the disutilities which such practices produce, e.g., the unhappiness caused by the discovery that such practices are performed.

Mill realizes that even if there is publicity, abuses may still occur unless the public is willing to pay attention and to act accordingly. "Publicity . . . is no impediment to evil nor stimulus to good if the public will not look at what is done; but how could they either check or encourage what they were not permitted to see?"[27]

An even better check on evil would be to assure through education and threatened severe punishments that the interests of government officials were coincident with the public interest. "The ideally perfect constitution of a public office is that in which the interest of the functionary is entirely coincident with his duty."[28]

We consider an example. It is generally accepted that governments are permitted not to reveal certain information, if the publication of that information would be to the severe detriment of the public. However, governments which abuse that privilege cause general insecurity and distrust.

Presumably, governmental lying can also be justified by appealing to considerations of the public good.[29] However, a government which lies at inappropriate times can cause a great deal of disutility, including the problems involved in a severe loss of credibility.

Some abuses of power will be prevented if we follow Mill's suggestion and try to assure that government officials' interests and the public interest coincide. However, even if we have adequate safeguard to assure that result, e.g., by setting up efficient 'watchdog' committees, we will have to hope that public officials are foresightful enough to do what really is in their own and the public interest.

On Guaranteeing that Rights Will Be Protected

Mill offers convincing reasons to show that individual liberties should be protected, even within a utilitarian framework. However, some theorists want a guarantee that utilitarianism will protect rights.[30] Thus, were utilitarianism to happen to protect rights adequately in our world, that would not establish that utilitarianism is a valid moral system.

One could develop a system which did not merely happen to protect rights adequately, but which *always* completely protected them. If one adopts a view of rights as never-overridable side constraints and one is sure that the rights are carefully delimited so that there cannot be a case in which one right conflicts with another, then one could guarantee the protection of rights in all possible worlds.[31]

Or, one might argue that rights should always be protected *except when certain specified conditions obtain*, e.g., unless great calamity would otherwise result. That rule might be held to be true *for all possible worlds*.

The claim that utilitarianism is invalid because it does not guarantee that rights will be respected is not as effective as it might first appear. A utilitarian might argue, "Rights are to be respected unless their abridgement would be utility-maximizing, including within that calculation all 'hidden' costs involved in right-abridgements." Or, a utilitarian might argue, "Rights should *never* be abridged." However, she might point out, since rights are based on utility, there *can never be a conflict between utility and the protection of rights*. The utilitarian rights theorist who maintains either of the positions above might claim that her position holds *in all possible worlds*.

In order for the 'all possible worlds' claim to be helpful, more would have to be said than merely that 'its implications for all possible worlds must be true'. We would need in addition some way to know which implications were 'true'. For example, one might argue that one 'true' implication would be that rights could never be overridden. However, unless one further posited that rights could not be based on utility, such a requirement *would not* preclude utilitarianism from being valid. Such a requirement *would* preclude a variety of deontological systems from being valid.[32] It is simply inappropriate to claim that the truth or falsity of a theory depends upon its implications for all possible worlds.[33]

Let us concentrate on *this* world. An important issue is when (if ever) rights may justifiably be overridden. If indeed they can be, then there must be some method by which to determine when those overridings would be justified. If utilitarianism would allow too many right-overridings, then it would seem to be an unappealing system.

Can Mill Guarantee that Justice Will Be Adequately Protected?

If the principle of utility is the ultimate moral principle, then utilitarianism would seem unable to guarantee that justice will be adequately respected. The protection of justice has a sacred aura around it (as Mill frequently points out). If utilitarianism can be shown not to protect justice, then utilitarianism will have been dealt a telling blow.

Before we can establish whether justice is respected by utilitarianism, we must determine what justice requires. If we say that justice requires that we treat relevantly similar beings similarly, we have not added enough content to be helpful. Justice would then depend upon how we define 'relevantly similar'.

Suppose that Jones, a young boy, is drowning. Smith and Robinson are on the shore watching. Mill would say that Smith, an expert swimmer, is morally obligated to help Jones. Robinson, who does not know how to swim, might be obligated to seek help but is not obligated to go in the water to save the boy. Smith and Robinson are relevantly dissimilar. Thus, merely because it is right for Smith to do something does not mean that it is right for anyone, e.g., Robinson, to perform that same action.

Sidgwick, when defining justice, describes an impartiality which "is merely a special application of the wider maxim that it cannot be right to treat two persons differently if their cases are similar *in all material circumstances* [my italics]."[34] However, the important question involves determining what exactly the material circumstances are.

Sidgwick, when talking about the essence of justice, seems to make a stronger claim. "The essence of Justice or Equity (insofar as it is clear and certain) is that different individuals are not to be treated differently except on grounds of universal application."[35] However, universal application is not as helpful as it first appears. If one allows all red-headed, one-eyed men, with warts on their cheeks and mermaids tattooed on their left forearms, to lie on Tuesdays, then one might come up with very different results than if one allows everyone to lie whenever they feel like it.[36]

Perhaps it would be easier to decipher 'relevantly similar' if we narrow our focus. Suppose that we limit our discussion to criminal punishment. Let us again consider the powerful tycoon who murders her husband. If brought to trial and convicted, she will see to it that many people will suffer much hardship. If she is not tried and convicted, the town will acquire a new hospital. The tycoon will never murder again, very few people know of the crime, etc. In short, there will much more benefit if the crime is simply ignored. Is it just to ignore the crime?

Can Some Foreseen Consequences Be Disqualified?

Perhaps the tycoon's threats should be ignored — she might be bluffing. Even if she is serious, if she is justly convicted, then her carrying out these threats would be immoral, since she would be causing undeserved hardship. However, immoral actions are still actions and these actions have consequences which will affect the happiness of various individuals.

It is possible that net utility would be produced by not punishing the tycoon.[37] If indeed utility would be produced by letting the tycoon go free (including all of the adverse effects on character, etc.) and if disutility would be produced by punishing her, then Mill would say that not punishing her would be just — what is normally just would not be just in this case.[38] Presumably, at least some deontologists would claim that the tycoon should be punished. However, as Mill points out, maintaining that the pursuit of justice can result in net disutility in the long run is not a particularly appealing position.

If rights do not promote human welfare, then one might ask why rights are important and why they must be respected.[39] The deontologist who maintains that rights must be upheld even if disutility is thereby produced may have much difficulty in convincing an impartial observer that rights must be respected.

Certainly, Mill is a great believer in the protection of individual rights and liberties. The "free development of individuality *is one of the leading essentials of well-being* [my italics]; ... it is not only a co-ordinate element with all that is designated by the terms civilization, instruction, education, culture, but is itself a necessary part and condition of all those things."[40] Mill is arguing that in order for humankind's utility to be promoted, there must be a free development of individuality. In order for there to be a free development of individuality, the necessary goods for successful agency must be present. Individuals cannot develop if they cannot make choices. In order to make choices, certain conditions must obtain, e.g., that one can actualize one's choices. Mill is in agreement with many deontologists about the paramount importance of individuality and the necessary goods for individual agency, although for different reasons.

Mill is unlike most utilitarians. His theory of obligation is based upon the promotion rather than the maximization of utility. Further, he does not merely want to promote the utility of a particular society. He instead wants to promote the utility of humankind. His using that standard allows him to judge attitudes as well as actions. Given certain facts about human nature, e.g., the importance of security, we can determine which attitudes will indeed promote utility. For example, one's attitudes must involve a great deal of respect for liberty. *On Liberty* is written to convince people of the importance of the preservation of the freedom to act without external constraint (within certain spheres). Thus, if we are to decide whether a right should be abridged, we must judge as people who appreciated the importance of liberty would judge. Presumably, competent judges would appreciate the importance of liberty (although competent judges would not be competent by virtue of their ability to appreciate the higher pleasures — authoritarian individuals might appreciate the higher pleasures but not have the proper respect for liberty).

Mill is confident, perhaps too confident, that he can tell which attitudes are utility-producing for people to hold. He believes that we can determine those attitudes and actions because "social phenomena [e.g., what makes people happy] conform to invariable laws."[41] If these invariable laws exist, then we must discover them. We can do so by examining our history and seeing which rules and actions promote the most happiness.[42]

Our history has been long enough and varied enough to indicate which actions and attitudes will indeed promote utility. By studying history, we can infer how we can better ourselves. Indeed, "intellectual progress [is] in no other way so beneficial as by creating a standard to guide the moral sentiments of mankind, and a mode of bringing those sentiments effectively to bear on conduct."[43]

Thus, Mill has the idealistic notion that there are certain laws which regulate the world which, if discovered and followed, would enable us to live much more happily. Human nature is very malleable. People can bring about changes in their own attitudes to enable themselves to live in accord with these laws. Eventually, a long time in the future, humankind will live in a sort of utopia composed of extremely benevolent and caring creatures. However, in the "comparatively early state of human advancement in which we now live, a person cannot . . . feel that entireness of sympathy with all others which would make any real discordance in the general direction of their conduct in life impossible."[44] Some day in the future, however, we will feel this almost boundless sympathy.

In such a world, only in very rare circumstances would right-abridgements be justified. In such cases, a great deal of utility would be produced for humankind — enough to outweigh all of the various disutilities of the abridgement. Were we to characterize Mill as a rule-utilitarian, we would not understand this aspect of his thought, viz., that rule-abridgements are permissible in very rare cases. In the case of a justified right-abridgement, Mill would say that the 'right' was not really a right. What was normally a right was not a right in this particular case. In this way, Mill hopes to avoid the problems faced by both deontologists and utilitarians in those few instances in which the protection of rights would promote disutility.

To assure that all just actions promote utility, Mill says that in those rare cases in which the normal dictates of justice promote disutility the normal dictates of justice do not apply. Were Mill a rule-utilitarian, he would have said that because the normal dictates of justice generally promote utility, the normal dictates of justice must be followed all of the time — even in those cases in which the dictates are harmful.

Mill does not avail himself of the rule-utilitarian option — he is unwilling to countenance (morally) an agent's following a rule when the agent knows that doing so will be harmful. Mill maintains that only utility-producing actions are morally correct.

Rights Are Not Superfluous

Some critics charge that within utilitarianism the notion of a right seems superfluous.[45] According to standard act-utilitarianism, one is morally required to act in a utility-maximizing fashion. If one can only have rights to that which is utility-maximizing, and the utility-maximizing action should be performed whether or not one has a right to it, then one's having a right would not seem to entitle one to anything that one would not have gotten anyway.

Even if one only had rights to that which was utility-maximizing, rights would still serve a function in our world. Were we living in a perfect world where all calculations of utility could be made easily and with great exactness, the point about superfluousness would be accurate. In such a world, there would be no need for rights. Everyone would be treated exactly as he or she should be treated.[46]

Unfortunately, our world is not perfect. Rights serve a few functions within a world such as ours. My having a right indicates to the State, to society, and to myself that it is utility-maximizing for me to be allowed to perform or have performed the action in question. Anyone who is even considering abridging the right must very carefully examine the utilities involved. There is a strong, *prima facie* case against abridging it — because I have a right to an Object, there is a very good guide indicating that an abridgement of that right would not be utility-maximizing.

When 'guide' is used here, it is being used in the same way that Mill wants to use the notion of a secondary moral principle. A guide is not *merely* a rule of thumb which may be ignored relatively easily. Nor is it an inviolable principle. A guide may in principle be ignored, but one must be quite sure that ignoring the guide would maximize utility before doing so.

My having a right should serve as a flag to any would-be abridger that she is very likely going to be acting immorally if she actually abridges my right. Both the would-be abridger and the agent realize that an agent's having a right serves as an indicator that the abridgement would be disutility-producing. The agent begins to count on her being able to perform or have performed the action in question. Abridging the right thus becomes even more costly than the abridger might first have anticipated, since the agent would have had higher expectations as a result of having had the right and thus would suffer even more were the right abridged.

Utilitarians, like other people, like to make life-plans. However, the leaders of society have access to more and better information than most agents have. Thus, even if an individual knew that the State and society would act in the best possible manner, the individual might not be able to make specific plans. She would not know which particular actions the State and society would prevent or allow. (While the agent might be able to make some very good guesses, she probably would not feel very secure about them.)

If the agent has rights, she will feel much more secure that certain activities will be protected. The agent will be better able to plan and will live a happier life.

Certainly, within standard act-utilitarianism one's having a right would not entitle one to an object which society should not have allowed one to have had, had one not had a right to it. *In general, the possession of a right would only make that which is utility-maximizing for society to protect, even more beneficial for society to protect.* Basically, then, from the standard act-utilitarian point of view, rights make even more obvious the various objects which one should be protected in acquiring, should one desire to acquire them. In a fallible world, rights significantly lessen the number of non-utility-maximizing actions, i.e., the withholding of objects which society should not withhold and the granting of objects which society should not grant, since the difference between almost utility-maximizing and utility-maximizing becomes greater when rights are involved.

Even within a standard act-utilitarian society, rights are not superfluous. They provide a margin of safety which helps prevent society from making mistakes which it otherwise might have made. Thus, members of society can lead lives which are happier and more secure.

Mill writes, "When, indeed, the question arises, *what is* justice? — that is, what are those claims of others which we are bound to respect? and *what is* the conduct required by 'regard to the common good'? the solutions which we can deduce from our foresight are not infallible."[47] If we have a system of rights, where rights make more obvious those freedoms which should be respected, then we will reduce the number of mistaken right-abridgements due to improper foresight of consequences.

Rights serve several functions in Mill's system, since in his system one does not *only* have the right to perform utility-maximizing actions but also the right to perform a variety of utility-producing actions. Of course, one does not have a right to perform *any* act which will promote utility, since rights are based on the sliding scale which changes as society progresses. Nor does one have the right to perform an act merely because one *believes* it would promote the requisite amount of utility. (One might have miscalculated the relevant utilities.) Rights serve the function of distinguishing those acts which one could perform without fear of rightful (external) interference from those acts for which the imposition of external sanctions might be appropriately imposed.

In Mill's system, the possession of rights would indeed promote security. The extra margin of safety which the possession of rights affords is a feature which both Mill and standard act-utilitarians cite in their explanations of why the possession of rights promotes utility.

Mill's system does not hold that the (set of) rights which one holds at one time in history would be identical to the (set of) rights which one might hold a century later. As society progresses, the amount of utility required to justify the existence of a right would increase. On the one hand, a right the protection of which would be barely sufficiently utility-producing in one century might not meet the relevant standard the next century. On the other hand, because uncommon virtue in one society might become common virtue in that same society one century later, one might have certain rights in the latter society which one would not have in the former.

The Right to Act Immorally

Most deontologists claim that the protection of rights promotes utility. For example, Dewey comments, "Would there be any use or sense in moral acts if they did not tend to promote welfare, individual and social? If theft uniformly resulted in great happiness and security of life, if truth-telling introduced confusion and inefficiency into men's relations, would we not consider the first a virtue, and the latter a vice?"[48] Nonetheless, most deontologists deny that the protection of rights *always* produces utility. Further, they make that claim without at all relying on the difficulties posed by knowledge and time constraints. Mill disagrees. If one knows that the protection of a right would be disutility-producing, then Mill would say that what we thought was a right was not really a right. The right in question would have been improperly described — it would not include the object in question. The right to free speech does not include the right to describe corndealers as robbers of the poor to an angry crowd that is in front of the corndealer's house.[49]

Mill gives several very convincing arguments showing why it is productive of utility for society to respect certain rights. Yet, one might still have nagging doubts about the correctness of Mill's position, since I might spend my time in disutility-producing ways if I am given the right to make choices for myself. A deontologist might ask Mill why a utilitarian society should not ignore my right to spend my time as I see fit and instead, for example, force me to help feed the hungry.

The question is a good one. It elicits a seemingly paradoxical response. Mill believes that the protection of rights promotes utility. However, he does not believe that the exercise of one's rights is always productive of utility. Individuals have the right to perform disutility-producing actions. Even if my writing this book is disutility-producing, society should neither prevent me from writing it nor allow others to prevent me from writing it.

The deontologist might demand that Mill explain this confusing position. Individuals, like society, should perform those actions which promote utility and should refrain from performing those actions which are disutility-producing. If both individuals and society are required to perform utility-promoting actions, then how can it be possible, the deontologist might inquire, for it to be productive of utility for society to allow someone to perform a disutility-producing action?

Yet, this seeming paradox is not a paradox at all. Every interference by society has costs.[50] These costs must be considered when one makes a calculation about what society should do. For example, it would be very costly for society to try to force me to feed the starving rather than allow me to act in a way which did not produce quite enough utility. There would be costs in locating me, in keeping track of what I was doing, in trying me (court costs), etc. The costs would be sufficiently prohibitive to make society's forcing me to feed the hungry a disutility-producing course of action.

I have a right to act in somewhat disutility-producing ways rather than feed the hungry, even if my feeding them would promote utility. If I have a right to perform a disutility-producing action and all disutility-producing actions are morally wrong, then Mill must be suggesting that I have a right to perform morally wrong actions.

Mill believes that society should protect my rights if protecting them would promote the utility of humankind. Certainly, empirically, it may be difficult to establish what would promote humankind's utility. He gives us some helpful suggestions. He points to the security produced by granting rights. He points to the importance of liberty in the development of intellectual and cultural growth. He points to the likelihood that society will abridge rights at improper times if society is to go about abridging them, etc. However, he fails to point to one of the surprising implications of his theory of rights, viz., that one has a right to do wrong.[51]

Mill has a very good reason for being reluctant to mention that his theory rests on one's right to do wrong (the right to perform foreseeably disutility-producing actions). Intuitively, such a claim is not very appealing, although as long as utilitarians are trying to mold attitudes rather than reflect them, that one's intuitions are not in accord with a utilitarian's is not particularly damning. However, the problem is more serious than that posed by a conflict of intuitions.

According to Mill, to say that an action is wrong is to say that it is blameworthy. To say that an action is blameworthy is to say that one's conscience should punish the action. To say that one's conscience should punish an action is to say that a properly functioning conscience would punish the action.

My having a right involves my having something which society should defend me in the possession of. Just as society must pay certain costs if it is going to force me to feed the poor, society must pay certain costs (costs involved in maintaining police or in providing an education) if it is going to defend me in my right to perform slightly disutility-producing actions. Society's defending me in the possession of an object, e.g., my being allowed to act in those ways if I so desire, involves:

1.   society's preventing anyone's interfering with me while I am performing the action, and
2.   society's preventing anyone from punishing me for performing the action. (If someone punishes me because I performed the action, I will be discouraged from performing that action in the future.)

If I have a right to perform disutility-producing actions and all disutility-producing actions are wrong, then I have a right to do wrong. If I have a right to do wrong, then I have a right to perform actions which are blameworthy. If I have a right to perform blameworthy actions, then society should prevent my being blamed (punished) for performing blameworthy actions. However, if I perform a wrong action, my conscience should blame me. Even if the sanctions of law or public opinion should not be imposed, the sanctions of conscience should be imposed. If none of the sanctions should be imposed, then I have not acted wrongly.

According to Mill, the conscience is not innate. It is developed. Society helps to develop it. We now see why the notion of a right to do wrong is so difficult to understand. Society ends up being pitted against itself. Society seeks to develop disinterested consciences and is thus acting to assure that sanctions will be imposed against anyone who acts wrongly. Yet, society is also supposed to defend the agent in the possession of his rights. In cases in which the agent exercises his right to do wrong, society is supposed to prevent the imposition of sanctions. Yet, these sanctions are precisely the sanctions the imposition of which society has promoted.

When I have a *legal* right to X, society must prevent others from interfering with me in my X-ing. Society must prevent the imposition of any external sanctions against me.

The *moral* right to do X also involves society's preventing the imposition of any external sanctions against me. Indeed, society might require others to help me to X. However, on at least *some* notions of a moral right, the *moral* right to X entails *more* than merely that no external sanctions be imposed against me. The *moral* right to X entails that there be *no* sanctions imposed against me for my X-ing, not even internal sanctions.

My having a moral right to something means that society must protect me in acquiring and keeping that something for as long as I desire it. Society only does part of its job by protecting the agent from external sanctions. Society must do the other part and protect the agent from the imposition of internal sanctions.

Now we have a problem. We can say that consciences should not impose sanctions in cases in which the agent is exercising her right to act wrongly — we can say that a properly developed conscience will not impose sanctions against an agent for exercising her right to do wrong. Yet, if a conscience should not impose sanctions (i.e., if a properly developed conscience would not impose sanctions) against someone who has performed a wrong action, then the word 'wrong' loses its meaning.

Mill does not want to change the meaning of 'wrong'. He wishes to preserve the sting of that evaluative term. Yet, to talk about one's right to do wrong robs 'wrong' of its sting.

Mill is faced with a dilemma. On the one hand, he can say that one only has a right to perform utility-producing actions. Such a position would limit both the number of rights that humans have and the breadth of those rights. While the position is not necessarily invalid in that we must be able to show which rights people "should" have before we can show that a system is invalid or inadequate due to its dearth of rights,[52] such a position would entail that many of the rights argued for by Mill are not really rights.

On the other hand, Mill can say that we have a right to do wrong. Such a position *seems to be* contradictory. My having a right to an object means that I should be allowed to pursue that object without interference. Further, my having a right to an object means that I should not be punished for pursuing that object. Yet, my performing a wrong action entails that I should be punished if only by conscience, since wrong actions are blameworthy and should have some sanction imposed against them. Thus, if I exercise my right to do wrong, I both should and should not be punished.[53]

One reason that Mill has difficulty in talking about a right to do wrong involves society's contradictory roles with respect to such rights. *If a moral right to do wrong only implied that society should not interfere with an agent's exercise of that right and that society should prevent others from interfering with the exercise of that right,* then Mill would have no problem. *Mill's only problem involves the proper role of conscience in those cases in which an agent exercises her right to do wrong.*[54]

Even if society does nothing to Kathy when she exercises her right to *X*, and even if society prevents anyone else from interfering with Kathy in her attempt to *X*, Kathy may not have a *moral* right to *X*. Kathy's having a *legal* right to *X* requires that society prevent itself and other individuals from interfering with her exercise of that right. However, on at least *some* notions of a moral right, an agent's having a moral right to *X* is not equivalent to society's having a moral duty to prevent itself and others from interfering with the agent. If the agent has a moral right to X, then she should be free from *all* interference in her exercise of that right, *even interference from her own conscience.* If Kathy's conscience should punish her for *X*-ing, then Kathy should not *X* — she does not have a *moral* right to *X* even though no one other than Kathy should interfere with her should she decide to *X*.

Mill is quite aware of the distinction pointed to here. Indeed, he suggests that many of the confusions and difficulties surrounding rights are produced by a conflation of some of the different meanings of a 'right'.

> Speaking morally, you are said to have a right to do a thing, if all persons are morally bound not to hinder you from doing it. But, in another sense, to have a right to do a thing is the opposite of having *no* right to do it, i.e., of being under a moral obligation to forbear doing it. In this sense, to say that you have a right to do a thing, means that you may do it without any breach of

duty on your part; that other persons not only ought not to hinder you, but have no cause to think you worse for doing it. This is a perfectly distinct proposition from the preceding. The right which you have by virtue of a duty incumbent upon other persons, is obviously quite a different thing from a right consisting in the absence of any duty upon yourself. Yet the two things are perpetually confounded. Thus a man will say he has a right to publish his opinions; which may be true in this sense, that it would be a breach of duty in any other person to interfere and prevent the publication: but he assumes thereupon, that in publishing his opinions, he himself violates no duty; which may be true or false, depending, as it does, on his having taken due pains to satify himself, first, that the opinions are true, and next, that their publication in this manner, and at this particular juncture, will probably be beneficial to the interests of truth on the whole.[55]

Thus, there are two notions of a 'right' which must be kept distinct:

1.   a right to X implies that one should be free from external interference in one's X-ing, and
2.   a right to X implies that one does not have a duty to refrain from X-ing.

In the next chapter, we shall see how these different meanings of a 'right' affect contemporary deontological and utilitarian theories of rights.

The Challenge for Mill

In order for Mill to show that we have all of the moral rights which he claims that we have, he must show:

1.   that our having rights promotes utility, and
2.   that one can have a right to do wrong.

Mill argues convincingly that #1 is true. He and *all moral theorists* have a much more difficult task in showing that #2 is true (where my having a moral right to X implies not only that others would be wrong to interfere with my X-ing but *also* that my X-ing would not be a violation of duty). If a moral right to X implies that one's X-ing is not a violation of Duty, then people will not have many of the *moral* rights which Mill believes that they have. We will not have the right to free speech, where free speech entails being able to make a vast variety of utterances. We will only have the right to make utility-promoting utterances. We will not have the right to freedom of religion, where freedom of religion entails being able to worship as one chooses.[56] We will only have the right to 'choose' the utility-promoting religions and worship in utility-promoting ways.

If my having a right implies that I should not be punished for exercising that right and if my acting wrongly implies that I should be punished for so acting, then I cannot have a right to do wrong. If I cannot have a right to do wrong, then I cannot within an act-utilitarian framework have a right to perform foreseeably disutility-producing actions. I can only have a right to perform that which promotes utility.

Deontologists often attack Mill on empirical grounds, claiming that Mill does not adequately protect rights because, too often, there is more utility in abridging rights than in protecting them. Defenders of Mill counterclaim that all of the utilities have not been counted in the examples posed by the deontologists. Were one to take all of the relevant utilities into account, one would see that the rights protected by the deontological systems are also protected by utilitarian systems.

Were deontologists to criticize Mill on analytic grounds, i.e., by claiming that a right to do wrong is a contradiction in terms and thus that agents only have the right to perform utility-producing actions, the defenders of Mill would be forced to admit that *on that definition of a right* all of the rights protected by (some) deontological systems are not protected by Mill's utilitarianism. However, Mill still can and does offer convincing arguments which show why society must protect certain liberties. Deontologists are wrong to claim that a utilitarian society would necessarily protect fewer *liberties* than would a deontological society.

One is correct to accuse Mill of being unable to account for rights *only if one adopts the definition of a 'right' presented here, i.e., that a moral right to X entails that the agent should not be punished even by her own conscience for X-ing.* Mill cannot claim that an agent can exercise her right to do wrong without deserving to have any sanctions imposed against her. However, those sanctions would be imposed by her conscience. No one *external to the agent* could rightfully impose sanctions against her for having exercised her right to do wrong.

Yet, if Mill's system is impugned because of his notion of a right, then so are a variety of deontological systems. As we shall see in the final chapter, a variety of rights theorists claim that one can and must have a moral right to do moral wrong.

Further, Mill may not need to argue that we have moral rights, especially if the sense of a right is used where one's having a right implies that *no* interference is appropriate. For the most part, Mill believes that rights are important because they produce security. Yet, there might be other ways to produce security besides maintaining a system of rights. In the final chapter, we will examine the implications of a society in which the members are as secure as the members in our society are, even though that other society does not have a system of rights.

NOTES

1. Rawls, *A Theory of Justice*, p. 27.
2. See H. L. A. Hart, "Between Utility and Rights" in *The Idea of Freedom*, ed. Alan Ryan (Oxford: Oxford University Press, 1979), p. 79.
3. See R. M. Hare, "Ethical Theory and Utilitarianism" in *Utilitarianism and Beyond*, p. 27. But see Hart, "Between Utility and Rights," p. 79.
4. Smart suggests that there are very few (if any) instances in which an equal distribution of wealth would produce exactly as much utility as would an unequal distribution of wealth. He implies that we need not worry about this issue (what to do in cases in which two different distributions would produce exactly as much utility), because the question would hardly ever arise. He suggests that if we can produce even slightly more utility by an unequal distribution of wealth, then we should do so. Smart and Williams, *Utilitarianism For and Against*, pp. 35-37. For related discussion, see Hardin, p. 174.
5. *Utilitarianism*, Ch. 5, Par. 10, p. 244.
6. Even if Julia is a standard act-utilitarian who believes that she and others *should* act in utility-maximizing ways, she might not *actually* be motivated to produce as much as she would have, were she to have been awarded the wages herself. Unfortunately, people are not always motivated to act in the way which they believe to be morally

correct. See my discussion of "election" in my *Francis Hutcheson's Moral Theory*, Chapter 5.

7. See Robert Nozick, *Anarchy, State and Utopia* (New York: Basic Books, 1974), p. 33.

8. See John Rawls, "Social Unity and Primary Goods" in *Utilitarianism and Beyond*, p. 182; Gewirth, "Can Utilitarianism Justify Any Moral Rights?," p. 151.

9. For related comments, see Thomas Scanlon, "Preference and Urgency," *Journal of Philosophy* 72 (1975), p. 658.

10. *Utilitarianism*, Ch. 5, Par. 25, p. 251.

11. For related comments, see Narveson, *Morality and Utility*, pp. 155 ff. Narveson is somewhat sympathetic to the claim that innocents must be protected, even if doing so would promote disutility. He does not seem to appreciate the force of the utilitarian response to such criticisms, *viz.*, that if the punishment of the innocent really would foreseeably promote utility, including all of the hidden costs, e.g., increased insecurity, then perhaps the innocent should be punished in such circumstances.

12. *A System of Logic*, Book 5, Ch. 4, Sec. 4, Par. 11, pp. 780-781.

13. For related comments, see *On Liberty*, Ch. 2, Par. 12, p. 235.

14. See Brian Barry, "Justice and the Common Good," *Analysis* 21 (1961), p. 87.

15. See Gewirth, "Can Utilitarianism Justify and Moral Rights?," p. 154. But see Narveson, "Rights and Utilitarianism," p. 145, who denies that rights are abridged *too* easily.

16. Even if we limit 'everyone' to professional philosophers, we still will not achieve an accord about what is morally correct. It would be most surprising if Nozick and Sartorius were always in agreement about which actions were morally correct.

17. "Whewell on Moral Philosophy," p. 194.

18. See Smart and Williams, *Utilitarianism For and Against*, p. 6.

19. Even Rawls admits that his criticism of utilitarianism does not invalidate the system — he just wants to point out the consequences of utilitarianism as compared to the consequences of his own system. Rawls, "Social Unity and Primary Goods," p. 183. For related comments, see Leslie Mulholland, "Rights, Utilitarianism and the Conflation of Persons," *Journal of Philosophy* 83 (1986), p. 324.

20. See Samuel Scheffler, *The Rejection of Consequentialism* (Oxford: Clarendon Press, 1982), p. 9; and Williams's comments in Smart and Williams, *Utilitarianism For and Against*, p. 116. But see Hare, "Ethical Theory and Utilitarianism," p. 297. See also Nagel, *The View From Nowhere*, p. 192. Williams and Scheffler may be criticizing utilitarianism because it "requires agents to discount their own projects in a way which disregards the personal point of view." (Brink, p. 423) For an analysis of that claim, see David Brink's discussion in his "Utilitarian Morality and the Personal Point of View," *Journal of Philosophy* 83 (1986), pp. 417-438.

21. "Auguste Comte and Positivism," p. 337.

22. *Ibid.*, p. 306.

23. *Utilitarianism*, Ch. 5, Par. 2, p. 240.

24. "Auguste Comte and Positivism," p. 337.

For further discussion of this and related issues, see Adrian Piper, "Moral Theory and Moral Alienation," *Journal of Philosophy* 84 (1987), pp. 102-118; and Loren Lomasky, *Persons, Rights and Moral Community*, especially pp. 28 ff and 52 ff. Some of the criticisms offered here against Mill's critics seem appropriately directed against Lomasky's position as well.

25. Sidgwick, *The Methods of Ethics*, p. 489. See also J. D. Mabbott, "Punishment" in *Mill: Utilitarianism with Critical Essays*, p. 91.

26. For a general discussion of secrecy, see Sissela Bok, *Secrets* (New York: Pantheon Books, 1982).

27. *Considerations on Representative Government*, Ch. 2, Par. 21, p. 391.

28. *Ibid.* See also Rawls on the importance of publicity, especially with respect to the protection and enforcement of rights. John Rawls, "Kantian Constructionalism in Moral Theory," *Journal of Philosophy* 77 (1980), pp. 538 ff.

29. Even Sissela Bok countenances some governmental lying. See her *Lying* (New York: Vintage Books, 1978).

30. Donagan claims that "whether a moral theory is true or false depends on whether its implications for all possible world are true. Hence whether utilitarianism is true or false cannot depend on how the actual world is." Alan Donagan, "Is There a Credible Utilitarianism?" in *Contemporary Utilitarianism*, ed. Michael Bayles (Garden City: Anchor Books, 1968), p. 193.

31. Gray describes but does not advocate this position. See his "Indirect Utility and Fundamental Rights," p. 89. For a discussion of

rights as side constraints, see Nozick, *Anarchy, State and Utopia*, pp. 27 ff.

32. Since Dworkin, Feinberg, and a variety of other deontologists argue that rights are sometimes justifiably overridden, their theories would thus be invalidated.

33. Rawls argues, "If we require principles to hold in all possible worlds, and so allow the domain to include all conceivable possibilities, then moral theory may be condemned to futility from the start." Rawls, "The Independence of Moral Theory," p. 11.

34. Sidgwick, pp. 441-42.

35. *Ibid.*, p. 496.

36. This is Harrison's example.   Jonathan Harrison, "Utilitarianism, Universalization, and Our Duty to Be Just" in Gorovitz ed., *Mill: Utilitarianism with Critical Essays*, p. 156.

37. It is possible that because of the circumstances of the particular case there would be utility in society's doing this secretly. Further, it is possible that the utility produced by occasional secret performances (like this) would more than offset the fear produced by everyone's knowing about the possibility of (such) secret actions, although such a scenario would require extremely trustworthy and perspicacious leaders.

38. *Utilitarianism*, Ch. 5, Par. 37, p. 259.

39. See Gewirth, "Can Utilitarianism Justify Any Moral Rights?" p. 144. See also Hardin, "Morality Within the Limits of Reason," p. 76; T. M. Scanlon, "Rights, Goals and Fairness" in Jeremy Waldron ed., *Theories of Rights* (Oxford: Oxford University Press, 1984), p. 137.

40. *On Liberty*, Ch. 3, Par. 2, p. 261.

41. "Auguste Comte and Positivism," p. 290.

42. *Utilitarianism*, Ch. 2, Par. 23, p. 224.

43. "Auguste Comte and Positivism," pp. 322-23.

44. *Utilitarianism*, Ch. 3, Par. 11, p. 233.

45. For related somments, see Gewirth, "Can Utilitarianism Justify Any Moral Rights?" p. 152.

46. R. G. Frey argues that rights in *this* world are superfluous. See his *Interests and Rights: The Case Against Animals* (Oxford: Oxford University Press, 1980), especially the first chapter.

47. "Sedgwick's Discourse," p. 64.

48. John Dewey and James Tufts, *Ethics* (New York: Henry Holt and Co., 1914), p. 234.

49. *On Liberty*, Ch. 3, Par. 1, p. 260.

50. It is precisely because of these costs that we should not agree with Sumner that "a moral duty is . . . a morally justified conventional duty." See Sumner, *The Moral Foundation of Rights*, p. 135. If a morally justified conventional duty is a duty which society would be morally justified in enforcing (a duty whose enforcement would produce utility), then some 'duty candidates' would not be actual duties because their being enforced would not produce utility. For example, imperfect duties will presumably be non-actual duties because their enforcement by society would produce disutility.

51. For a more detailed discussion of the right to do wrong, see my "Hutcheson on External Rights." Numerous theorists support such a right. See Dworkin, "Taking Rights Seriously," p. 96; Jeremy Waldron, "A Right to Do Wrong," *Ethics* 92 (1981), p. 38. See also Sumner, *The Moral Foundation of Rights*, footnote on p. 48.

52. See Sumner on the difficulty of achieving pre-analytic agreement about which things really count as rights. *The Moral Foundation of Rights*, p. 50.

53. I do not believe that the moral right to do moral wrong is necessarily a contradiction in terms. However, in order for such a right not to be self-contradictory, we would have to be willing to deny that my having a moral right to X entails that my X-ing is morally permissible, assuming that X's being wrong entails that X is morally impermissible. For a discussion of these points and an argument as to why the definition of 'right' offered here seems to be better than the definition often used in which a right is merely viewed as involving one's deserving protection from *others*, see my "Conscience and the Right to Do Wrong."

54. R. G. Frey implies that standard act-utilitarians have difficulty in accounting for rights, even excluding the role of conscience described here. "The situation, then, is this: consequentialism prevents the act-utilitarian from allowing moral rights a hand in deciding the rightness of acts, but anything less than this will mean that the rights an act-utilitarian incorporates into his theory will be theoretically nonbasic, appendage rights." See R. G. Frey, "Act-Utilitarianism, Consequentialism and Moral Rights" in the collection he edits entitled *Utility and Rights* (Minneapolis: University of Minnesota Press, 1984), p. 66. However, as numerous theorists argue, an action's being wrong does not justify society's or others' interfering with the performance of that action. Thus, moral rights need not have a 'hand' in determining the rightness of an agent's action in order to have a function. Since rights are concerned with

freedoms from interference or punishment and since wrong actions may not deserve interference or punishment from others, even standard act-utilitarianism may not have the problem with rights which Frey implies that it does.

55. *A System of Logic*, Book 5, Ch. 7, Sec. 1, Par. 25, p. 818.

56. Again, the account of rights offered here differs from Sumner's account. Sumner argues that the "claim that we have the moral right to worship freely is equivalent to the claim that the legal right to do so is morally justified." See Sumner, *The Moral Foundation of Rights*, p. 149.

Often, one has legal rights to that to which one has moral rights. However, the two are not necessarily co-extensive. We must be careful to keep separate the contents of our moral rights and the contents of our morally justified legal rights. See my *Francis Hutcheson's Moral Theory*, Ch. 8, especially the discussion of imperfect and external rights.

CHAPTER TEN

The Value and Function of Rights

Insofar as one's possessing a moral right to X merely implies that one's X-ing should be free from external interference, Mill's system accounts for a variety of rights. Insofar as one's possessing a moral right to X not only implies that one should be free from external interference in one's X-ing but also that one's X-ing is morally permissible and is not a violation of Duty, Mill cannot account for the wealth of rights which we normally think people have. However, Mill can account for what I shall call "external rights" (which will be useful in *both* utilitarian and deontological systems). Before we examine external rights, however, we shall examine whether rights in themselves have value.

Rights As Producing Psychological Benefit

Many theorists claim that the possession of a right entails possessing a right against someone.[1] A world in which individuals have rights is a world in which there are conflicting interests — individuals have claims *against* other parties.[2] Rights are desirable, at least in part, because our possessing rights makes us more secure that our interests will be respected should there be a conflict of wills — we believe that our having rights is effective in reducing the probability that others will successfully deprive us of what we should have.

Suppose that rights did not either make us more secure that our interests would be respected or, in fact, make our interests more likely to be respected.[3] Would they still have value?

We imagine two societies, one in which the members have rights and the other in which the members do not. If the members in the first society are not more secure that their interests will be respected and if, in fact, those interests are not more likely to be respected, would the possession of rights nonetheless be beneficial? Some suggest that the answer is 'Yes'.

Let us consider Nowheresville, a town in which the inhabitants are as attractive and virtuous as humanly possible.[4] In that town, individuals have moral duties but do not have any rights. People still deserve things in that society. However, desert operates much differently in Nowheresville than it does in our society, since people there cannot claim to have a right to what they deserve. Instead, they may try to get what they want in other ways, e.g., resort to force and trickery.[5]

Certainly, this world is not particularly inviting. If people cannot make righteous demands against each other and must instead resort to trickery and deceit to get what they deserve, one might not want to live in such a place. However, there might be another city, Nowheresville$_1$, in which people *could* make demands. Unfairly treated individuals might not be able to claim their due *by right*, but they could complain just as loudly as anyone else if someone had wronged them.[6]

Nowheresville is a town in which individuals cannot demand what they deserve. Nowheresville$_1$ is a town in which such demands can be made, but not as a matter of right. Neither of these towns should be confused with the type of town in which some people have rights and other similarly situated people do not.[7] This latter society is greatly offensive in large part because of the *inequality* which obtains there. There are haves and have-nots with respect to something as fundamental as rights.

Nowheresville is a society in which there is no conception of rights — there are no haves and have-nots with respect to rights. However, the question here is whether Nowheresville is not merely less offensive than a society in which only some have rights, but is not offensive at all.

Before we can decide whether Nowheresville is completely inoffensive, we must establish whether it is plausible to believe that people there could only get what they deserved by deceit and trickery. We consider the strident voices of certain members of our society who want to proclaim that certain sexual practices (performed by *others* who are consenting adults) are immoral. The protesters' fervor is not based on their having been deprived of something which was their due. Instead, they are claiming that the practices in question are morally impermissible. Yet, if these individuals can stand up and complain loudly about these matters, one wonders why they would be unwilling to speak loudly when someone else had not given them their due.

We consider the bigot who objects to certain religous practices. He is not protesting loudly and vigorously because he has a right to these religious groups' not practicing their religions. Indeed, he is assertive *despite their rights to practice their religion.*

Perhaps Nowheresvillians would not loudly inveigh against others who had failed to fulfill their duties. However, that forbearance would not be due to their lacking rights. The citizens of the sister city Nowheresville₁ might loudly inveigh against wrongdoers, perhaps not by claiming, "You owe me that," but rather by claiming, "You have a duty to do that," or even, "You have a duty to give me that."

We can easily understand why it is objectionable that some individuals are accorded rights when other relevantly similar individuals are not. In that kind of society, some individuals can make certain kinds of claims which other relevantly similar individuals cannot. However, it is not at all clear that Nowheresville will have the negative attribute often ascribed to it, *viz.*, that no one will be able to make any demands of any kind.

Indeed, Nowheresville may have a positive attribute which our society lacks. Since individuals in Nowheresville do not have rights, they may be less likely to view their own and others' actions solely in terms of how those actions affect their own particular interests. They may be more likely instead to view their own and others' actions in terms of whether those actions will be in accord with the interests of society as a whole. These individuals could still praise and blame each other. They simply would not use their own interests as the *ground* of those praisings and blamings.

Mill disapproves of each person's thinking in terms of his own interests. "[E]very person who lives by any useful work, should be habituated to regard himself not as an individual working for his private benefit, but as a public functionary; and his wages, of whatever sort, not as the remuneration or purchase money of his labor, which should be given freely, but as the provision made by society to enable him to carry it on, and to replace the materials and products which have been consumed in the process."[8]

Indeed, Mill sees this change in attitude (where people seek to promote the interests of society) as quite important. "Until laborers and employees perform the work of industry in the spirit in which soldiers perform that of an army, *industry will never be moralized*, and military life will remain, what in spite of the anti-social character of its direct object, it has hitherto been — *the chief school of moral co-operation* [my italics]."[9] Nowheresville might be a place in which people had this community spirit.

On the interpretation of Mill's system presented in this book, all (foreseeably) disutility-producing actions are wrong. Insofar as one's moral rights are limited to those actions which are morally permissible, one could not have a right to perform a (foreseeably) disutility-producing action. This sense of a 'right' corresponds to one of the senses of a 'right' discussed by Mill, *viz.*, the sense in which one's having a right to *X* implies that one does not have an obligation to refrain from *X*-ing. Using this sense of a 'right', critics are correct that the only kind of right for which Mill can offer an account is a right to do that which is (foreseeably) utility-producing. Since in Mill's ideal society Duty would require that one perform actions which produced a great deal of utility, his envisioned society might look something like Nowheresville, a society in which there were no or very few rights.

Yet, we must be very careful before trying to establish that rights have value by arguing that we would prefer to live in our own world than in Nowheresville. For example, one might claim that she would rather live in our world because she would be happier and more secure here than she would be in Nowheresville. However, we then would not know whether she was choosing our world because she could have rights in it or because she would be happier and more secure in it. Further, we would not know whether she would be judging what would make her happier and more secure in light of her current attitudes or in light of the attitudes which she would have were she living in that society. Precisely because Mill links one's duty to the society in which one lives, most people would *not* feel that Mill's ideal society made unfair demands, *were they indeed living in that society.*

In order for our choosing our own world over Nowheresville to be indicative of some value which the possession of rights has:

a.   we will have to choose our own world even when the people of Nowheresville are as happy and secure as we are, or

b.   we will have to show why some of the happiness and security which we have and Nowheresvillians lack is securable *only* through the possession of rights.

Mill makes clear that one can have duties to perform or refrain from performing certain actions (e.g., making charitable contributions), even if no one has rights to the performance or non-performance of those actions. I might have a duty to produce utility without someone else's having a right to my performing utility-producing actions. I may be blameworthy for not having promoted utility, even if no one else has a right to my promoting utility. Just as I am blameworthy for not having fulfilled my duties to myself and yet I do not have a right to the performance of those actions,[10] I am sometimes blameworthy for not having promoted utility even if no one has a right to my so acting.

The point here *is not* that rights are superfluous, since (in current systems and practices) rights seem to have a variety of functions that duties do not. The point here *is* that moral systems may be able to do without rights or, at least, without a wealth of rights. We can account for many of the functions of (claim) rights by appropriately specifying the contents of duties, and we can account for some (if not all) of the other functions by positing a system of external rights, a term which will be defined later in this chapter.

A complete account of rights is beyond the scope of this chapter or this book. It is hoped nonetheless that the present account will contribute to an understanding of (claim) rights and how they function within moral systems.

The Right to Do Wrong

The above discussion assumes that one can only have a right to do that which is morally permissible. That assumption is by no means uncontroversial. Some argue that a failure to recognize a right to do wrong will eventually cause us to have very few rights.[11] Others make an even stronger claim by arguing that the right to do wrong is a necessary part of any system of rights.[12]

If indeed one can have a right to X even if one's X-ing would be morally impermissible, then Mill's claiming that we have a duty to promote utility cannot be used to show why Mill cannot account for a variety of rights. The notion of a 'right' in which one can have a right to do wrong corresponds to the second sense of 'right' discussed by Mill — that a right to X implies that external *but not necessarily internal* interference would be inappropriate, i.e., that it would be wrong for the State or society or others to interfere with the exercise of that right.

External Rights

At this point, a new term, 'external rights', will be introduced.[13] An external right corresponds to the second sense of a 'right' mentioned above. If an agent has an external right to X, then not only will the agent be entitled to X without external interference, he will sometimes be entitled to aid from others. The only difference between rights and external rights is that an agent will have neither external nor internal sanctions appropriately imposed against her for the exercise of her rights, whereas the agent will have no external sanctions but may have internal sanctions (feelings of guilt or regret) appropriately imposed against her for the exercise of her external rights.

There are distinct advantages to talking about external rights. Before those advantages are addressed, one point must be made about what external rights are *not*.

Berlin discusses two types of liberty, where "negative" liberty is the freedom *from* the interference of others and "positive" liberty is the freedom *to* act, e.g., in accord with reason.[14] An external right is neither a positive nor a negative liberty. An external right not only involves the absence of interference from others, but also may have a 'positive' aspect — one's having an external right may sometimes involve one's having a claim against others for assistance. This 'positive' aspect is *not* what is meant by positive liberties. "Positive" liberties are used to justify one's being forced to act against one's current goals and desires if, for example, they are not in accord with reason and are thus unacceptable.

Insofar as a negative liberty involves a freedom from the interference of all punishers, a moral negative liberty would involve the freedom from the interference of others *and* from the interference of one's own conscience. A moral external right, however, only involves the freedom from the interference of others.

Mill offers two definitions of a right — one which involves an agent's not having a duty to refrain from performing the action which she has a right to perform and one which involves the absence of appropriate interference with the performance of that action. If these definitions are not co-extensive and if an agent might have a moral right to *X* on one account and not on the other, it would not be better (at least for the sake of clarity) to have different terms for these distinct meanings of a 'right'.

There are advantages in addition to clarity to restricting a 'right' (*simpliciter*) to only one of the meanings mentioned above. Traditionally, we make a tri-partite distinction between those actions which we are required to perform, those actions which we are permitted although not required to perform, and those actions which we are prohibited from performing. We can make this same tri-partite distinction in terms of the appropriateness of the imposition of punishment. Those actions which we are required to perform are those actions the not-doing of which deserves punishment. Those actions which we are permitted but not required to perform are those actions the doing or not-doing of which deserves no punishment. Those actions which we are prohibited from performing are those actions the doing of which deserves punishment.

Within this schema, at least traditionally, we have rights to perform those actions which are in the first two categories. However, a wrong action is one which deserves punishment, if only by conscience. If we talk about a right to do wrong, we will no longer be able to fit rights neatly into this schema.

The problem here is *not* that we cannot have co-extensive definitions of a 'right' if, on the one hand, we talk about one's not having a duty to refrain and, on the other hand, we talk about the absence of appropriate punishment. Indeed, insofar as we define rights in terms of permissible actions and permissible actions in terms of:

a.   actions which we have no duty to refrain from performing, *or*
b.   actions the performance of which deserves no punishment,

we would expect that either definition would be appropriate for a 'right'. If that is true, however, then we should suspect that right-to-do-wrong theorists have overlooked something important.

Critics note that a right to do wrong involves the permissibility of one's performing the impermissible.[15] Certainly, that paradox should be avoided if at all possible.

When we talk about one's possessing a right as involving the inappropriateness of external interference, we are too vague about who may not appropriately interfere. This vagueness has led to an important misunderstanding about rights.

Suppose that a group of youngsters formed a club. One of the rules of the club was that a member might swear as much as he wanted and that no sanctions would be appropriately imposed against him for doing so. One day, Ms. Smith happens to be attending one of the club meetings and her son swears. She reprimands him. He says that he has a right to swear. She responds that the club's granting him a right to swear implies that no sanctions may be imposed against him *by the club*. However, *she* is not prevented from imposing a punishment merely because the club has granted this right. By the same token, had the club granted its members a right to murder, this would not have prevented society or the State from appropriately imposing sanctions against a member for having committed a murder.

When one has a right to X, one should be free from the interference of all *relevant* punishers. Insofar as a club gives one a right to X, one should be free from interference from the club, but not necessarily from others. When one has a moral right, one should be free from all relevant punishers, i.e., law, public opinion, and *conscience* (on Mill's account). Insofar as one should be punished by one's conscience for exercising one's 'right' to do wrong, one should not be free from *all* relevant punishers. Thus, if it is correct to define one's possessing a right as one's deserving to be free from all *relevant* punishers and if all moral wrongs should be punished by at least one of the relevant punishers, *viz.*, conscience, then one cannot have a moral right to do moral wrong.[16]

On the account here, we can define rights *either* in terms of one's not having an obligation to act in a certain way *or* in terms of one's not deserving punishment for exercising one's rights. At the same time, we can talk about certain kinds of actions, the performance of which does not deserve the imposition of *external* sanctions but may deserve the imposition of *internal* sanctions.

Deontological Criticisms of Utilitarian Rights Theory

Basically, deontologists make two criticisms of utilitarian theories of rights:

a.   utilitarian theories do not capture all of the rights which should be captured, and
b.   utilitarian theories cannot give an adequate account of the ways in which rights function in moral deliberation and argument.[17]

Insofar as one claims that utilitarianism does not capture all of the rights which a moral system *should* capture, one should provide a list of rights which should be captured or, at least, some rights which utilitarianism does not capture. One further should provide some rationale to establish why those rights must be captured.

It is *not* claimed here that utilitarians protect all rights which deontologists protect. It simply is not clear whether there are any rights within deontological systems which are not also protected within utilitarian systems. Many of the rights which deontologists claim that utilitarianism does not protect are protected by utilitarians because of the hidden costs of abridging rights. Critics too quickly dismiss that general insecurity will be produced if innocents are punished. Further, it is not easy to perform actions without anyone else's finding out about them. Many people have been severely disappointed because their secret actions became public, as certain former presidents might testify.

In many of the cases in which utilitarianism would clearly dictate that the rights be abridged — those cases in which 'the heavens would fall' unless the rights were abridged, most deontologists would also agree that the rights should be abridged. Thus, it is not clear that citizens of a utilitarian society would have markedly fewer external rights or rights (if we can exclude the role of conscience when talking about rights) than citizens in a deontological society.

Perhaps it is true that some deontologists would protect some rights which utilitarians would not protect. For example, maximizing act-utilitarians may reject that one has a right to save one's own life at the cost of five other lives.[18]

Since Mill is not a maximizing utilitarian, the above example would have to be modified in order for it to be applicable. (He would argue that one's sacrificing one's life to save the lives of others would be meritorious rather than obligatory.) Nonetheless, suppose that the example could be appropriately modified so that even Mill would have to call the sacrifice a duty. What would follow from that?

The right to save one's own life at the expense of others' is a right which many of us feel that we have. However, our intuitions may be in need of correction on this point. Further, not only consequentialist systems make demands which are extremely difficult to meet. Deontological systems may also be open to that charge. Some argue *on deontological grounds* that we may have a duty to give so much aid to others that we would thereby secure our own deaths.[19] Finally, it may be that utilitarians have a external right, not a right (*simpliciter*), to save their own lives at the expense of others' — their doing so is *not* something for which they would deserve to be subject to *external* sanctions.

Deontologists are taking a risk when they impugn utilitarianism by pointing out that it does not protect all of the rights which deontological systems protect. The deontologists may be guilty of miscalculating the relevant utilities. Or, the deontologists may merely be pointing out that deontological systems protect too many rights rather than that utilitarian systems protect too few rights. Or, the deontologists may conveniently be forgetting that some of the rights which they charge utilitarianism with being unable to protect *are also not protected within various deontological systems.*

Mill argues that "the strongest of all arguments against the interference of the public with purely personal conduct, is that when it does interfere, the odds are that it interferes wrongly, and in the wrong place."[20] There are a variety of external rights which would be protected by Mill's utilitarian system. Even if Mill cannot protect an "adequate" number of *rights*, he may be able to protect more than enough actions from external interference or punishment.

On The Functions Of Rights

It is somewhat difficult to say whether utilitarians cannot give an adequate account of how rights function. Since some theorists ascribe to rights certain functions and other theorists ascribe to rights other functions, we will need some way to determine which functions rights must perform.

For example, a utilitarian theory will be unable to account for rights insofar as they are supposed to be the *foundation* of the system.[21] By the same token, a rights-based theory cannot account for the promotion of human interests or the promotion of human happiness insofar as either is supposed to be the *foundation* of the system.[22]

The claim here is neither that morality *must be* right-based nor that it *cannot* be right-based. The claim here is merely that when theorists argue that utilitarians cannot account for some of the functions of rights, they must not support that claim by arguing that rights must be the basis of that system. Were that the case, many moral theories would be ruled out of court, e.g., interest-based theories, duty-based theories, etc.

By the same token, it would be question-begging to rule rights-based theories out of court. Here, we will examine the 'appropriate' functions of rights without assuming that they either must or cannot be the foundation of the moral system.

Rights as Grounds of Duties

One might not believe that rights must be the foundation of any valid moral system, but nonetheless believe that duties must be based on rights.[23] If rights must be the *grounds* of duties, then Mill's utilitarianism does not adequately account for rights, since he claims that duties and rights are both grounded on the principle of utility.

Yet, it is not clear what is gained by requiring that rights ground duties. Further, there are underappreciated costs associated with setting up one's system that way. ·

Duties limit one's range of action — either one must refrain from doing something one might have wanted to do or one must do something one might not have wanted to do. (True. Some duties are not at all psychologically burdensome because we want to fulfill them. Those will not be discussed here because they are irrelevant to the issue at hand.) On some deontological accounts, one's range of activities is limited because the rightholder will thereby benefit,[24] whereas on utilitarian accounts one's range is limited because society as a whole will benefit.

The existence of rights suggests that people in society have conflicting interests. There are winners and losers. It is bad enough that there must be winners and losers, but it is still worse that a loser loses because it is in the *winner's* interest that he lose rather than in society's interest that he lose. At least the loser should have the consolation that his losing promotes society's good rather than merely some other individual's good. If one wishes to have a cohesive, amiable society, exactly the *wrong* message is conveyed when one is told that one should fulfill one's duty because the *right-holder's* rather than *society's* good will thereby be promoted.

Were there really a net benefit to basing duties on rights, utilitarians might offer a system *in which rights were based on the principle of utility and duties were based on those rights.*[25] In such a system, rights would be fundamental in the sense that duties would be based on them, but not foundational in the sense required by some deontologists. It is not at all clear that utilitarians cannot offer an account in which rights perform all of their 'proper' functions.

The Extra Margin Of Protection

Perhaps the most frequently made criticism of utilitarian theories of rights is that they do not adequately protect rights.[26] Such a criticism implicitly assumes a standard which indicates when rights may appropriately be abridged. Understandably, critics have not specifically stated or even described that standard.[27]

We must be careful to distinguish between obvious costs and hidden costs. The utilitarian believes that the hidden costs must also be considered before rights can be abridged. Mill argues that in order to see the effects of a particular action "[w]e must look at [the action] multiplied, and in large masses,"[28] precisely because he understands that some of the effects of a right-abridgement would be difficult to discern were we to consider that abridgement in isolation.

The claim here is *not* that the hidden costs of overriding rights would always prevent their being overridden. The claim here is *not even* that the exercise of rights within utilitarian systems would be protected from outside interference as often as would the exercise of rights within deontological systems. Neither deontologists nor utilitarians are specific enough about when rights would be protected and when they would be overridden for us to be able to make such a determination. It should be noted, however, that one of the greatest defenders of liberty, *viz.*, Mill, defends the protection of liberty on utilitarian grounds.[29]

Further, if deontologists protect rights even when the utilities (*including* the hidden costs) dictate otherwise, then those rights are being protected at disutility-producing times. Deontologists would then be open to two questions:

1.   why should we protect rights when their protection would be disutility-producing?
2.   what would happen to general happiness and security were people to realize that the interests of some are sometimes furthered, even when the interests of everyone are not furthered by that protection?

Cost/Benefit Analyses of Rights and External Rights

The Nowheresville thought-experiment demonstrates that some theorists attach a sacred aura to the protection and preservation of rights even if we could secure the objects of the rights in some other way which would not involve our having rights. In Nowheresville, people can do whatever we can do in our society. The only difference is that we have rights and they do not. Nowheresvillians feel every bit as secure as we do. Indeed, they may feel even more secure than we do, because people might help each other more often in that society than people do in our society. (People there are at least as compassionate and helpful as are people in our society.[30])

It is by no means clear why rights are necessary if they do not secure or assure some Object which we would not otherwise have. Mill believes that the possession of rights promotes security. He thus offers a *utilitarian* reason for the protection of rights — he is not offering a reason to believe in the intrinsic value of rights.

If my having a right to an object implicitly promotes the attitude that my interests are different from and possibly more important than other people's interests, then rights in and of themselves are somewhat undesirable. Unless we can show that the possession of rights secures advantages which we would not otherwise have, rights are actually undesirable, since it would be difficult to show that (*ceteris paribus*) it is better to have a society in which members view their own interests as more valuable than, rather than as valuable as, those of other members.

When we talk about rights as securing advantages which we could not otherwise have, we are making a consequentialist argument. We are not talking about the rights, *per se*. We are talking about considerations which a utilitarian would take into account, since we are talking about the *benefits* of rights.

Deontologists cannot discredit utilitarianism by saying that it yields undesirable consequences. For example, utilitarianism is not open to the charge that, by not sufficiently protecting rights, it will cause much insecurity and unhappiness. Such a criticism merely implies that the action which utilitarianism would allegedly allow (abridging a right) would not in truth be allowed.

Deontologists can discredit utilitarianism in the eyes of some by showing that it does not protect as many rights as deontological systems do. These people would presumably be those who would benefit from the existence of the right, even though the existence of the right would not benefit society as a whole.

Even the stronger line of attack, *viz.*, that utilitarianism does not guarantee that moral agents will have *any* rights, does not invalidate utilitarianism. Utilitarianism will protect rights for as long as the possession of rights promotes security and well-being. Utilitarianism will not protect rights merely for the sake of protecting rights. It is not clear, however, that a right in and of itself is valuable. What does seem clear is that the object of the right is valuable.

It is not at all clear that rights have a necessary place within morality. If a moral system can somehow account for all of the functions that rights perform without making use of the notion of rights, then we would not only have a moral system, but we would have as 'good' a moral system as any rights-based system. Indeed, *ceteris paribus*, a moral system based on rights seems 'worse' than a moral system based on a common goal, e.g., promoting general utility. The former engenders selfishness in people while the latter engenders impartiality in people. Insofar as moral systems are designed to promote peace and harmony, the latter system (*ceteris paribus*) would seem to be preferable.

When we are trying to decide whether utilitarianism protects too few rights or whether deontological systems protect too many rights, we should discuss the costs and protections of various external rights or, in general, the costs and benefits of the protection of the Objects of rights rather than talk about the protection of rights, *per se.* Too many theorists attach a significance to rights which goes far beyond what is appropriate. Particular rights may not be significant or desirable, except insofar as they secure or assure benefits. Even the possession of rights in general may not be intrinsically valuable.

The notion of an external right has been employed in this chapter to help utilitarians explain how they can account for the protection of a variety of liberties while nonetheless admitting that those liberties might involve morally impermissible actions. This notion is helpful for both *deontological and consequentialist theories.* When Mill argues that we do not call an action wrong unless it ought to be punished by law, public opinion, or conscience, he is not offering a definition which is peculiar to utilitarianism. He is offering a definition which deontologists might also adopt (although they might utilize a different standard to determine when sanctions should be imposed).

Deontologists and utilitarians face analogous problems. According to many deontologists, there are some actions for which the agent should not be held responsible by society or by individuals other than the agent herself which, nonetheless, *are wrong to perform.* Deontologists must also decide what to say about individuals who waste their money without ever contributing to charity. These theorists must also find a way to say that one has a right never to give charity in the sense that one should not be punished *by others or by society* for failing to donate, but not in the sense that one should be free from punishment *by one's own conscience* for always failing to donate. The notion of a external right is not merely a notion which utilitarians can employ to deflect the attacks of deontologists. An external right is a notion required by *any* moral system which holds:

1.   some actions which one should perform and should feel guilty for failing to perform are nonetheless not deserving of punishment *by others or by society,*

2.   a moral right entails that one does not deserve to be punished by *any* of the 'relevant' punishers, and

3.   an action is morally wrong if it should be punished by law, public opinion, or conscience.

The notion of a external right allows both deontologists and consequentialists to admit that some immoral actions do not deserve to be punished by others or by society, and yet deny that one can have a moral right to do moral wrong.

There is an additional point to consider. One of the points emphasized here is that even if others' or society's punishing an action would be inappropriate because the punishment itself would be counterproductive, the action might nonetheless be wrong. Deontologists might also want to prevent society and individuals other than the agent herself from imposing punishments if imposing those punishments would be counterproductive. Nonetheless, deontologists would also want to argue that even if the agent does not deserve to have *external* sanctions imposed against her, her action might nonetheless have been immoral. By adopting the position suggested here with respect both to external rights and to 'relevant punishers', deontologists can talk about an inseparable connection between immorality and the appropriateness of punishment *without* claiming that *external* sanctions should always be imposed regardless of the effect those punishments would have.

Conclusion

Mill argues that some pleasures are intrinsically superior to others. He includes the inherent quality of pleasures in utilitarian calculations, although he denies that the higher pleasures should be pursued even to the detriment of the interests of humankind.

Mill is an act-utilitarian who believes that the utility of humankind should be promoted. He is interested in evaluating both attitudes and actions according to the principle of utility. However, Mill is nervous about talking about secondary moral principles as 'mere rules of thumb', because he fears that doing so would result in too many inappropriate rule-breakings. Nonetheless, Mill is quite clear that rules should not be followed if doing so would clearly be disutility-producing.

By distinguishing between his theory of moral worth and his theory of moral obligation, Mill provides a system which maintains the utilitarian ideals and also does not impose 'unfair' demands on individuals. He can talk about the maximization of the happiness of humankind as the aim and goal of morality without imposing on individuals the duty to maximize utility on every occasion. By linking the standard of obligation to (some of) the currently existing attitudes of society, he can assure both that utility will be promoted and that individuals will not be subject to demands that are too strict. Further, he will not have to worry about a backlash, either with respect to the theory's acceptance or with respect to its practice.

If Mill wants to be consistent, then he must claim that all actions which do not (foreseeably) produce a sufficient amount of utility are wrong, although not necessarily blameworthy by others. Sometimes, because of existing circumstances, an agent should only be punished by her conscience for her wrong action. Even well-intended actions should be punished by conscience, although sometimes only slightly.

Mill argues that society's imposing sanctions against certain immoral actions is sometimes impermissible. He believes that 'the carrot is sometimes better than the stick' — that rewarding right actions is sometimes more efficacious than punishing wrong ones. However, that argument is relevant to whether external, *not internal*, sanctions can appropriately be imposed. If Mill wishes to be a type of act-utilitarian who claims that all (foreseeably) disutility-producing actions are morally wrong, and if wrongness is to be defined in terms of blameworthiness by law, public opinion, or conscience, then Mill cannot argue that some (foreseeably) disutility-producing actions deserve *no* punishment, not even from conscience.

Mill's ambivalence with respect to whether actions should be evaluated in terms of their actual or foreseeable conseqences reflects the ambivalence shared by many theorists with respect to that same question. To some extent, this problem can be resolved by appealing to those consequences which a reasonable person would have foreseen. However, these problems cannot be resolved completely that way.

Suppose that an agent acts exactly as a reasonable, benevolent agent would have acted, *given the information which she has.* However, suppose further that a reasonable agent would have had more or better information. The action performed is morally wrong, although the agent acted quite reasonably and quite benevolently.

Mill's method of distinguishing between the moral assessment of actions and the moral assessment of characters is helpful in this kind of case. He would argue that the action was wrong because a reasonable person would have known that it would be disutility-producing. However, the agent's character is praiseworthy because her action manifested the good character traits of reasonableness and benevolence.

If we distinguish between pangs of guilt and pangs of regret, then we can avoid at least some of the problems in maintaining that agents should be punished by conscience for their reasonable, well-intended actions. A benevolent person would feel at least somewhat badly for having produced a bad result. His feeling badly would not be *deserved*, as it would have been had he acted negligently. Rather, he would feel badly because a benevolent person would simply be the sort of person who would be sorry that unhappiness had resulted from one of his actions.

If utilitarians adopt a system like Mill's, they can account for imperfect duties and supererogatory actions and can also claim that individuals should be concerned about who receives their charity. The agent who gives his money to useless charities should feel guilty for doing so. However, in such a case it is the agent's conscience and not the State or society that should impose sanctions.

Mill, at least in principle, can show that utilitarian societies will protect a multitude of liberties. He offers convincing arguments which show why society will protect many of the liberties which deontologists claim will not be protected. His insoluble problem connected with rights involves showing how a person should not be punished, even by herself, for exercising her right to do wrong. If Mill does not have to worry about the sanctions imposed by conscience when discussing rights, then Mill *can* account for rights.

Perhaps, though, this result is not so damning. Even when we say that people do have the right not to give charity, we tend to feel that they should give it and that their consciences should bother them, at least a little, for not giving it. Mill's system accounts for our feeling that people should feel at least a little guilt or regret for not promoting utility. At the same time, his system accounts for why society should neither force nor allow others to force agents to perform certain utility-producing actions.

The notion of external rights offered here is important because it allows theorists to avoid the conceptual confusion involved in a moral right to do moral wrong. If rights may be defined in terms of permissible actions *or* in terms of the absence of appropriate sanctions from any of the *relevant* sources, then theorists cannot talk about a moral right to do moral wrong.

Yet, theorists can quite consistently talk about morally wrong actions which deserve punishment *only* by conscience. The notion of a external right allows theorists to explain why the exercise of what is normally called a right would be morally wrong and why nonetheless no one *external to the agent* should interfere with the exercise of that 'right'.

Critics are correct that there are numerous problems associated with Mill's moral system. Some of these problems are due to Mill's not having been sufficiently clear. Other problems, however, are associated with moral systems in general. Critics do not seem to appreciate that Mill, by relying on conscience so heavily, can help to explain and solve many of the problems which not only plague his own system, but which plague moral theory in general.

NOTES

1. See Gewirth, "Can Utilitarianism Justify Any Moral Rights?" p. 144, and Joel Feinberg, "The Nature and Value of Rights" in *Rights*, p. 91. See also Richard Brandt, "Utilitarianism and Moral Rights," *Canadian Journal of Philosophy* 14 (1984), p. 2. Sandel offers an analogous claim. "For there to be justice, there must be the possibility of conflicting claims." See his *Liberalism and the Limits of Justice*, p. 50.

2. See Carl Wellman, *A Theory of Rights* (Totowa: Rowman and Allanheld, 1985), p. 10.

3. For related comments, see Allen Buchanan, "What's So Special About Rights?" *Social Philosophy and Policy* 2 (1984), pp. 61-83.

4. The example is Feinberg's. See "The Nature and Value of Rights," p. 78.

5. *Ibid.*, p. 84.

6. See William Nelson, "On the Alleged Importance of Moral Rights," *Ratio* 18 (1976), p. 150.

7. See Richard Wasserstrom, "Rights, Human Rights, and Racial Discrimination," *Journal of Philosophy* 61 (1964), p. 640.

8. "Auguste Comte and Positivism," p. 340.

9. *Ibid.*, p. 341.

10. Rolf Sartorius claims that one can have rights against oneself and that, further, such rights may pose a problem for utilitarianism. See his "Utilitarianism, Rights and Duties to Self," *American Philosophical Quarterly* 22 (1985), pp. 241-249.

In many deontological and consequential systems, imperfect duties are not correlated with rights. Thus, the fact that one has duties to oneself would not entail that one had rights against oneself. See Sartorius' argument on pg. 247. Certainly, one would need much argument to establish that moral systems must countenance the possibility, much less the actuality, of one's having rights against oneself. Indeed, Mill discusses this very question in "Austin on Jurisprudence," pp. 178-179.

11. See Waldron, "A Right To Do Wrong," p. 55.

12. Theodore Benditt, *Rights* (Totowa: Rowman and Littlefield, 1982), pp. 39-40.

13. I am borrowing the notion of an external right from Hutcheson. For a discussion of his view of external rights, see my "Hutcheson on External Rights," *Philosophical Studies* 49 (1986), pp. 263-269.

14. See Isaiah Berlin, *Two Concepts of Liberty* (Oxford: Oxford University Press, 1958).

15. See, e.g., William Galston, "On the Right to Do Wrong: A Response to Waldron," *Ethics* 93 (1983), pp. 320-324.

16. For a discussion of 'relevant punishers', see my "Conscience and the Right to Do Wrong."

17. See Benditt, p. 20. For related comments, see Jeremy Waldron, "Rights in Conflict," *Ethics* 99 (1989), pp. 503-519.

18. See Derek Parfit, "Innumerate Ethics," *Philosophy and Public Affairs* 7, p. 288.

19. See, e.g., Richard Watson, "Reason and Morality in a World of Limited Food," reprinted in *Applying Ethics*, Barry ed., pp. 352-357.

20. *On Liberty*, Ch. 4, Par. 12, p. 283.

21. Mackie argues that "there cannot be an acceptable moral theory that is not right-based."J. L. Mackie, "Can There Be A Right-Based Moral Theory?" in Waldron ed., *Theories of Rights*, p. 176.

22. Raz implies that morality *cannot* be right-based. "It may be claimed that by defining rights as based on the well-being of individuals I have ruled out of court the view that morality is right-based." However, he would deny that he is arguing that rights are not fundamental, claiming that "the view that rights are fundamental can be explained in terms of [his] proposed account" in which rights are based on interests. J. Raz, "On the Nature of Rights," *Mind* 93 (1984), p. 213.

Raz is able to account for the fundamental nature of rights because of the way in which he defines 'fundamental'. "A right is a morally fundamental right if it is justified on the ground that it serves the right-holder's interest in having that right in as much as the value of that interest is considered to be of ultimate value, i.e., in as much as the value of that interest does not derive from some other interest of the right-holder or of other persons." Thus, on Raz's account, rights are fundamental in the sense that they are very important. They are also fundamental in the sense that they are based on certain kinds of interests. However, rights are not fundamental in the sense of being foundational — they do not provide the base upon which the moral system is erected. Indeed, Raz seems to realize this, since he admits that his account "makes it highly unlikely that morality is right-based." (p. 214.) For reasons to believe that moral theories are not right-based, see Raz's "Right-Based Moralities" in Waldron ed., *Theories of Rights.*

23. See Gewirth, "Why Rights Are Indispensable," *Mind* 95 (1986), p. 333.

24. *Ibid.*, p. 334.

25. For related comments, see Raz, "On the Nature of Rights," p. 199.

26. See David Lyons, "Utility and Rights" in Waldron ed., *Theories of Rights*, p. 113. But see Richard Flathman, "Moderating Rights," *Social Philosophy and Policy* 1 (1984), p. 162.

27. For example, Dworkin only gives us a rough idea of what that standard is when he argues, "There would be no point in the boast that we respect individual rights unless that involved some sacrifice, and the sacrifice in question must be that we give up whatever marginal benefits our country would receive from overriding these rights when they prove inconvenient." Dworkin, "Taking Rights Seriously," p. 100.

28. "Whewell on Moral Philosophy," p. 181.

29. See my "Mill and the Utility of Liberty."

30. See Feinberg, "The Nature and Value of Rights," p. 78.

WORKS CITED

Alexander, Larry (1985), "Pursuing the Good — Indirectly," *Ethics* 95, pp. 315-332.

Arneson, Richard (1980), "Mill Versus Paternalism," *Ethics* 90, pp. 470-489.

Aristotle, *Nicomachean Ethics*.

Bain, Alexander (1859), *The Emotions and the Will* (London: Parker).

Barnes, Gerald (1971), "Utilitarianisms," *Ethics* 82, pp. 56-64.

Barry, Brian (1961), "Justice and the Common Good," *Analysis* 21, pp. 86-90.

Barry, Vincent ed. (1985), *Applying Ethics* 2nd ed. (Belmont: Wadsworth Publishing).

Bayles, Michael ed. (1968), *Contemporary Utilitarianism* (Garden City: Anchor Books).

Benditt, Theodore (1982), *Rights* (Totowa: Rowman and Littlefield).

Bentham, Jeremy (1789) *An Introduction to the Principles of Morals*, Introduction Laurence LaFleur (New York: Hafner Publishing Co., 1948).

_____ (1825), *The Rationale of Reward* in *The Works of Jeremy Bentham*, John Bowring ed. (New York: Russell and Russell, 1962), Vol. 2.

Berger, Fred (1979), "John Stuart Mill on Justice and Fairness," in Cooper ed., *New Essays on John Stuart Mill and Utilitarianism*, pp. 115-136.

_____ (1984), *Happiness, Justice and Freedom: The Moral and Political Philosophy of John Stuart Mill* (Berkeley: University of California Press).

Bergstrom, Lars (1977), "Utilitarianism and future mistakes," *Theoria* 43, pp. 84-102.

Berlin, Isaiah (1958), *Two Concepts of Liberty* (Oxford: Oxford University Press).

Bok, Sissela (1978), *Lying* (New York: Vintage Books).

_____ (1982), *Secrets* (New York: Pantheon Books).

Bradley, F. H. (1876), "Pleasure for Pleasure's Sake" in *Ethical Studies*, Introduction Ralph Ross (Indianapolis: Bobbs-Merrill, 1951), pp. 29-80.

Brandt, Richard (1979), *A Theory of the Good and the Right* (Oxford: Clarendon Press).

———— (1982), "Two Concepts of Utility" in Miller ed., *The Limits of Utilitarianism*, pp. 169-185.

———— (1983), "Concept of a Moral Right," *Journal of Philosophy* 80, pp. 29-45.

———— (1984), "Utilitarianism and Moral Rights," *Canadian Journal of Philosophy* 14, pp. 1-19.

———— (1988), "Fairness to Indirect Optimific Theories in Ethics," *Ethics* 98, pp. 341-360.

Brink, David (1986) "Utilitarian Morality and the Personal Point of View," *Journal of Philosophy* 83, pp. 417-438.

Brock, Dan (1982), "Utilitarianism and Aiding Others" in Miller ed., *The Limits of Utilitarianism*, pp. 225-241.

Brown, D. G. (1974), "Mill's Act-utilitarianism," *Philosophical Quarterly* 27, pp. 67-68.

———— (1972), "Mill on Liberty and Morality," *Philosophical Review* 81, pp. 133-158.

———— (1982), "Mill's Criterion of Wrong Conduct," *Dialogue* 21, pp. 27-44.

Buchanan, Allen (1984), "What's So Special About Rights," *Social Philosophy and Policy* 2, pp. 61-83.

Castaneda, Hector-Neri (1972), "On the Problem of Formulating a Coherent Act-Utilitarianism," *Analysis* 32, pp. 118-124.

Cooper, Wesley; Nielsen, Kai; Patten, Steven eds. (1979), *Canadian Journal of Philosophy* 5, Supplement. *New Essays on John Stuart Mill and Utilitarianism* (Guelph: Canadian Association for Publishing in Philosophy).

Copp, David (1979), "The Iterated-Utilitarianism of J. S. Mill" in Cooper ed. *New Essays on John Stuart Mill and Utilitarianism*, pp. 75-98.

Cowling, Maurice (1963), *Mill and Liberalism* (Cambridge: Cambridge University Press).

Dahl, Norman O. (1973), "Is Mill's Hedonism Inconsistent?" in *Studies in Ethics*, American Philosophical Quarterly Monograph Series, Nicholas Rescher ed. (Oxford: Basil Blackwell, 1973), pp. 37-54.

Dennett, Daniel (1978), "Intentional Systems" in his *Brainstorms* (Montgomery: Bradford Books), pp. 3-22.

Dewey, John and Tufts, James (1914), *Ethics* (New York: Henry Holt and Co.)

Donagan, Alan (1968), "Is there a Credible Utilitarianism?" in Bayles ed. *Contemporary Utilitarianism*.

Donner, Wendy (1983), "John Stuart Mill's Concept of Liberty," *Dialogue* 22, pp. 479-494.

_____ (1987), "Mill on Liberty of Self-Development," *Dialogue* 26, pp. 227-237.

Dostoyevsky, Fyodor (1866), *Crime and Punishment*

Dryer, D. P. (1969), "Mill's Utilitarianism" in *CW*, Vol. 10, pp. lxiii-cxiii.

Dworkin, Ronald (1970), "Taking Rights Seriously" in Lyons ed., *Rights*, pp. 92-110.

Ebenstein, Larry (1985), "Mill's Theory of Utility," *Philosophy* 60, pp. 539-543.

Edwards, Rem B. (1979), *Pleasures and Pains: A Theory of Qualitative Hedonism* (Ithaca: Cornell University Press).

_____ (1985), "J. S. Mill and Robert Veatch's Critique of Utilitarianism," *Southern Journal of Philosophy* 23, pp. 181-200.

_____ (1986), "The Principle of Utility and Mill's Minimizing Utilitarianism," *Journal of Value Inquiry* 20, pp. 125-136.

Ellis, Brian (1981), "Retrospective and Prospective Utilitarianism," *Nous* 15, pp. 325-339.

Ezorsky, Gertrude (1968), "A Defense of Rule-Utilitarianism Against David Lyons Who Insists on Tieing it to Act-Utilitarianism, Plus a Brand New Way of Checking Out General Utilitarian Properties," *Journal of Philosophy* 65, pp. 533-544.

Feinberg, Joel ed. (1969), *Moral Concepts* (Oxford: Oxford University Press).

_____ (1970), "The Nature and Value of Rights" in Lyons ed., *Rights*, pp. 78-91.

_____ (1973), *Social Philosophy* (Englewood Cliffs: Prentice Hall).

_____ (1984), *Harm To Others* (New York: Oxford University Press).

Feldman, Fred (1974), "On the Extensional Equivalence of Simple and General Utilitarianism," *Nous* 8, pp. 185-194.

_____ (1986), *Doing the Best We Can* (Dordrecht: D. Reidel Publishing Co.).

Findlay, J. N. (1961), *Values and Intentions* (London: George Allen and Unwin, Ltd.).

Flathman, Richard (1984), "Moderating Rights," *Social Philosophy and Policy* 1, pp. 149-171.

Frey, R. G. (1980), *Interests and Rights: The Case Against Animals* (Oxford: Oxford University Press).

_____ (1984), "Act-Utilitarianism, Consequentialism and Moral Rights" in his *Utility and Rights* (Minneapolis: University of Minnesota Press), pp. 61-85.

Galston, William (1983), "On the Right to Do Wrong," *Ethics* 93, pp. 320-324.

Gaus, Gerald (1980), "Mill's Theory of Moral Rules," *Australasian Journal of Philosophy* 58, pp. 265-279.

Gauthier, David (1986), *Morals by Agreement* (Oxford: Oxford University Press).

Gewirth, Alan (1982), "Can Utilitarianism Justify Any Moral Rights?" in his *Human Rights: Essays on Justification and Applications* (Chicago: University of Chicago Press), pp. 143-162.

_____ (1986), "Why Rights Are Indispensable," *Mind* 95, pp. 329-344.

Gibbs, Benjamin (1986), "Higher and Lower Pleasures," *Philosophy* 61, pp. 31-59.

Goldman, A. I.; Kim, J. eds. (1978), *Values and Morals* (Dordrecht: D. Reidel Publishing Co.)

Goldman, Holly (1974), "David Lyons on Utilitarian Generalization," *Philosophical Studies* 26, pp. 77-95.

Gorovitz, Samuel ed. (1971), *Mill: Utilitarianism with Critical Essays* (Indianapolis: Bobbs-Merrill Co. Inc.)

Gray, John (1981), "John Stuart Mill on Liberty, Utility and Rights," *Nomos* 23 *Human Rights*, J. Roland Pennock and John W.

Chapman eds. (New York: New York University Press), pp. 80-116.

_____ (1983), *Mill and Liberty: a Defence* (London: Routledge and Kegan Paul)

_____ (1984), "Indirect Utility and Fundamental Rights" in *Human Rights*, Ellen Paul, Jeffrey Paul, Fred Miller, Jr. eds. (Oxford: Basil Blackwell, 1984), pp. 73-91.

Griffin, James (1982), "Modern Utilitarianism," *Revue Internationale de Philosophie* 36, pp. 331-375.

_____ (1986), *Well-Being* (Oxford: Oxford University Press).

Gruzalski, Bart (1981), "Foreseeable Consequence Utilitarianism," *Australasian Journal of Philosophy* 59, pp. 163-176.

Hampshire, Stuart ed. (1978), *Public and Private Morality* (Cambridge: Cambridge University Press).

Hardin, Russell (1988), *Morality Within the Limits of Reason* (Chicago: University of Chicago Press).

Hare, R. M. (1981), *Moral Thinking* (Oxford: Oxford University Press).

_____ (1982), "Ethical Theory and Utilitarianism" in Sen ed., *Utilitarianism and Beyond*, pp. 23-38.

Harrison, Jonathan (1974), "The Expedient, the Right and the Just in Mill's Utilitarianism" in *Canadian Journal of Philosophy* Supplementary Vol. 1, pp. 93-107.

Harsanyi, John (1977), "Rule Utilitarianism and Decision Theory," *Erkenntnis* 11, pp. 25-53.

_____ (1982), "Morality and the Theory of Rational Behavior" in Sen ed., *Utilitarianism and Beyond*, pp. 39-62.

Hart, H. L. A. (1979), "Between Utility and Rights" in Ryan ed., *The Idea of Freedom*, pp. 77-98.

_____ (1982), "Legal Rights" in his *Essays On Bentham* (Oxford: Clarendon Press), pp. 162-193.

Hill, Jr., Thomas (1973), "Servility and Self Respect," reprinted in Lyons ed., *Rights*, pp. 111-124.

Himmelfarb, Gertrude (1974), *On Liberty and Liberalism* (New York: Alfred A. Knopf, Inc.)

Holbrook, Daniel (1988), *Qualitative Utilitarianism* (Lanham:
University Press of America)
Honderich, Ted (1974), "The Worth of J. S. Mill *On Liberty,* "
Political Studies 22, pp. 463-470.
_____ (1982), "'On Liberty' and Morality-Dependent Harms,"
Political Studies 30, pp.504-514.
Horton, John and Mendus, Susan eds. (1985), *Aspects of Toleration*
(London: Methuen).
_____ (1985), "Toleration, Morality and Harm" in his *Aspects of
Toleration,* pp. 113-135.
Hutcheson, Francis (1755), *A Short Introduction to Moral Philosophy*
2nd ed. (Glasgow: Robert and Andrew Foulis).
Jones, Peter (1985), "Toleration, Harm and Moral Effect" in *Aspects
of Toleration,* Horton ed., pp. 136-157.
Kagan, Shelly (1984), "Does Consequentialism Demand Too Much?
Recent Work on the Limits of Obligation," *Philosophy and
Public Affairs* 13, pp. 239-254.
_____ (1989), *The Limits of Morality* (Oxford: Oxford University
Press)
Kant, Immanuel (1785), *Foundations of the Metaphysics of Morals,*
Lewis White Beck trans. (Indianapolis: Bobbs-Merrill Co., Inc.,
1959)
Kilcullen, John (1981), "Mill on Duty and Liberty," *Australasian
Journal of Philosophy* 59, pp. 290-300.
Levi, Albert William (1938), *A Study in the Social Philosophy of
John Stuart Mill,* University of Chicago doctoral dissertation.
_____ (1959), "The Value of Freedom: Mill's Liberty (1859-1959),"
Ethics 70, pp. 37-46.
Lippke, Richard (1984), "Why Persons are the Ground of Rights (and
Utility Isn't)," *Journal of Value Inquiry* 18, pp. 207-217.
Lomasky, Loren (1987), *Persons, Rights and Moral Community*
(New York: Oxford University Press)
Lyons, David (1965), *Forms and Limits of Utilitarianism* (Oxford:
Oxford University Press).
_____ (1976), "Mill's Theory of Morality," *Nous* 10, pp. 101-120.

_____ (1978), "Mill's Theory of Justice" in *Values and Morals*, A. I.
Goldman and J. Kim eds., pp. 1-20.

_____ ed. (1979), *Rights* (Belmont: Wadsworth Publishing Co.,
Inc., 1979)

_____ (1979), "Human Rights and the General Welfare" in his
Rights, pp. 174-186.

_____ (1982), "Utility and Rights," in Waldron ed., *Theories of
Rights*, pp. 110-136.

_____ (1982), "Benevolence and Justice in Mill" in Miller ed., *The
Limits of Utilitarianism*, pp. 42-70.

Mabbott, J. D. (1939), "Punishment," first appearing in *Mind* 48,
reprinted in Gorovitz ed., *Utilitarianism with Critical Essays*, pp.
88-98.

_____ (1956) "Interpretations of Mill's Utilitarianism" in
Schneewind ed., *Mill: A Collection of Essays*, pp. 174-186.

Mackie, J. L. (1978), "Can There Be A Right-Based Theory?" in
Waldron ed., *Theories of Rights*, pp. 168-181.

Marcus, Ruth Barcan (1980), "Moral Dilemmas and Consistency,"
Journal of Philosophy 77, pp. 121-136.

Martin, Rex (1972), "A Defense of Mill's Qualitative Hedonism,"
Philosophy 46, pp. 140-151.

_____ ; Nickel, James (1980), "Recent Work on the Concept of
Rights," *American Philosophical Quarterly* 17, pp. 165-180.

McCloskey, H. J. (1971), *John Stuart Mill: A Critical Study*
(London: Macmillan and Co., Ltd.)

McConnell, Terrance (1980), "Utilitarianism and Supererogatory
Acts," *Ratio* 22, pp. 36-38.

Mill, John Stuart (1825), "Law of Libel and Liberty of the Press,"
CW Vol. 21

_____ (1833), "Blakey's History of Moral Science," *CW* Vol. 10.

_____ (1833), "Remarks on Bentham's Philosophy," *CW* Vol. 10.

_____ (1835), "De Toqueville" (1), *CW* 18.

_____ (1835), "Sedgwick's Discourse," *CW* Vol. 10.

_____ (1836), "Civilization," *CW* 18.

_____ (1837), "Taylor's Statesman," *CW* Vol. 19.

_____ (1838), "Bentham," *CW*, Vol. 10.

_____ (1840), "De Toqueville" (2), *CW* 18

_____ (1843), *A System of Logic*, *CW* Vol. 7, 8.

_____ (1848), *Principles of Political Economy*, *CW* Vol. 2, 3.

_____ (1852), "Whewell on Moral Philosophy," *CW*, Vol. 10.

_____ (1859), *On Liberty*, *CW* Vol. 18.

_____ (1861), *Utilitarianism*, in *CW* Vol. 10

_____ (1861), *The Subjection of Women*, *CW* Vol. 21

_____ (1861), *Considerations on Representative Government*, *CW* Vol. 19.

_____ (1865), *An Examination of Sir William Hamilton's Philosophy*, *CW* Vol. 9.

_____ (1865), "Auguste Comte and Positivism," *CW* Vol. 10.

_____ (1869), "Thornton on Labor and Its Claims," *CW* Vol. 5.

_____ (1863), "Austin on Jurisprudence," *CW* Vol. 21.

_____ (1873), *Autobiography*, in *CW* Vol. 1.

_____ (1874), *Three Essays on Religion*, *CW* Vol. 10.

_____ (1879), "Chapters on Socialism," *CW* 5.

_____ Later Letters 1849-1873, *CW* Vol. 17.

Miller, Harlan; Williams, William eds. (1982), *The Limits of Utilitarianism* (Minneapolis: University of Minnesota Press).

Montague, Phillip (1985), "The Nature of Rights: Some Logical Considerations," *Nous* 19, pp. 365-377.

Montefiore, Alan ed. (1973), *Philosophy and Personal Relations* (London: Routledge and Kegan Paul).

Moore, G. E. (1903), *Principia Ethica* (Cambridge: Cambridge University Press, 1971).

_____ (1912), *Ethics* (Oxford: Oxford University Press, 1971).

Morris, Herbert (1968), "Persons and Punishment," *The Monist* 52, pp. 475-601.

Mulholland, Leslie (1986), "Rights, Utilitarianism and the Conflation of Persons," *Journal of Philosophy* 83.

Nagel, Thomas (1986), *The View From Nowhere* (New York: Oxford University Press).

Narveson, Jan (1967), *Morality and Utility* (Baltimore: Johns Hopkins University Press)

_____ (1976), "Utilitarianism, Group Actions and Co-ordination," *Nous* 10, pp. 173-194.

_____ (1979), "Rights and Utilitarianism" in Cooper ed., *New Essays on John Stuart Mill and Utilitarianism*, pp. 137-160.

Nelson, William (1976), "On the Alleged Importance of Moral Rights," *Ratio* 18, pp. 145-155.

Nozick, Robert (1974), *Anarchy, State and Utopia* (New York: Basic Books Inc, Publishers).

Packe, Michael (1954), *The Life of John Stuart Mill* (London: Secker and Warburg)

Parfit, Derek (1973), "Later Selves and Moral Principles" in Montefiore, *Philosophy and Personal Relations*, pp. 137-169.

_____ (1978), "Innumerate Ethics," *Philosophy and Public Affairs* 7, pp. 285-301.

_____ (1984), *Reasons and Persons* (Oxford: Oxford University Press).

Piper, Adrian (1987), "Moral Theory and Moral Alienation," *Journal of Philosophy* 84, pp. 102-118.

Postow, B. C. (1977), "Generalized Act Utilitarianism," *Analysis* 37, pp. 49-52.

Radcliff, Peter ed. (1966), *Limits of Liberty* (Belmont: Wadsworth Publishing Co., Inc.).

Rawls, John (1951), "Outline of a Decision Procedure for Ethics," *Philosophical Review* 60, pp. 177-197.

_____ (1955), "Two Concepts of Rules," first appearing in *Philosophical Review* 64, reprinted in Gorovitz ed., *Utilitarianism with Critical Essays*, pp. 175-194.

_____ (1971), *A Theory of Justice* (Cambridge: Harvard University Press).

_____ (1974-1975), "The Independence of Moral Theory," *American Philosophical Association Proceedings and Addresses* 48, pp. 5-22.

_____ (1980), "Kantian Constructionalism in Moral Theory," *Journal of Philosophy* 77, pp. 515-572.

_____ (1982), "Social Unity and Primary Goods" in Sen ed., *Utilitarianism and Beyond*, pp. 159-186.

Raz, J. (1982), "Right-Based Moralities" in Waldron ed., *Theories of Rights*, pp. 182-200.

_____ (1984), "On the Nature of Rights," *Mind* 93, pp. 194-214.
Rees, John (1960), "A Rereading of Mill on Liberty" in Radcliff ed.,
    Limits Of Liberty, pp. 87-107.
_____ (1985), *John Stuart Mill On Liberty* (Oxford: Oxford
    University Press).
Regan, Donald (1980), *Utilitarianism and Co-operation*, (Oxford:
    Oxford University Press).
Riley, Jonathan (1988), *Liberal Utilitarianism* (Cambridge: Cambridge
    University Press).
Robson, John ed. (1969) *Collected Works of John Stuart Mill* (referred
    to as *CW*) (Toronto: University of Toronto Press).
Ross, William David (1930), *The Right and the Good* (Oxford: Oxford
    University Press).
Ryan, Alan (1970), *John Stuart Mill* (New York: Pantheon Books).
_____ ed. (1979), *The Idea of Freedom* (Oxford: Oxford University
    Press).
Sandel, Michael (1982), *Liberalism and the Limits of Justice*
    (Cambridge: Cambridge University Press).
Sartorius, Rolf (1975), *Individual Conduct and Social Norms* (Encino:
    Dickenson Publishing Co., Inc.)
_____ (1985), "Utilitarianism, Rights and Duties to Self," *American
    Philosophical Quarterly* 22, pp. 241-249.
Scanlon, T. M. (1975), "Preference and Urgency," *Journal of
    Philosophy* 72, pp. 655-669.
_____ (1978), "Rights, Goals and Fairness" in Hampshire ed.,
    Public and Private Morality, pp. 93-111.
_____ (1982), "Contractualism and Utilitarianism" in Sen ed.,
    Utilitarianism and Beyond, pp. 103-128.
Scheffler, Samuel (1982), *The Rejection of Consequentialism* (Oxford:
    Oxford University Press).
Schneewind, J. B. ed. (1968), *Mill: A Collection of Critical Essays*
    (Garden City: Anchor Books).
Sedgwick, Adam (1833), *A Discourse on the Studies of the University*
    (New York: Humanities Press, 1969).
Semmel, Bernard (1984), *John Stuart Mill and the Pursuit of Virtue*
    (New Haven: Yale University Press).

Sen, Amartya (1982), *Choice, Welfare and Measurement* (Oxford: Basil Blackwell).

———; Williams, Bernard eds. (1982), *Utilitarianism and Beyond* (Cambridge: Cambridge University Press).

Sidgwick, Henry (1867, 7th ed. 1907), *The Methods of Ethics* (Indianapolis: Hackett Publishing Co., 1981).

Sikora, R. I.; Barry, Brian eds. (1978), *Obligations to Future Generations* (Philadelphia: Temple University Press)

——— (1979), "Utilitarianism, Supererogation and Future Generations," *Canadian Journal of Philosophy* 11, pp. 461-466.

Singer, Marcus (1977), "On Rawls, On Mill, On Liberty and So On," *Journal of Value Inquiry* 11, pp. 141-148.

——— (1977) "Actual Consequence Utilitarianism," *Mind* 86, pp. 67-77.

——— (1982), "Incoherence, Inconsistency, and Moral Theory: More on Actual Consequence Utilitarianism," *Southern Journal of Philosophy* 20, pp. 375-391.

——— (1983), "The Paradox of Extreme Utilitarianism," *Pacific Philosophical Quarterly* 64, pp. 242-248.

——— (1984), "Consequences, Desirability and the Moral Fanaticism Argument," *Philosophical Studies* 46, pp. 227-237.

Singer, Peter (1972), "Famine, Affluence and Morality," originally in *Philosophy and Public Affairs* 1, reprinted in Barry ed., *Applying Ethics*, pp. 342-352.

Slote, Michael (1984), "Satisficing Consequentialism," *Proceedings of the Aristotelian Society* Supplementary Volume 58, pp. 139-164.

——— (1985), *Common-sense Morality and Consequentialism* (London: Routledge and Kegan Paul).

——— (1985), "Utilitarianism, Moral Dilemmas and Moral Cost," *American Philosophical Quarterly* 22.

Smart, J. J. C. (1956), "Extreme and restricted utilitarianism" in Gorovitz ed., *Mill: Utilitarianism with Critical Essays*, pp. 195-203.

———; Williams, Bernard eds. (1973), *Utilitarianism For and Against* (Cambridge: Cambridge University Press).

Sobel, Jordan (1976), "Utilitarianism and past and future mistakes,"
    Nous 10, pp. 195-219.
Stegenga, James (1973), "J. S. Mill's Concept of Liberty and the
    Principle of Utility," *Journal of Value Inquiry* 7, pp. 281-289.
Stephen, James Fitzjames (1873) *Liberty, Equality, Fraternity* White,
    R. J. ed. (Cambridge: Cambridge University Press, 1967)
Strasser, Mark (1984), "Mill and the Utility of Liberty,"
    Philosophical Quarterly 34, pp. 63-68.
_____ (1986), "Hutcheson on External Rights," *Philosophical
    Studies* 49, pp. 263-269.
_____ (1987), "Guilt, Regret and Prima Facie Duties," *Southern
    Journal of Philosophy* 25, pp. 133-146.
_____ (1987), "Hutcheson on the Higher and Lower Pleasures,"
    Journal of the History of Philosophy 25, pp. 517-531.
_____ (1987), "Conscience and the Right to Do Wrong,"
    Philosophia 17, pp. 411-420.
_____ (1988), "Frankfurt, Aristotle and PAP," *Southern Journal of
    Philosophy* 26, pp. 235-246.
_____ (1989), "Actual vs. Probable Consequence Utilitarianism,"
    Southern Journal of Philosophy 27, pp. 585-598
_____ (1990), *Francis Hutcheson's Moral Theory: Its Form and
    Utility* (Wakefield: Longwood Academic).
Sumner, L. Wayne (1987), *The Moral Foundation of Rights* (Oxford:
    Oxford University Press).
Ten, C. L. (1980), *Mill on Liberty* (Oxford: Clarendon Press).
Thomas, D. A. Lloyd (1980), "Liberalism and Utilitarianism," *Ethics*
    90, pp. 319-334.
Thomson, Judith (1986), "Self Defense and Rights" in her *Rights,
    Restitution, and Risk* (Cambridge: Harvard University Press), pp.
    33-48.
Urmson, J. O. (1953), "The interpretation of the moral philosophy of
    J. S. Mill" in Gorovitz ed., *Mill: Utilitarianism with Critical
    Essays*, pp. 168-174.
_____ (1958), "Saints and Heroes" in *Moral Concepts*, Feinberg ed.,
    pp. 60-73.
Waldron, Jeremy (1981), "A Right to Do Wrong," *Ethics* 92, pp. 21-
    39.

_____ ed. (1984), *Theories of Rights* (Oxford: Oxford University Press).

_____ (1989), "Rights in Conflict," *Ethics* 99, pp. 503-519.

Wasserstrom, Richard (1964), "Rights, Human Rights, and Racial Discrimination," *Journal of Philosophy* 61, pp. 628-641.

Watson, Richard (1977), "Reason and Morality in a World of Limited Food" in Barry ed., *Applying Ethics*, pp. 352-357.

Weale, Albert (1985), "Tolerations, Individual Differences and Respect for Persons" in *Aspects of Toleration*, pp. 16-35.

Wellman, Carl (1985), *A Theory of Rights* (Totowa: Rowman and Allanheld, Publishers)

West, Henry (1976), "Mill's Moral Conservatism," *Midwest Studies in Philosophy* 1, pp. 71-80.

Whewell, William (1845), *Elements of Morality including Polity* (New York: Harper and Brothers).

Williams, Bernard (1973), "Ethical Consistency" in his *Problems of the Self* (Cambridge: Cambridge University Press), pp. 166-186.

Wolf, Susan (1982), "Moral Saints," *Journal of Philosophy* 79, pp. 419-439.

Wolff, Robert Paul (1968), *The Poverty of Liberalism* (Boston: Beacon Press)

Wollheim, J. (1973), "J. S. Mill and the Limits of State Action," *Social Research* 40, pp. 1-30.

INDEX